Ghidra Essentials: The Complete Guide to Reverse Engineering

Claudiox Mastrangelo

Reverse engineering is a critical skill in today's technology-driven world. Whether you're uncovering vulnerabilities in software, analyzing malicious code, or understanding legacy systems, reverse engineering enables you to break down complex binaries into understandable components. It's a discipline that combines technical expertise, analytical thinking, and creativity to uncover hidden insights.

This book, **Ghidra Essentials: The Complete Guide to Reverse Engineering**, is your gateway to mastering one of the most powerful tools available for reverse engineering—Ghidra. Developed by the National Security Agency (NSA) and released to the public in 2019, Ghidra is a free and open-source reverse engineering suite that has quickly become a favorite among security researchers, analysts, and software developers. Its user-friendly interface, robust feature set, and extensibility make it an indispensable tool for tackling some of the most challenging reverse engineering tasks.

Why This Book?

This book is designed to cater to a wide range of readers—from beginners taking their first steps in reverse engineering to seasoned professionals looking to deepen their understanding of Ghidra. The chapters are structured to guide you through Ghidra's core features and advanced capabilities while providing practical examples and real-world applications.

You'll start with the basics, learning how to navigate the tool and analyze simple binaries. From there, you'll delve into advanced topics such as decompilation, debugging, scripting, and automation. You'll also explore practical applications like malware analysis, firmware reverse engineering, and solving crackme challenges. Along the way, you'll gain insights into Ghidra's architecture and learn how to extend its functionality with custom plugins and scripts.

What You'll Learn

By the time you finish this book, you'll be able to:

- Navigate and effectively use Ghidra's powerful suite of tools.
- Analyze binaries, understand disassembly, and work with decompiled code.
- Identify functions, track data flow, and map control structures.
- Debug and emulate code to uncover runtime behaviors.

Automate repetitive tasks with scripting and extend Ghidra's capabilities with plugins. Tackle real-world challenges like malware analysis and firmware reverse engineering.

Who This Book Is For

Whether you're a cybersecurity professional, a software developer, or a curious hobbyist, this book is for anyone who wants to explore the world of reverse engineering with Ghidra. No prior experience with reverse engineering is required, though a basic understanding of programming and computer architecture will be helpful.

The Journey Ahead

The chapters are organized to provide a logical progression, starting with fundamental concepts and gradually introducing more complex topics. Each chapter includes detailed explanations, practical examples, and actionable insights to help you build a solid foundation and grow your expertise.

So, let's dive in and unlock the potential of Ghidra. Welcome to the exciting world of reverse engineering!

Claudiox Mastrangelo is a seasoned cybersecurity professional, reverse engineer, and technology enthusiast with years of experience unraveling the mysteries of software and systems. With a deep passion for understanding how things work under the hood, Claudiox has dedicated his career to dissecting binaries, analyzing malware, and solving complex reverse engineering challenges.

Claudiox's journey into the world of reverse engineering began out of sheer curiosity—an insatiable desire to break down complex systems and uncover their secrets. Over the years, this curiosity has evolved into expertise, as Claudiox has worked with global organizations to enhance their security posture, identify vulnerabilities, and defend against emerging cyber threats.

As an avid user and advocate of Ghidra, Claudiox appreciates its unique blend of power, flexibility, and accessibility. His firsthand experience with the tool has made him a trusted resource for those looking to master Ghidra and apply it to real-world scenarios. Through this book, Claudiox shares his knowledge, insights, and best practices to help others succeed in their reverse engineering endeavors.

When not reverse engineering code or writing, Claudiox can often be found exploring the latest advancements in cybersecurity, participating in Capture the Flag (CTF) competitions, and contributing to the open-source community.

This book is a reflection of Claudiox's passion for teaching and empowering others in the field of reverse engineering. Whether you're new to the field or a seasoned professional, Claudiox's approachable style and wealth of knowledge make this guide an invaluable resource on your journey with Ghidra.

Part I: Introduction to Ghidra

The first step in any journey is understanding the terrain, and Part I of this book is designed to familiarize you with the foundational concepts of reverse engineering and introduce you to the powerful capabilities of Ghidra. Here, you'll learn what reverse engineering entails, explore the ethical considerations surrounding it, and discover how Ghidra fits into the broader landscape of reverse engineering tools. From installing and setting up the software to navigating its user-friendly interface and core features, this section ensures you're well-prepared to dive into more advanced topics. Whether you're a newcomer or seeking a refresher, Part I lays the groundwork for everything that follows.

Chapter 1: Understanding Reverse Engineering Fundamentals

Reverse engineering is both an art and a science, blending technical skills with creative problem-solving to deconstruct and analyze software. This chapter introduces you to the essential principles that define reverse engineering, its applications in cybersecurity, and the critical role it plays in understanding and improving software systems. You'll explore common use cases like malware analysis, vulnerability discovery, and legacy system maintenance, while also addressing the ethical and legal boundaries that come with this powerful practice. By the end of this chapter, you'll have a solid grasp of the key concepts and challenges in reverse engineering, setting the stage for your journey with Ghidra.

1.1 The Role of Reverse Engineering in Cybersecurity

Reverse engineering plays a critical role in the field of cybersecurity, serving as a cornerstone for discovering vulnerabilities, understanding malware, and enhancing software defenses. The process of reverse engineering involves deconstructing software or hardware to uncover its components, structure, and behavior, often to identify potential security risks or gain insights into its functionality. This practice is essential for professionals working to protect systems from cyber threats, as it helps them dissect malicious code, uncover hidden vulnerabilities, and develop more secure applications.

Understanding Reverse Engineering

At its core, reverse engineering is the process of analyzing software, hardware, or systems to extract design, architecture, or functionality information. In software, this often involves analyzing the binary code of programs to understand how they work internally. Unlike forward engineering, where developers design systems from scratch using high-level specifications, reverse engineering aims to work backward from an existing system to uncover its secrets.

For cybersecurity experts, reverse engineering is a vital tool for dissecting malicious software (malware), understanding security flaws, and finding ways to strengthen system defenses. It is a practice employed by various cybersecurity specialists, including ethical hackers, penetration testers, incident response teams, and malware analysts.

Reverse Engineering in Malware Analysis

One of the most significant applications of reverse engineering in cybersecurity is malware analysis. Malicious software can be used for a variety of nefarious purposes, including data theft, system compromise, espionage, and more. Malware is often designed to hide its true intent and avoid detection by traditional security measures, such as antivirus software. Reverse engineering allows security professionals to break down the malware to understand its behavior, code structure, and how it interacts with the infected system.

By reverse engineering a malware sample, analysts can identify the attack vector (how the malware entered the system), the payload (the actual malicious action carried out by the malware), and the behavioral patterns (how it operates once inside the system). This analysis is crucial for creating defenses against the malware. For example, by understanding how a virus or Trojan communicates with its command-and-control server, an analyst can develop network filters to block that communication, neutralizing the threat.

Additionally, reverse engineering malware can help uncover zero-day vulnerabilities—flaws in software or hardware that have not been previously discovered or patched. By discovering these vulnerabilities, security experts can warn organizations and software vendors before the flaw is exploited by cybercriminals. Without reverse engineering, many sophisticated threats would remain undetected and continue to wreak havoc on vulnerable systems.

Identifying and Exploiting Vulnerabilities

Another critical application of reverse engineering in cybersecurity is identifying and exploiting vulnerabilities in software systems. When reverse engineers examine a program, they can often uncover security flaws that were not identified during the initial development process. These flaws can range from buffer overflows and format string vulnerabilities to race conditions and memory leaks. By analyzing how a program processes user inputs and handles memory, reverse engineers can pinpoint areas where an attacker might inject malicious code or take advantage of a flaw.

For example, in a buffer overflow attack, an attacker sends more data to a program than it can handle, causing the program to overwrite its own memory. This can lead to the execution of arbitrary code, allowing attackers to control the program. By reverse engineering the application, cybersecurity professionals can identify whether a vulnerability exists and if so, understand how to fix it. This knowledge can be used to design more secure applications, patch existing software, and create defensive strategies that prevent such attacks from succeeding.

Reverse engineering also plays an essential role in vulnerability research. In this context, reverse engineers disassemble and analyze software to uncover potential vulnerabilities that can be exploited. These vulnerabilities may not always be immediately apparent in the code, especially if the software has been intentionally obfuscated or designed to be resilient against static analysis. Through reverse engineering, security researchers can identify hidden vulnerabilities, such as those in encryption algorithms, authentication mechanisms, and network protocols. Once a vulnerability is discovered, researchers can work on patches or defensive tools to mitigate the risk.

Penetration Testing and Ethical Hacking

Penetration testing, or ethical hacking, is another area where reverse engineering is crucial. Penetration testers use reverse engineering techniques to simulate real-world cyberattacks, with the goal of identifying security weaknesses before malicious hackers can exploit them. By reverse engineering the target system, testers can identify attack surfaces, evaluate how well security measures are working, and find ways to bypass protections like firewalls, intrusion detection systems, and encryption protocols.

For example, in a reverse-engineered web application, a penetration tester may deconstruct the software to identify logic flaws, misconfigurations, or hidden features that could lead to a breach. By exploiting these vulnerabilities in a controlled environment, the tester provides valuable insights into the system's overall security posture. The insights gained from reverse engineering can then be used to harden the system and ensure it is resistant to real-world attacks.

Reverse engineering is also fundamental for testing defensive tools. For instance, reverse engineers might examine an antivirus program to discover how it detects malicious code and identify any weaknesses in its detection mechanisms. This analysis can help improve the effectiveness of security software by allowing vendors to patch vulnerabilities in their tools or adapt them to detect newer forms of malware.

Enhancing Software Security

Reverse engineering is not only about breaking into systems; it is also about building stronger defenses. Software developers and cybersecurity professionals use reverse engineering to improve the security of their own systems by analyzing potential weaknesses. For example, code review and security audits frequently involve reverse engineering software to ensure that security best practices have been implemented and that no vulnerabilities remain.

Furthermore, reverse engineering can help developers detect and mitigate software piracy and cracking attempts. By understanding how cracking tools work and reverse engineering their methods, developers can implement more robust protections against illegal modifications to their software.

Legal and Ethical Considerations

While reverse engineering is an essential tool in cybersecurity, it also raises legal and ethical concerns. Many software vendors explicitly prohibit reverse engineering in their end-user license agreements (EULAs), claiming that it infringes on intellectual property rights. However, in many jurisdictions, reverse engineering is allowed for specific purposes, such as interoperability, security research, and vulnerability discovery. Cybersecurity professionals need to be mindful of these legal frameworks and ensure that their activities comply with applicable laws and regulations.

Ethically, reverse engineers must also consider the potential impact of their work. While analyzing malware or uncovering vulnerabilities can help protect systems, the same techniques could be used by cybercriminals for malicious purposes. Therefore, ethical reverse engineers often work in collaboration with organizations, security vendors, and law enforcement agencies to ensure that their research is used responsibly and for the greater good.

In conclusion, reverse engineering plays an indispensable role in cybersecurity by enabling professionals to understand the inner workings of software, identify vulnerabilities, and counteract cyber threats. Whether used for malware analysis, vulnerability discovery, penetration testing, or enhancing software security, reverse engineering is a powerful tool in the cybersecurity arsenal. As cyber threats become more sophisticated and pervasive, the ability to reverse engineer malicious code and software systems will remain a key skill for defending against and mitigating these evolving risks. By mastering reverse engineering, cybersecurity professionals can stay ahead of attackers and build more secure, resilient systems.

1.2 Exploring Common Use Cases: Malware Analysis, Software Debugging, and More

Reverse engineering is a versatile and powerful skill, widely used in cybersecurity and software development. It involves deconstructing software or hardware to understand its structure, functionality, and vulnerabilities. While reverse engineering is often associated with cybersecurity, its applications span multiple domains, each with its own specific needs and challenges. In this section, we explore some of the most common use cases of reverse engineering, including malware analysis, software debugging, and other critical areas such as vulnerability research, license cracking, and digital forensics. Understanding these use cases helps highlight the broad scope of reverse engineering's potential in improving security, software quality, and overall system reliability.

Malware Analysis

One of the most significant and widely recognized applications of reverse engineering is in malware analysis. Malware analysis is the process of dissecting malicious software (such as viruses, worms, ransomware, Trojans, and spyware) to understand its behavior, propagation methods, and payloads. Malware is often designed to conceal its true intentions and avoid detection by traditional security measures like antivirus programs, making reverse engineering an essential tool for identifying, neutralizing, and defending against these threats.

The role of reverse engineering in malware analysis can be divided into several steps:

Static Analysis: Reverse engineers first examine the malware without executing it. They inspect the binary file's structure, extracting metadata, analyzing file headers, and reviewing code patterns. Using tools like Ghidra, IDA Pro, or Binary Ninja, analysts can disassemble the binary code and attempt to understand its logic, including identifying hidden functionalities, embedded files, or obfuscated code.

Dynamic Analysis: Once static analysis has been completed, the next step is to execute the malware in a controlled environment, such as a virtual machine or sandbox. Dynamic analysis helps researchers observe how the malware behaves during execution. This can reveal how the malware interacts with the system, what files it manipulates, what network traffic it generates, and how it attempts to evade detection. Dynamic analysis can also help uncover malware's persistence mechanisms, rootkit capabilities, and its attempts to exfiltrate data or encrypt files.

Behavioral Analysis: After understanding the execution flow and impact of the malware, reverse engineers can focus on how the malware uses system resources, including processes, files, and network connections. By reverse engineering malware's internal structures, experts can develop signatures for intrusion detection systems or methods to block the malware from infecting systems.

Through malware analysis, reverse engineers help organizations identify security gaps, develop detection signatures, and craft defenses to protect against evolving threats.

Software Debugging

Another critical use case of reverse engineering is in software debugging, where engineers use reverse engineering techniques to troubleshoot and correct software bugs, vulnerabilities, or unintended behaviors. Software debugging is essential to ensure that applications run smoothly, securely, and without errors. Reverse engineering helps developers pinpoint bugs that might be difficult to identify through normal testing or direct code inspection.

Key applications of reverse engineering in software debugging include:

Uncovering Hidden Bugs: When standard debugging methods fail, reverse engineering can help uncover hidden bugs, especially in complex software that interacts with various system components, hardware, or third-party libraries. Through reverse engineering, a developer can examine how the software behaves at the machine code level and identify faulty behavior not visible at higher layers of abstraction.

Understanding Legacy Code: In many cases, developers are tasked with maintaining or updating legacy systems without access to the original source code. Reverse engineering allows developers to understand how a legacy application works by disassembling and decompiling the binary code. This is particularly useful for legacy systems that are no longer actively maintained by their original developers or for proprietary software with no source code available.

Performance Optimization: Reverse engineers may also analyze the performance of applications by understanding how code is executed at the assembly level. This allows them to identify inefficient routines, memory leaks, or excessive CPU usage, which can be addressed to optimize the software for better performance.

Bypassing Software Protection: Some software may be intentionally obfuscated or protected against debugging in order to prevent reverse engineers from understanding or modifying its behavior. Reverse engineering can help bypass these protections, which is particularly useful when debugging software with anti-debugging or anti-tampering mechanisms.

Vulnerability Research and Exploitation

Reverse engineering is an essential tool for vulnerability research, where security experts analyze software and systems to find weaknesses that could be exploited by attackers. Vulnerabilities like buffer overflows, race conditions, and improper memory handling are often difficult to detect without a deep understanding of the system's inner workings. Reverse engineers play a crucial role in discovering these vulnerabilities before attackers can exploit them.

Buffer Overflows: A buffer overflow occurs when a program attempts to write more data to a block of memory than it can hold. By reverse engineering an application, security researchers can identify buffer overflow vulnerabilities and create exploit code that takes advantage of these flaws to execute arbitrary code.

Privilege Escalation: Reverse engineers often analyze systems to identify weaknesses in privilege escalation mechanisms, where an attacker could gain unauthorized access to higher-level privileges or administrative rights. By analyzing software interactions with the operating system, reverse engineers can pinpoint vulnerabilities in user permission management and exploit them.

Cryptographic Weaknesses: Many reverse engineers focus on uncovering flaws in cryptographic algorithms. This includes studying weak encryption or hashing techniques that can be exploited to break security measures, decrypt sensitive information, or tamper with data integrity.

Through vulnerability research, reverse engineers help improve software security by discovering and patching weaknesses, preventing potential exploits that could lead to data breaches or system compromise.

License Cracking and Software Piracy

Another common use case for reverse engineering is license cracking and software piracy, where individuals may reverse engineer applications to bypass licensing protections or crack activation mechanisms. This is often done to allow unauthorized use of paid software, potentially leading to financial losses for developers.

Cracking License Validation: Many applications implement license validation mechanisms that check whether the software is legitimately purchased and activated. Reverse engineers can bypass or disable these checks to allow the software to run without a valid license, enabling unauthorized users to access premium features.

Copy Protection: Reverse engineers can also target copy protection schemes that prevent users from distributing software illegally. By reverse engineering the protection mechanism, attackers can create cracked versions of the software that can be freely distributed.

While software piracy is illegal and unethical, reverse engineering in this domain is also critical for software protection and digital rights management (DRM). By understanding how attackers bypass these systems, developers can improve security measures and create more resilient protections against illegal distribution.

Digital Forensics

Reverse engineering plays a key role in digital forensics, where investigators analyze digital evidence to solve cybercrimes, recover data, or uncover hidden information. Digital forensics often involves examining digital devices, analyzing data remnants, and tracing actions taken by cybercriminals. Reverse engineering helps investigators understand how malicious actions were carried out and uncover evidence that can be used in legal proceedings.

Examples include:

File Recovery: Reverse engineers may analyze corrupted or partially deleted files to recover information lost during a cyber attack or system failure. By inspecting file structures and data remnants, they can reconstruct lost data.

Attribution: In the case of cybercrimes, reverse engineering can help investigators trace malware back to its source, uncovering attack methods, origin points, and attacker tactics.

Reverse engineering is an indispensable tool in a wide range of fields, from malware analysis and software debugging to vulnerability research, license cracking, and digital forensics. Each of these areas relies on reverse engineering to uncover hidden information, identify vulnerabilities, and develop solutions for improving security. As cybersecurity threats become more sophisticated, reverse engineering will continue to be a vital skill for understanding and defending against complex, evolving attacks.

1.3 Legal and Ethical Considerations

Reverse engineering is an essential skill in cybersecurity, software development, and various other technical fields. However, as powerful as reverse engineering is, it comes with significant legal and ethical considerations that practitioners must navigate carefully. Understanding these aspects is crucial for reverse engineers, as their work can easily stray into illegal or unethical territory if proper care is not taken. In this section, we explore the primary legal and ethical concerns surrounding reverse engineering, including intellectual property rights, software licenses, privacy, and responsible disclosure.

Legal Considerations in Reverse Engineering

Reverse engineering can often involve the deconstruction of proprietary software, hardware, or systems, which raises concerns about intellectual property (IP) rights, copyright, and patent law. The legality of reverse engineering depends largely on the jurisdiction and the purpose behind the activity.

Copyright Law and End User License Agreements (EULAs):

One of the primary legal challenges faced in reverse engineering is the potential violation of copyright law. Copyright protects the original expression of ideas, which includes software code. Software vendors typically use End User License Agreements (EULAs) to impose restrictions on how their software can be used. These EULAs may explicitly prohibit reverse engineering, disassembly, or decompilation of the software. Violating these terms could expose reverse engineers to legal liability, including lawsuits and fines.

However, many jurisdictions, such as the United States, allow reverse engineering under specific conditions. For instance, the Digital Millennium Copyright Act (DMCA) in the U.S. has exemptions that permit reverse engineering for purposes like interoperability or security research. The key point is that reverse engineering for personal learning, vulnerability research, or ensuring compatibility is often legal, but doing so to circumvent protections or create pirated versions can breach copyright law.

Patents and Trade Secrets:

Reverse engineering could potentially infringe on patents or reveal trade secrets. Patents protect specific technological inventions, and reverse engineering a patented product to copy or exploit its functionality without permission is illegal. Similarly, trade secrets (such as proprietary algorithms or confidential design information) are protected by law, and reverse engineering to uncover these secrets with the intent to benefit from them can lead to legal consequences.

It's also important to note that reverse engineering for the purpose of discovering vulnerabilities or understanding how a product works for ethical reasons (e.g., security research) is generally treated more leniently under the law. However, exploiting that knowledge for malicious intent, such as exploiting a vulnerability to harm users, is a clear violation of legal standards.

Jurisdictional Differences:

Laws regarding reverse engineering vary significantly between countries. For example, in the European Union, the EU Software Directive permits reverse engineering for the purpose of interoperability (e.g., ensuring different software applications can work together), but this is heavily regulated and restricted to specific use cases. In contrast, some countries have more stringent rules regarding reverse engineering, with little to no exceptions for research or security purposes.

Reverse engineers must be aware of the local laws governing their activities. This is especially important when conducting research on software or hardware from vendors based in different countries. In some instances, international trade regulations and sanctions may prohibit the reverse engineering of products from certain nations or companies, adding a further layer of legal complexity.

Ethical Considerations in Reverse Engineering

Beyond the legal framework, reverse engineering also presents numerous ethical dilemmas that practitioners must consider. These ethical considerations often focus on whether the intent behind reverse engineering aligns with professional conduct, integrity, and the broader well-being of users and society.

Intent and Purpose:

A central ethical question in reverse engineering is the intent behind the activity. Reverse engineering can be used for legitimate purposes such as security research, educational learning, or improving the functionality of existing software. For instance, a security researcher may reverse engineer malware to identify how it operates and create signatures to defend against it. Similarly, reverse engineering can be used to improve interoperability or extend the life of legacy systems.

On the other hand, reverse engineering can also be used unethically, such as for bypassing copy protections, cracking software, or stealing trade secrets. The intent to harm, exploit, or profit from malicious purposes is clearly unethical. Therefore, ethical reverse engineers must always ensure that their activities are done with the right motives, such as contributing to security, education, or enhancing systems, rather than for personal gain or causing harm.

Responsible Disclosure:

One of the core ethical principles in reverse engineering—especially in the context of security research—is responsible disclosure. When reverse engineers discover vulnerabilities or security flaws, they are ethically obligated to disclose them responsibly. This often means reporting the vulnerability to the vendor or developer before making it public, providing the organization with time to address the issue and release a patch.

Irresponsible disclosure, where vulnerabilities are publicly revealed without giving the vendor or developer time to fix the issue, can expose users to unnecessary risks and damage the reputation of the reverse engineer. This practice is widely regarded as unethical because it prioritizes personal recognition or attention over user safety and responsible handling of sensitive information.

Privacy and Confidentiality:

Privacy is another ethical consideration in reverse engineering, particularly when dealing with systems that contain personal or confidential information. Reverse engineers may encounter sensitive data during their analysis, either by deconstructing a software application or by conducting dynamic analysis of a system. Ethical reverse engineers must respect privacy and confidentiality, ensuring that personal or proprietary data is not exposed or misused.

For example, when analyzing malware or conducting penetration tests, reverse engineers should avoid exploiting or leaking private information unless necessary for the research or security improvements. In cases where sensitive data is uncovered (e.g., credentials, private communications, or financial data), it must be handled with integrity and in accordance with privacy laws and ethical guidelines.

Impact on Users and Society:

Ethical reverse engineers should always consider the broader impact of their actions on the user base and society. While uncovering vulnerabilities or flaws in a system can be valuable for improving security, releasing exploit code or malware publicly can have devastating consequences. The ethical responsibility extends beyond legal compliance to ensuring that the research and reverse engineering work does not inadvertently harm the public, damage businesses, or create security risks for users.

For example, releasing a proof-of-concept (PoC) exploit for a vulnerability without responsible disclosure could lead to widespread attacks, impacting millions of users. In contrast, working with the software vendor to patch the vulnerability first and then responsibly disclosing it ensures that the vulnerability is fixed before it is publicly available, protecting users.

Best Practices for Legal and Ethical Reverse Engineering

To navigate the complexities of legal and ethical reverse engineering, practitioners should adhere to the following best practices:

Understand the Laws: Always be aware of the legal framework governing reverse engineering in your jurisdiction, and seek legal counsel when in doubt. Pay particular attention to copyright law, patent law, and trade secret protections.

Document Intent: Clearly define the purpose of the reverse engineering process, ensuring that it aligns with ethical goals, such as security research or educational purposes, rather than malicious activities.

Adhere to Responsible Disclosure: If you discover vulnerabilities or security issues, follow responsible disclosure practices, such as notifying the vendor first and giving them time to fix the issue before making it public.

Respect Privacy: Handle sensitive data with care and respect privacy regulations, such as GDPR, when performing reverse engineering activities that may involve personal information.

Contribute to Security: Use reverse engineering skills to contribute positively to the security community, whether by developing patches, improving defenses, or educating others.

Reverse engineering is a powerful tool, but it requires careful consideration of both legal and ethical frameworks. By understanding the complexities of copyright law, intellectual property rights, responsible disclosure, and privacy, reverse engineers can ensure that their work remains legal, ethical, and beneficial to society. Ethical reverse engineering should always prioritize the greater good—enhancing security, improving software functionality, and protecting users—while avoiding malicious intent and harm. By adhering to both legal and ethical guidelines, reverse engineers can navigate the challenges of their work while contributing to a safer and more secure digital world.

1.4 Key Concepts: Assemblers, Decompilers, and Debuggers

In the field of reverse engineering, understanding the essential tools and concepts is critical to the success of analyzing software and systems. Reverse engineers rely on a variety of software tools that help them disassemble, decompile, and debug applications to uncover their underlying code and behavior. Three of the most fundamental tools for reverse engineering are assemblers, decompilers, and debuggers. Each plays a unique and important role in the reverse engineering process, providing the means to inspect and manipulate binaries, understand how they function, and uncover vulnerabilities or hidden behaviors. In this section, we will explore these key concepts in more detail.

Assemblers

An assembler is a tool that translates assembly language into machine code, the low-level code that is executed by the computer's CPU. Assembly language is a human-readable representation of machine code, where each instruction corresponds to a specific operation that the CPU can execute. However, assembly language is still closely tied to the underlying architecture of the machine, such as the x86 or ARM instruction sets.

In reverse engineering, the primary purpose of an assembler is to disassemble a binary file. This means converting the machine code of a program back into its assembly language representation so that reverse engineers can analyze the instructions executed by the CPU. Assembling code allows reverse engineers to examine the low-level details of the program, including its control flow, data manipulation, and interactions with system resources.

Key points about assemblers in reverse engineering:

- **Disassembly**: Assemblers are often used in reverse engineering tools (like Ghidra, IDA Pro, or Radare2) to convert machine code into assembly code, which can then be manually examined or further analyzed.
- **Instruction Mapping**: Each line of assembly code represents a single CPU instruction. By analyzing the sequence of instructions, reverse engineers can infer how the program functions, identify critical functions, and locate potential vulnerabilities.

- **Processor-Specific**: Assemblers are closely tied to the architecture they are designed for. For example, x86 and ARM architectures have different instruction sets, so an assembler must be tailored to the specific platform.

For example, if reverse engineers are analyzing a Windows executable file compiled for x86 architecture, an assembler would help transform the executable's machine code into x86 assembly code, making it more understandable.

Decompilers

A decompiler is a tool that translates machine code or assembly code back into higher-level programming languages, such as C or C++. Decompilation is a more complex process than disassembly because it tries to reconstruct the original source code (or an approximation of it) from the compiled binary. While an assembler merely translates the machine code into assembly language, a decompiler attempts to recreate the program's logic at a higher level, making it easier to understand the program's structure and flow.

Decompilers are essential for reverse engineers because they offer a higher-level view of a program's functionality. While disassembled code can show the raw instructions being executed, a decompiled version attempts to recover higher-level structures such as functions, loops, and conditionals, making the code more readable and easier to analyze.

Key points about decompilers in reverse engineering:

- **Restoring Logic**: Decompilers attempt to reconstruct higher-level programming constructs like variables, functions, and control flow structures that are abstracted away in the compiled binary.
- **C/C++ Source Approximation**: Many decompilers try to reformat the binary code into C or C++ code, which is familiar to most reverse engineers. While it may not be identical to the original source code, it provides a good approximation of the original logic.
- **Obfuscation Handling**: Some compilers use obfuscation techniques to make decompilation harder, such as inlining functions, renaming variables, or removing certain debug symbols. Advanced decompilers can handle some of these techniques, but there are limits to how much can be recovered.
- **Popular Decompilers**: Tools like Ghidra, Hex-Rays (IDA Pro's decompiler), and RetDec are popular in the reverse engineering community for decompiling programs.

Decompilers are invaluable for analyzing software when the source code is unavailable, as they allow reverse engineers to recover an understandable version of the program. However, the quality of decompilation may vary depending on the complexity of the code and the compiler used, and the result is often not as clear or usable as the original source code.

Debuggers

A debugger is a tool used to monitor and control the execution of a program. It allows reverse engineers to inspect the program while it is running, step through the code line by line, set breakpoints, and examine variables and memory. Debuggers provide deep insight into how a program behaves during execution, which is invaluable for understanding its runtime dynamics, identifying bugs, and uncovering vulnerabilities.

In reverse engineering, debuggers are essential for dynamic analysis, where the focus is on observing the behavior of the program as it interacts with the system and external resources. By using a debugger, a reverse engineer can watch the program in action, trace how data is manipulated, and track how it interacts with the operating system, hardware, or other software components.

Key points about debuggers in reverse engineering:

- **Breakpoint Management**: Debuggers allow users to set breakpoints at specific points in the code, stopping the execution of the program to examine the state of the system. This is useful for tracing the flow of execution or investigating specific conditions.
- **Step Execution**: Debuggers allow reverse engineers to step through a program one instruction at a time, observing how the code changes state with each step. This is critical for understanding how a program handles input, makes decisions, and processes data.
- **Memory Inspection**: Debuggers can inspect the program's memory space, providing a view of the data in use at any given time. This is particularly helpful for identifying buffer overflows, malicious data manipulation, or unauthorized memory access.
- **Handling Obfuscation and Anti-Debugging**: Some programs incorporate anti-debugging measures to prevent debugging or make it more difficult (e.g., checking for the presence of a debugger or detecting breakpoints). Skilled reverse engineers can often bypass these techniques with specialized tools and methods.
- **Popular Debuggers**: Tools like OllyDbg, x64dbg, GDB (GNU Debugger), and WinDbg are commonly used for dynamic analysis and debugging. They offer

features like live debugging, memory inspection, and disassembly, making them indispensable for reverse engineers.

Debuggers are a critical tool for reverse engineers working on vulnerability research, malware analysis, and understanding the behavior of complex software systems. They provide an interactive and real-time view of a program's execution, allowing engineers to investigate how the program operates, find bugs, or uncover malicious actions.

Summary of Key Concepts

To recap, assemblers, decompilers, and debuggers each play a vital role in reverse engineering:

- Assemblers are used to convert machine code into assembly language, which allows reverse engineers to inspect low-level instructions and gain insights into how a program operates at the CPU level.
- Decompilers attempt to convert compiled binaries back into high-level source code (like C or C++), providing reverse engineers with a more readable, structured version of the program, which is useful for understanding its logic and flow.
- Debuggers enable reverse engineers to observe a program while it runs, step through the code, and inspect its behavior, memory, and data in real time. Debuggers are invaluable for dynamic analysis and discovering runtime behaviors, such as vulnerabilities or exploits.

Together, these tools form the foundation of reverse engineering, providing multiple approaches to analyzing and understanding software. While disassemblers offer insight into the binary structure, decompilers help restore high-level logic, and debuggers allow for dynamic investigation during execution. Reverse engineers use these tools in combination to gain a deep understanding of programs, uncover vulnerabilities, and secure systems against threats.

1.5 Challenges and Limitations in Reverse Engineering

Reverse engineering, while a powerful tool in cybersecurity and software analysis, comes with a set of challenges and limitations that can complicate the process of understanding complex software and systems. These challenges can arise from the inherent complexity of modern software, as well as from technical, legal, and ethical considerations. In this section, we will explore the primary obstacles faced by reverse engineers, including technical difficulties, obfuscation techniques, legal concerns, and the limitations of reverse engineering tools themselves.

1.5.1 Technical Challenges

Reverse engineering involves a detailed examination of compiled binary code, which is far more difficult to understand than high-level source code. Some of the primary technical challenges in reverse engineering include:

Code Obfuscation:

Many software developers use code obfuscation techniques to make reverse engineering more difficult. Obfuscation involves altering the program's code in ways that make it harder to understand or analyze while preserving its functionality. This can include techniques like renaming variables and functions to meaningless strings, inserting dummy code, or using complex control flow structures. Such techniques can significantly increase the difficulty of reverse engineering, as the original logic of the program is intentionally obscured, making it harder to identify vulnerabilities or understand how the software works.

Additionally, some programs may use anti-reverse engineering techniques specifically designed to detect and prevent reverse engineering tools from functioning correctly, such as checking for debuggers or detecting breakpoints.

Complex Code Structures:

Modern software applications can be incredibly complex, with millions of lines of code, sophisticated algorithms, and interdependent modules. Reverse engineers must often deal with a large number of files and libraries, which may be compiled into various machine code formats depending on the operating system and architecture. This complexity can lead to significant analysis overhead, as it becomes time-consuming and error-prone to manually trace through vast amounts of code.

Additionally, modern software often relies on dynamic execution, multi-threading, and complex memory management techniques, making it even harder to reverse engineer and understand the program's runtime behavior. Tracking every function, loop, and call in large software applications can overwhelm even experienced reverse engineers.

Lack of Debugging Information:

In many cases, the binaries that reverse engineers work with are stripped of debug symbols and other metadata that can significantly aid in analysis. Debug symbols, which include information about function names, variable names, and source file locations, are often removed during the compilation process to reduce the size of the executable and protect intellectual property. Without this information, reverse engineers must rely on disassembly and decompilation techniques to infer the program's structure and behavior, which can be a slow and tedious process.

This lack of high-level information can make it difficult to understand the program's intended functionality or pinpoint specific areas of interest (e.g., security vulnerabilities).

Cross-Platform and Cross-Architecture Challenges:

Software can be written and compiled for a wide range of platforms and architectures, such as x86, ARM, or MIPS. Each architecture has its own set of instructions, registers, and memory layouts, which can make reverse engineering more challenging when dealing with software intended for multiple platforms. Tools like Ghidra and IDA Pro offer support for various architectures, but translating code from one architecture to another (e.g., from x86 to ARM) often requires significant expertise and experience.

Furthermore, modern software often relies on dynamic linking—where parts of the software are linked at runtime—complicating analysis. Reverse engineers need to consider not only the software itself but also its interactions with external libraries, drivers, and hardware components.

1.5.2 Obfuscation and Anti-Reverse Engineering Techniques

As reverse engineering has become more common, software developers and attackers have developed anti-reverse engineering and anti-debugging techniques to make it harder to analyze their code. These techniques are used both to protect proprietary software from being copied or modified and to prevent security researchers from identifying vulnerabilities.

Control Flow Obfuscation:

One common obfuscation technique involves altering the flow of control in the program. Instead of having a straightforward sequence of instructions, control flow obfuscation inserts jumps or branches that make it difficult to follow the execution path. This may involve the use of opaque predicates (conditions that always evaluate to true or false but are hard to predict) or unreachable code to confuse the reverse engineer.

Code Virtualization:

In code virtualization, the program is transformed into an intermediate language or a virtual machine bytecode. This bytecode is then interpreted by a custom virtual machine at runtime. This makes the program's execution harder to follow because the code is no longer directly executed by the CPU but rather interpreted by a layer of virtual code.

Packed and Encrypted Binaries:

Many applications use packers to compress or encrypt their binary files to make it harder for reverse engineers to examine the original code. A packed binary is one where the executable is compressed or encrypted and needs to be unpacked at runtime before the program can execute. Reverse engineers often need to use unpacking tools or reverse engineer the unpacking process itself to examine the original code.

Anti-Debugging and Anti-Analysis Techniques:

Many programs use techniques to detect whether they are being debugged or analyzed. These techniques can include checking for the presence of debugger-specific processes, monitoring for breakpoints, or checking whether certain registers or memory areas are altered. If the program detects a debugger, it might alter its behavior or even refuse to run altogether. Overcoming these techniques requires specialized knowledge and tools that can bypass or disable anti-debugging features.

1.5.3 Legal and Ethical Constraints

While technical challenges dominate the reverse engineering process, legal and ethical constraints can further limit what reverse engineers can and cannot do. For example, the Digital Millennium Copyright Act (DMCA) in the United States prohibits reverse engineering software for certain purposes, such as cracking software or circumventing copy protection. This presents a significant challenge, as reverse engineers may face legal action if they are found to have violated intellectual property laws, even if their work is aimed at improving security or learning.

Additionally, reverse engineers working with malware, proprietary software, or confidential information must exercise caution to avoid disclosing sensitive data or violating privacy regulations. Ethical guidelines around responsible disclosure—when security vulnerabilities are found in a program—must be adhered to, ensuring that vulnerabilities are reported to the software vendor first before being made public. Reverse engineers must also be careful to avoid using the knowledge gained from reverse engineering to create or distribute malicious software.

1.5.4 Limitations of Reverse Engineering Tools

Reverse engineering tools, while invaluable, have their own set of limitations. Even sophisticated tools like Ghidra, IDA Pro, and Radare2 can be limited in their ability to completely decompile or analyze complex software. Some of these limitations include:

Decompilation Accuracy:

Decompilers can generate a higher-level version of a program, but the decompiled output is often not perfect. It may miss certain control structures, variables, or logic, or introduce errors that are difficult to identify. In some cases, the decompiled code can be far from the original, making it hard to reconstruct the program's original structure or logic accurately.

Obfuscation Resistance:

Many reverse engineering tools struggle with advanced obfuscation techniques. While they may offer some support for detecting common forms of obfuscation, they often struggle with more sophisticated methods like code virtualization, advanced packing, or custom encryption algorithms. In these cases, reverse engineers may need to resort to manual analysis, which is time-consuming and error-prone.

Memory and Performance Limitations:

Working with large software systems or analyzing malware that requires a lot of memory and processing power can overwhelm the capabilities of reverse engineering tools. In particular, tools that analyze large binaries in real-time or perform dynamic analysis can consume significant system resources, slowing down the process and making the analysis more difficult.

Reverse engineering, while an indispensable technique for cybersecurity, software analysis, and vulnerability research, is not without its challenges. Technical hurdles like obfuscation, complex code structures, and the lack of debug symbols can make the analysis process incredibly difficult. Furthermore, the increasing use of anti-reverse engineering techniques by developers, along with the legal and ethical considerations involved, add layers of complexity to the practice. Despite these obstacles, reverse engineering remains a crucial skill in understanding and securing software, and with the right tools, techniques, and knowledge, reverse engineers can successfully navigate these challenges and make valuable contributions to the field of cybersecurity.

Chapter 2: Getting Started with Ghidra

Ghidra is a versatile and feature-rich reverse engineering toolkit, and in this chapter, you'll learn how to set it up and start using it effectively. We'll begin with a step-by-step guide to installing Ghidra on your system, followed by a walkthrough of creating and managing projects. You'll familiarize yourself with Ghidra's workspace, including its intuitive interface and essential tools, and learn how to import and organize binary files for analysis. With tips on customizing the interface and leveraging shortcuts for efficiency, this chapter ensures you have a strong foundation to confidently navigate Ghidra and prepare for deeper exploration in the chapters ahead.

2.1 Installation Guide for Different Operating Systems

Ghidra is a powerful, open-source reverse engineering platform developed by the National Security Agency (NSA). It provides a comprehensive suite of tools for analyzing binaries, decompiling code, debugging programs, and performing security research. Installing Ghidra correctly is essential for ensuring a smooth reverse engineering experience. In this section, we will walk through the installation process for Ghidra on various operating systems, including Windows, macOS, and Linux. Each operating system requires different steps, so let's explore the installation process for each.

2.1.1 Installing Ghidra on Windows

Windows is one of the most popular platforms for running Ghidra, and its installation process is straightforward. Follow these steps to install Ghidra on Windows:

Download the Ghidra Installer:

- Visit the official Ghidra website (https://ghidra-sre.org) and navigate to the Download section.
- Download the latest stable version of Ghidra (usually available as a .zip file).

Extract the Files:

- Once the .zip file is downloaded, locate it in your file system and extract it to a folder of your choice. Right-click the .zip file and select Extract All… or use a third-party tool like 7-Zip to extract the contents.

Ensure Java is Installed:

- Ghidra is written in Java and requires a Java Runtime Environment (JRE) to run. Before proceeding with the installation, make sure Java is installed on your system.
- To check if Java is installed, open a Command Prompt window (press Windows + R, type cmd, and hit Enter), then type java -version. If Java is not installed, you can download the latest version of the Java Development Kit (JDK) from Oracle's website or from AdoptOpenJDK.
- Ghidra typically works with Java 11 or later, but refer to the Ghidra documentation for the specific Java version required for your version of Ghidra.

Running Ghidra:

- In the folder where you extracted the Ghidra files, locate the ghidraRun.bat file and double-click it to start Ghidra.
- If you encounter any issues related to Java, you may need to manually set the JAVA_HOME environment variable or update the PATH variable to include the location of the Java installation. You can do this by:
- Right-clicking This PC > Properties > Advanced System Settings > Environment Variables.
- Add a new System Variable with the name JAVA_HOME and the path to your Java installation (e.g., C:\Program Files\Java\jdk-11.x.x).

Configuring Ghidra:

- The first time you launch Ghidra, it will prompt you to configure your user preferences. You can choose the directory for your project files and configure other settings, but the default settings are usually sufficient for most users.
- You may also want to review the system requirements and update the default memory allocation for Ghidra, particularly if you are working with large files.

Additional Steps (Optional):

- You can also add Ghidra to your system's PATH variable to launch it from the command line by adding the Ghidra folder to the environment path in System Properties.
- Optionally, you can create a shortcut for easier access to the ghidraRun.bat script.
- Once the installation is complete, Ghidra should be ready for use on your Windows system.

2.1.2 Installing Ghidra on macOS

Installing Ghidra on macOS is similar to the installation process on Windows but requires a few platform-specific steps. Follow these steps to install Ghidra on macOS:

Download the Ghidra Installer:

- Visit the official Ghidra website (https://ghidra-sre.org) and download the latest .zip file for macOS.

Extract the Files:

- Once the .zip file is downloaded, locate it in your Downloads folder and double-click it to extract the files. A new folder will be created with the name "ghidra" or a similar variation, depending on the version.

Ensure Java is Installed:

- Ghidra requires Java 11 or later to run. macOS often comes with Java pre-installed, but it may not be the version required by Ghidra.
- To check your Java version, open the Terminal and run java -version. If you don't have the required version, you can install the JDK via Homebrew or download it from AdoptOpenJDK.

To install Java via Homebrew, run the following command in Terminal:

brew install openjdk@11

After installation, set the correct version by adding the following lines to your .bash_profile or .zshrc:

export JAVA_HOME=/usr/local/opt/openjdk@11
export PATH=$JAVA_HOME/bin:$PATH

Reload the profile by running:

source ~/.bash_profile # or source ~/.zshrc if using zsh

Running Ghidra:

- Navigate to the folder where Ghidra was extracted.
- Open Terminal in that folder (you can right-click inside the folder and choose New Terminal at Folder or use the cd command to navigate to the folder).

Execute the following command to start Ghidra:

./ghidraRun

Configuring Ghidra:

- Upon first launch, Ghidra will ask for a user preferences configuration. You can configure the installation path and project directory settings as desired.
- Make sure to review the memory allocation settings if you plan to work with large files.

Additional Steps (Optional):

To launch Ghidra more easily, you can create an alias in your shell configuration file by adding the following to your .bash_profile or .zshrc:

alias ghidra='/path/to/ghidra/ghidraRun'

Reload the shell configuration using source ~/.bash_profile (or source ~/.zshrc), and you can now launch Ghidra by typing ghidra in Terminal.

Once these steps are completed, Ghidra should be successfully installed on macOS.

2.1.3 Installing Ghidra on Linux

Installing Ghidra on Linux involves a similar process to the other operating systems but may require additional dependencies depending on your distribution. Follow these steps to install Ghidra on Linux:

Download the Ghidra Installer:

Go to the official Ghidra website (https://ghidra-sre.org) and download the .zip file for Linux.

Extract the Files:

After downloading the .zip file, navigate to the folder where it was downloaded and extract it using the following command in the Terminal:

unzip ghidra_*.zip

This will create a folder with the Ghidra installation files.

Ensure Java is Installed:

Ghidra requires Java 11 or later. To check if Java is installed, run the following command:

java -version

If Java is not installed or the version is incorrect, you can install it using your package manager. For Ubuntu, for example, run:

sudo apt install openjdk-11-jdk

Running Ghidra:

In the Terminal, navigate to the extracted Ghidra folder and run:

./ghidraRun

Configuring Ghidra:

- On the first run, Ghidra will ask you to configure the default directories for projects and other settings. These can be left as default or customized.
- Adjust memory settings as needed based on the size of the files you plan to analyze.

Additional Steps (Optional):

To simplify the launch of Ghidra, you can create an alias in your shell profile by adding the following to ~/.bashrc or ~/.zshrc:

alias ghidra='/path/to/ghidra/ghidraRun'

After editing the profile, reload it using:

source ~/.bashrc # or source ~/.zshrc

Ghidra should now be installed and ready to run on your Linux system.

Ghidra is a versatile reverse engineering tool that can be installed on Windows, macOS, and Linux systems. While the installation process is relatively straightforward, each operating system has its specific steps, such as ensuring the correct version of Java is installed and handling platform-specific dependencies. By following the appropriate steps for your system, you will be able to successfully install Ghidra and begin using it for reverse engineering tasks.

2.2 Setting Up Your First Project in Ghidra

Ghidra provides a robust environment for reverse engineering tasks, offering tools for disassembling, decompiling, and analyzing binaries. One of the first steps in working with Ghidra is setting up a project, which serves as the foundation for all your analysis activities. A project in Ghidra is where you store all the files related to a specific reverse engineering task, including binaries, analysis results, and scripts.

This section will walk you through the process of creating your first project in Ghidra, configuring it, and importing a binary for analysis.

2.2.1 Launching Ghidra

Start Ghidra:

- Launch Ghidra by running the ghidraRun script (or the ghidraRun.bat file on Windows) that was included when you installed Ghidra.
- When you open Ghidra, you will be presented with the Ghidra Project Window. This is where you can create new projects or open existing ones.

Selecting or Creating a Project:

- In the Ghidra Project Window, you will see options to Create a New Project or Open an Existing Project.
- If you're starting from scratch, click on the New Project button to begin.

2.2.2 Creating a New Project

Choosing Project Type:

- Ghidra offers two types of projects: Non-Shared Projects and Shared Projects.
- **Non-Shared Projects**: These are local to your machine and are stored in a single folder. This is the most common project type for individual users.
- **Shared Projects**: These are designed for collaborative work and store project data in a database that can be accessed by multiple users. For now, we'll focus on Non-Shared Projects.

Naming Your Project:

- Enter a Project Name in the appropriate field. This could be something descriptive like "MyFirstProject" or "MalwareAnalysis".
- Choose a location on your filesystem where the project files will be stored. Ghidra will create a new folder in this directory to hold all project-related data.

Creating the Project:

Once you've named your project and selected a location, click OK. Ghidra will create the new project and open it in the Ghidra Project Window.

2.2.3 Importing Your First Binary

With the project created, it's time to import a binary for analysis. Ghidra supports a variety of binary formats, including ELF, PE, Mach-O, and raw binaries.

Importing the Binary:

- To begin importing a binary, click on File > Import File from the top menu.
- Navigate to the binary file you want to analyze (for example, a compiled executable like program.exe, sample.bin, or myfile.elf).
- Select the file and click Open.

Setting Import Options:

- Ghidra will display a dialog showing the selected file and providing options to adjust the import settings.
- For most standard file types (like Windows executables, Linux ELF binaries, or macOS Mach-O files), Ghidra will automatically detect the format and provide appropriate settings.

- You may be asked to select the processor architecture (e.g., x86, ARM) or other details, depending on the binary format.
- Once the options are set, click OK to continue.

Analyzing the Binary:

- After the binary is imported, Ghidra will ask you whether to analyze the file immediately.
- Automatic Analysis is typically recommended as it helps Ghidra identify functions, strings, and other key elements in the binary. You can choose to Analyze the binary now or adjust the analysis settings if you want to control what gets analyzed.

Choosing Analysis Options:

- Ghidra will present a dialog with analysis options. You can choose whether to analyze code and data, identify functions, recognize references, or enable other analysis tasks. For your first project, the default options are usually sufficient.
- Click OK to begin the analysis.

2.2.4 Navigating the Project

Once the binary has been successfully imported and analyzed, Ghidra will display its contents in the Code Browser window. This is the primary interface for exploring and interacting with your project. The Code Browser includes several key components:

Code Browser Window:

- This is where most of your analysis work will take place. It contains the Listing Window (disassembled code), Decompiler Window (higher-level C-like representation), and other useful views like Symbol Tree, Function Graph, and Memory Map.
- The Listing Window will show the disassembled binary code, where each instruction corresponds to a byte in the original binary file. You can click on various lines of code to examine specific sections in more detail.

Symbol Tree:

This window provides an overview of all the symbols (functions, variables, labels, etc.) in the program. It helps you quickly locate specific functions or areas of interest.

Decompiler Window:

This window displays a decompiled version of the binary's code, which is often much easier to read than raw assembly. This can be invaluable for understanding the logic of the program.

Function Graph:

Ghidra can generate a function graph to visualize the flow of control between functions in a binary. This tool is useful for understanding how different functions interact with one another.

2.2.5 Project Organization and Management

With your first binary loaded into Ghidra, it's important to keep your project well-organized. As your analysis progresses, you might want to add notes, create bookmarks, or define custom functions and labels.

Adding Comments and Labels:

- You can annotate the disassembled code by adding comments or changing labels. Right-click a location in the Listing Window and select Add Comment or Rename to add descriptions and make the code easier to understand.
- You can also rename functions and variables to provide more meaningful names.

Creating Bookmarks:

To mark important areas of interest, you can add bookmarks in the code. This allows you to quickly return to certain locations during analysis.

Exporting Data:

If you want to save specific analysis results or data from the project, you can export your findings into formats like XML, CSV, or HTML. You can do this by going to File > Export and selecting your desired format.

2.2.6 Saving and Managing Your Project

After you've set up your project and performed some analysis, be sure to save your work regularly. Ghidra stores your project data in the .ghidra folder, which contains all your analysis results, scripts, and configuration settings.

Saving Your Project:

- Ghidra automatically saves your work as you go, but you can manually save your project at any time by selecting File > Save Project from the top menu.
- It's important to periodically back up your project files, especially if you're working with large or complex binaries.

Closing Your Project:

- Once you're done working for the session, you can close the project by going to File > Close Project. If you have unsaved changes, Ghidra will prompt you to save before closing.

By following these steps, you've successfully set up your first project in Ghidra and imported a binary for analysis. You're now ready to dive into more complex tasks, such as identifying vulnerabilities, reverse engineering malware, or understanding proprietary software. Ghidra provides a powerful and flexible environment for reverse engineering, and setting up projects properly is the first step in utilizing this tool to its full potential. As you continue using Ghidra, you'll become more familiar with its various features and gain deeper insights into the software you're analyzing.

2.3 Overview of the Ghidra Workspace

Ghidra is a comprehensive reverse engineering tool that offers a wide array of features designed to facilitate the analysis of binaries, disassembly, decompilation, debugging, and more. Once you have set up a project and imported a binary for analysis, understanding the Ghidra Workspace is critical for navigating and utilizing the platform effectively. The workspace is where all your analysis takes place, and it consists of various windows and components designed to give you a detailed and organized view of your target binary. In this section, we will walk you through the key elements of the Ghidra workspace, so you can make the most out of the tool's features.

2.3.1 The Ghidra User Interface

When you open a project in Ghidra and load a binary for analysis, the Ghidra User Interface (UI) will present multiple windows and panels that allow you to interact with the binary in various ways. The workspace can be customized to suit your preferences, and it provides you with the tools to explore different aspects of the binary, such as the disassembly, functions, data, and more.

The main components of the Ghidra workspace include:

Code Browser Window

This is the central interface for interacting with the binary in Ghidra. The Code Browser window is the primary tool for viewing and analyzing your binary. It contains several sub-panels, including:

- **Listing Window**: Displays the disassembled code, showing assembly instructions, memory addresses, and other important details about the binary. This is where you will spend much of your time interacting with the code.
- **Decompiler Window**: Shows a higher-level, more readable representation of the code, written in a C-like syntax. This helps to understand the logic of the program without manually analyzing raw assembly.
- **Symbol Tree**: A panel that shows the functions, variables, labels, and other symbols in the binary. This helps you quickly navigate to specific areas of the binary, such as functions or global variables.
- **Function Graph**: A graphical representation of function calls, showing how functions interact with each other. This is particularly helpful for understanding the flow of execution in the binary.

Program Tree

The Program Tree is located in the Symbol Tree panel and provides an organized hierarchy of the components in your program. It contains nodes for functions, variables, strings, and more. This makes it easy to locate specific items and explore their relationships. For example, you can click on a function name to navigate to its implementation in the Listing or Decompiler Window.

Listing Window

The Listing Window is the main area where you can see the assembly code of the binary. The code is displayed in a linear fashion, with each line corresponding to a specific instruction in the binary. The Listing Window provides multiple views, including:

- **Disassembly**: The raw assembly code of the binary.
- **Hex View**: Displays the raw bytes of the binary in hexadecimal format.
- **Function View**: Focuses on the functions defined in the binary and shows the related assembly code.

You can interact with the code by adding comments, renaming functions, or creating bookmarks to mark important sections of the code.

Decompiler Window

- The Decompiler Window provides a higher-level view of the binary, converting the assembly instructions into a readable C-like representation. This allows you to understand the program's logic without having to work with raw assembly.
- The decompiler does not always produce perfect results, but it can be a valuable tool for getting a general understanding of how functions behave. The decompiler window is especially useful when analyzing more complex binaries and understanding their high-level operations.

Memory Map

The Memory Map is another important part of the workspace, showing the layout of memory in the binary. This map helps you understand how different sections of the binary are arranged in memory (e.g., text segment, data segment, etc.). The memory map is useful for locating specific sections, such as code, data, and variables.

2.3.2 Additional Workspace Components

Beyond the core panels, Ghidra provides several other components that enhance your reverse engineering experience:

Toolbars and Menus

- At the top of the Ghidra workspace, you will find toolbars and menus that provide quick access to various functions, such as project management, analysis controls, and script execution. The toolbar typically contains icons for common tasks, such as saving your project, opening files, or running analysis.
- The Menus include options for detailed control over analysis, viewing, and manipulating the data in the workspace. The menus are organized into categories like File, Edit, Search, Window, and Help.

Search Functionality

The Search functionality in Ghidra allows you to find specific items, such as functions, strings, or addresses, within the binary. You can use the search to quickly locate known symbols, references, or instructions. The search panel can be customized to search for specific types of data or symbols.

Navigation Tools

Ghidra's Navigation Tools are helpful for moving around large binaries. You can use the Go To feature to jump directly to specific addresses, functions, or data. This is useful when analyzing large files with many functions or sections.

Bookmarks and Comments

To keep track of important areas within the binary, Ghidra allows you to add bookmarks and comments. Bookmarks are used to mark specific locations in the code that are of interest, while comments allow you to annotate specific lines of code or sections in the Listing and Decompiler Windows. This is especially useful for documenting your analysis and findings.

Log and Console Window

The Log Window keeps track of the activities performed within Ghidra, such as analysis tasks, errors, or warnings. The Console Window provides a space to execute and view the output of scripts, making it useful for automation and testing custom functionality.

2.3.3 Customizing the Workspace Layout

Ghidra's workspace is highly customizable, allowing you to modify the layout of the panels and windows to suit your workflow. You can:

Dock and Undock Panels

Ghidra supports docking and undocking of various panels. For example, you can dock the Listing Window to the left side of the screen and the Decompiler Window to the right, or you can choose to undock them into separate windows for a more flexible layout.

Resizing Panels

Panels within the workspace are resizable, meaning you can adjust the size of the Code Browser, Symbol Tree, Decompiler, and other components to give you more space for the sections that are most important for your analysis.

Changing Panel Views

Within each window, Ghidra allows you to toggle between different views. For example, the Listing Window can display assembly instructions, hexadecimal values, or function signatures. You can adjust these views based on your analysis needs.

Saving Workspace Layout

Once you've customized your workspace layout, Ghidra allows you to save the arrangement so that you can load it again the next time you work on your project. This ensures that you maintain a consistent working environment for long-term analysis.

2.3.4 Workspace Shortcuts and Productivity Tips

To enhance productivity, Ghidra offers a variety of keyboard shortcuts and tips that can speed up your analysis process:

Keyboard Shortcuts

Learn common keyboard shortcuts to navigate Ghidra more efficiently. For example, you can use Ctrl+F to open the search dialog, Ctrl+G to go to a specific address, and Ctrl+E to jump to the decompiler.

Automation with Scripts

The Script Manager allows you to write and run scripts to automate common tasks. Ghidra supports scripts written in Java, Python, and JavaScript, and the Script Manager makes it easy to organize and execute these scripts directly from the workspace.

The Ghidra Workspace is the heart of the platform, providing a customizable and efficient environment for reverse engineering. Understanding the layout and components of the workspace is essential for using Ghidra effectively, as it allows you to analyze binaries in a well-organized and systematic manner. By familiarizing yourself with the different windows, panels, and tools available in the workspace, you can streamline your reverse engineering process and maximize your productivity. As you become more comfortable with Ghidra, you'll find that the workspace offers a powerful suite of features to handle even the most complex reverse engineering tasks.

2.4 Importing and Managing Files in the Project Tree

In Ghidra, the Project Tree plays a central role in organizing and managing the files and assets you use for reverse engineering. This tree structure is designed to help you maintain an orderly workspace, making it easier to access, manage, and manipulate the files and projects associated with your analysis. Importing and managing files in the Project Tree is essential for keeping your analysis organized and ensuring that all related files (such as binaries, scripts, and documentation) are easily accessible.

This section will guide you through the process of importing files into the Project Tree, as well as how to manage and organize them effectively throughout your analysis.

2.4.1 The Project Tree Overview

The Project Tree is a panel within the Ghidra workspace that provides a hierarchical view of all files and resources associated with your project. This includes:

- **Binaries**: The main files you import for analysis, typically executable files like .exe, .bin, .elf, or .out.
- **Scripts**: Custom scripts used to automate tasks or extend Ghidra's functionality, written in languages like Java, Python, or JavaScript.
- **Saved Analysis Data**: This includes annotations, comments, renamed functions, bookmarks, and other analysis results.
- **Project Files**: These include the project configuration, settings, and any other files you choose to include in your project for reference.

The Project Tree allows you to easily navigate between different elements and perform operations like importing new files, organizing existing files, or deleting files that are no longer needed.

2.4.2 Importing Files into the Project Tree

When you begin a reverse engineering project in Ghidra, you'll typically import a binary file (or multiple files) to start the analysis. Here's how you import files into the Project Tree:

Open the Project:

Launch Ghidra and open the project where you want to import the files. If you have not yet created a project, follow the steps in 2.2 Setting Up Your First Project in Ghidra.

Accessing the Import Function:

- To import a file into the project, go to the File menu at the top of the Ghidra workspace and select Import File.
- Alternatively, you can right-click within the Project Tree panel and select Import File from the context menu.

Selecting the File to Import:

- A file dialog will open, allowing you to navigate to the file you want to import. This can be a binary, a script, or any other file relevant to your project.
- Select the file and click Open. If you're importing a binary, Ghidra will automatically recognize the file type (such as .exe, .elf, .bin, etc.) and apply the appropriate analysis configuration.

Import Settings:

- Ghidra will often prompt you to confirm certain settings when importing a file. For example, if you're importing a binary, it might ask you to select the processor architecture (e.g., x86, ARM) or set options for how the binary should be analyzed.
- After confirming these settings, click OK to complete the import. The file will now appear in the Project Tree under the File System node.

Adding Other Files:

- You can import additional files as needed, such as custom scripts or related documentation. Just repeat the import process for each file.
- Scripts are particularly useful if you plan to automate specific tasks within Ghidra, and they will be stored alongside your binaries in the Project Tree.

2.4.3 Managing Files in the Project Tree

Once files have been imported into the Project Tree, it's essential to organize them effectively so you can easily access and manage your data as your project progresses. Ghidra offers several tools for managing files in the tree:

Renaming Files:

- You can rename any file in the Project Tree to make it more descriptive or to reflect its role in the project. For example, if you imported multiple versions of a binary, you could rename them to clearly distinguish between the versions.
- To rename a file, right-click on it in the Project Tree and select Rename. Enter the new name and press Enter to save the changes.

Organizing Files into Folders:

- To keep your project well-organized, you can create custom folders within the Project Tree. For example, you might want to group all binary files in one folder and all scripts in another.
- To create a folder, right-click on the Project Tree and select New Folder. Enter a name for the folder, and then drag and drop files into it.
- You can also create subfolders within folders, allowing you to organize files in a hierarchical structure. This is especially useful when working on complex projects with many different assets.

Viewing and Opening Files:

- Double-click on any file in the Project Tree to open it for analysis. For example, double-clicking on a binary will open the Code Browser where you can begin disassembling and decompiling the file.
- If you import a script, you can double-click it to open it in the Script Manager, where you can edit, run, or debug the script.

Deleting Files:

- If you no longer need a file in your project, you can delete it from the Project Tree. Right-click on the file and select Delete. Keep in mind that this will only remove the file from the project, not from your file system (unless you select the option to delete the file permanently).
- Deleting unnecessary files helps keep your project organized and avoids clutter, especially if you're working with multiple large binaries or scripts.

2.4.4 Managing Binary Analysis Data

Once you have imported a binary file into the project and started analyzing it, Ghidra generates a range of analysis data that you may need to manage throughout the process.

This can include functions, labels, comments, and other data that you generate during your analysis. Here's how to manage this data:

Function Names and Labels:

- As you analyze the binary, you may want to rename functions or variables to make them more meaningful. For example, a function identified as sub_401000 might be renamed to process_data.
- You can also create labels for specific memory addresses or code locations, which will appear in the Listing Window and help you navigate the code more easily.

Comments and Bookmarks:

- As you make progress in your analysis, you can add comments to the code to explain what you've found or to document your analysis steps. Comments are stored as part of the project and will be accessible every time you open the project.
- Additionally, you can create bookmarks to mark specific locations or areas of interest within the binary. Bookmarks are helpful when you need to quickly return to a particular section.

Exporting Analysis Data:

- Ghidra allows you to export analysis data, such as function definitions, comments, or disassembled code, into various formats (e.g., XML, CSV, HTML). This can be useful for documentation or sharing your findings with others.
- To export data, go to File > Export and choose the appropriate format and settings for your export.

2.4.5 Best Practices for Managing Files in Ghidra Projects

Here are a few best practices for managing files and data in the Project Tree:

- **Regularly Save and Back Up**: Always save your work frequently and back up your project data to ensure that you don't lose any critical information during the analysis process.
- **Use Descriptive Names**: Use clear and descriptive names for your files and folders in the Project Tree. This will help you stay organized, especially when working with multiple binaries or projects.

- **Group Related Files Together**: Organize files into folders based on their type or purpose. For example, keep all related scripts in a separate folder, and group different binary files by their versions or platforms.
- **Delete Unnecessary Files**: As your analysis progresses, remove files that are no longer needed. This helps to reduce clutter in your project and makes it easier to focus on the important data.

The Project Tree in Ghidra is an essential part of the platform that helps you organize and manage all the files and assets associated with your reverse engineering project. By understanding how to import, manage, and organize files effectively, you can streamline your workflow, improve productivity, and keep your project structured. Whether you're working with multiple binaries, scripts, or analysis data, the Project Tree provides the tools you need to maintain an efficient and organized environment for your reverse engineering tasks.

2.5 Keyboard Shortcuts and Customizing Your Workflow

Ghidra, being a powerful reverse engineering tool, provides a wealth of features designed to streamline the analysis process. One of the most effective ways to enhance productivity and efficiency while using Ghidra is through mastering keyboard shortcuts and customizing your workflow. These shortcuts allow you to navigate quickly, execute commands with minimal effort, and tailor the interface to suit your needs. In this section, we will explore how to leverage keyboard shortcuts and customize your workflow to make the most out of Ghidra.

2.5.1 Keyboard Shortcuts in Ghidra

Ghidra supports a wide range of keyboard shortcuts that allow you to perform common tasks quickly without needing to navigate through menus. These shortcuts are designed to save you time and make your reverse engineering tasks more efficient. Below are some of the essential shortcuts and how they can improve your workflow:

General Navigation Shortcuts:

- **Ctrl + N**: Open a new project.
- **Ctrl + O**: Open an existing project.
- **Ctrl + S**: Save the current project.
- **Ctrl + W**: Close the currently active window.

- **Ctrl + F:** Open the search dialog for finding functions, symbols, or other items in the project.
- **Ctrl + G**: Go to a specific address or function in the disassembly or decompiled view.
- **Ctrl + E:** Open the decompiler view.
- **Ctrl + L**: Toggle between the Listing and Decompiler views for quick analysis.

These general navigation shortcuts help you move efficiently between different views and tasks within Ghidra, without wasting time on manual navigation.

Disassembly and Listing Window Shortcuts:

- **Space**: Toggle between disassembly and graph view.
- **Ctrl + L**: Toggle between Listing View and Decompiler View (useful for quick context switching).
- **F3**: Go to the next function in the disassembly.
- **Shift + F3**: Go to the previous function in the disassembly.
- **Ctrl + Shift + F**: Find a function in the Listing Window.
- **Ctrl + B**: Toggle the Bookmark for the current line in the Listing Window (helpful for tracking important sections of code).

These shortcuts allow you to move between functions, navigate the disassembly, and quickly find code locations while you are analyzing the binary. They can drastically reduce the time spent in finding the relevant code and improving your workflow.

Decompiler Shortcuts:

- **Ctrl + D:** Open the Decompiler window.
- **Ctrl + Shift + D:** Update the decompiler view with any changes in the disassembly or analysis.
- **Ctrl + Shift + G:** Go to the decompiled function corresponding to the current location in the Listing Window.
- **Ctrl + Shift + E:** Refresh the Decompiler window with the latest data from the Listing Window.

The Decompiler is often central to understanding the high-level logic of a program. These shortcuts allow you to seamlessly sync between the Listing and Decompiler views, ensuring that you can rapidly identify the structure and behavior of the binary.

Searching and Navigation Shortcuts:

- **Ctrl + F:** Open the search dialog to search for a string, function, or symbol in the current binary.
- **Ctrl + Shift + F:** Search within the Listing Window for specific patterns, instructions, or functions.
- **Alt + G:** Go to a specified address or label directly.
- **Ctrl + H:** View the symbol tree (functions, variables, etc.) for quick navigation to specific parts of the binary.
- **Ctrl + M**: Open the memory map for quick access to the layout of different segments of memory.

These search and navigation shortcuts are essential for efficiently moving through large binaries and locating specific items like functions, variables, or strings. When dealing with large datasets, these shortcuts are crucial for rapidly zooming in on points of interest.

2.5.2 Customizing Your Workflow in Ghidra

In addition to using keyboard shortcuts, Ghidra also allows you to customize your workflow by adjusting the layout, using advanced scripting options, and setting up personalized hotkeys. Here are some ways to make Ghidra work better for your needs:

Customizing the Layout:

- Ghidra's workspace is highly customizable, enabling you to adjust the layout of panels and windows. You can undock, resize, or rearrange various windows, such as the Listing Window, Decompiler Window, and Symbol Tree, to create a layout that suits your workflow. For example, you can dock the Code Browser on one side and the Decompiler on the other side to view both disassembled and decompiled views simultaneously.
- You can also save your customized layout by going to Window > Save Window Layout. This allows you to reopen your project in the same layout every time, ensuring a consistent workspace for your analysis.

Using Scripting to Automate Tasks:

- Ghidra supports scripting in languages like Java, Python, and JavaScript. You can write custom scripts to automate repetitive tasks or extend Ghidra's functionality. For example, you could write a script to automate the renaming of functions, perform custom analyses, or even automate the extraction of certain data from a binary.

- Scripts are easy to integrate into your workflow, and Ghidra's Script Manager provides a simple interface for writing, running, and managing scripts. You can even assign specific scripts to keyboard shortcuts for quick execution.

Configuring Custom Hotkeys:

- For power users, Ghidra allows you to configure custom keyboard shortcuts for commands and actions that are most important to you. This is especially useful when you find yourself repeatedly using certain commands that are not included in the default shortcut set.
- To configure custom hotkeys, go to Edit > Tool Options, then navigate to the Key Bindings section. Here you can assign your own shortcuts to actions that might not have default bindings or for functions that you frequently use. For example, you could assign a hotkey for a script you run regularly or a common disassembly command.

Saving and Sharing Workflows:

- If you have developed a particular workflow that you find effective for specific types of analysis (e.g., malware analysis or firmware reverse engineering), you can save it as a template and use it across multiple projects. This might include a customized layout, commonly used scripts, and preconfigured analysis options.
- You can also export your custom layouts, scripts, and preferences and share them with teammates or colleagues. This ensures that everyone is working with the same setup, which can be crucial for collaborative projects.

Using the Command Palette:

Ghidra has a Command Palette that provides quick access to a range of commands and functions, even if they aren't mapped to a specific keyboard shortcut. You can bring up the Command Palette by pressing Ctrl + Shift + P and typing the command you need. This feature is useful when you're unsure of the exact location of a function or when you want to avoid navigating through menus.

2.5.3 Best Practices for Customizing Your Workflow

To maximize productivity when using Ghidra, it's essential to tailor the software to your specific needs. Here are some best practices to consider when customizing your workflow:

Prioritize Frequently Used Features:

Identify the tasks or features you use most frequently and assign keyboard shortcuts for those actions. This will minimize the time spent searching through menus and help you stay focused on the analysis itself.

Streamline Your Layout:

Create a layout that allows you to view the disassembly, decompiler, and symbol tree simultaneously without overwhelming your screen. This ensures that you can quickly jump between different views without losing context.

Leverage Scripting for Repetitive Tasks:

Automate repetitive tasks, such as renaming functions, analyzing specific patterns, or extracting specific data, with custom scripts. Writing reusable scripts can save significant time and effort, especially for tasks you perform frequently across different projects.

Document and Share Your Workflow:

Once you've developed an optimized workflow, document it and share it with colleagues. This can help improve the consistency and quality of analysis, especially in team environments.

Customize Shortcuts for Long-Term Use:

Once you've customized the keyboard shortcuts to your liking, make a habit of sticking to them. The more consistent you are with your shortcuts, the faster you will become at navigating Ghidra.

Mastering keyboard shortcuts and customizing your workflow are crucial steps in maximizing productivity and efficiency when using Ghidra. By understanding the default keyboard shortcuts and setting up your environment to suit your needs, you can drastically reduce the time spent navigating and increase your focus on the analysis itself. Customizing the layout, using scripts for automation, and creating a personalized set of hotkeys will make Ghidra a more powerful tool in your reverse engineering toolkit. With the right setup, Ghidra can be adapted to fit your specific reverse engineering tasks, allowing you to work smarter and faster.

Chapter 3: Key Features and Tools in Ghidra

In this chapter, we dive into the powerful tools and features that make Ghidra an indispensable resource for reverse engineers. You'll get an in-depth look at CodeBrowser, the core interface that allows you to view and analyze disassembled code. We'll explore other key components of Ghidra's tool suite, such as the Decompiler for high-level code analysis, the Debugger for dynamic analysis, and the Function and Data Graphs for visualizing code flow. You'll also discover how to use Ghidra's collaborative features for working on multi-user projects, and how to customize Ghidra to suit your specific workflow. By the end of this chapter, you'll be comfortable with Ghidra's most important tools and ready to dive deeper into its analysis capabilities.

3.1 Ghidra's CodeBrowser Overview

Ghidra's CodeBrowser is one of the most powerful and essential components of the platform. It serves as the primary interface for analyzing and navigating the disassembled code, as well as examining the decompiled output of binary files. Whether you're working with executables, libraries, or firmware images, the CodeBrowser allows you to interact with the underlying assembly or high-level code in a way that is intuitive and efficient.

In this section, we will provide an overview of the CodeBrowser, explaining its key features, user interface, and how it helps streamline the reverse engineering process. By understanding the layout and functionality of this tool, you can begin to leverage it effectively for your analysis.

3.1.1 Introduction to CodeBrowser

The CodeBrowser in Ghidra is designed to provide a unified view of the binary being analyzed. It displays the disassembled code (assembly language) and optionally shows the decompiled code in a separate window, making it easier to understand the functionality of a program at both the low and high levels. The CodeBrowser allows you to:

- **Explore the disassembled code**: View the assembly instructions of the binary to understand its low-level operations.
- **View the decompiled code**: Automatically translated high-level code (usually C-like) that is easier to read than raw assembly.

- **Navigate functions and data**: Navigate easily through functions, variables, and memory addresses.
- **Inspect control flow**: Visualize the flow of execution through the program with features like the control flow graph (CFG).
- **Annotate and document findings**: Add comments and labels to the code to document your analysis and findings.

The CodeBrowser is essential for conducting static analysis and reverse engineering, enabling you to disassemble, annotate, and understand the program's structure in a detailed and organized way.

3.1.2 CodeBrowser Interface Layout

The CodeBrowser is divided into several key panels and views, each offering a specific function to aid in the analysis of a binary. Understanding how these panels interact will significantly improve your productivity when using Ghidra.

Listing Window:

- The Listing Window is where you'll see the disassembled code. This window displays the raw assembly instructions for the binary, showing the address, machine code, and corresponding assembly instruction for each line of code.
- You can navigate through the Listing Window by scrolling or searching for specific functions, addresses, or labels. Each line of code is accompanied by its address and can be annotated for better understanding.

Decompiler Window:

- The Decompiler Window is an optional but highly useful window that displays the high-level C-like code corresponding to the assembly instructions. It helps you see the logic behind the disassembled code in a more understandable format.
- The decompiled code is generated dynamically based on the analysis, and it's especially useful when you're trying to understand the program's logic or reverse engineer complex algorithms.
- You can switch between the Listing and Decompiler views at any time, making it easy to compare low-level and high-level representations of the code side by side.

Symbol Tree:

- The Symbol Tree provides a structured overview of all the symbols (such as functions, variables, and data structures) in the binary. It allows you to easily locate functions, global variables, and other important data elements.
- By expanding nodes within the Symbol Tree, you can quickly jump to relevant functions or variables in the Listing Window or Decompiler View.

Function Graph:

- The Function Graph is a visual representation of the control flow within a function. It helps you visualize the relationships between different blocks of code within the function and understand the flow of execution.
- This view is especially useful when dealing with complex functions or code that has numerous branches, loops, or conditional statements.

Memory Map:

- The Memory Map shows the memory layout of the binary, including the location of different segments (code, data, heap, stack, etc.) and provides a visual representation of how the binary is structured in memory.
- The Memory Map helps you understand where different parts of the program reside in memory and allows for easy navigation between memory segments.

3.1.3 Key Features of CodeBrowser

The CodeBrowser provides a wealth of features that enhance the reverse engineering experience. Here are some of the key features that you should be familiar with:

Disassembly View:

- The Listing Window allows you to see the disassembly of a binary. Ghidra's disassembler automatically analyzes the binary, translates machine code instructions into human-readable assembly, and presents them in a navigable format.
- You can interact with the disassembly by right-clicking on instructions to rename functions, variables, or even entire blocks of code. This helps improve the clarity of your analysis, as you can annotate important code locations with meaningful names.

Decompiler View:

- The Decompiler View provides a high-level view of the binary's functionality in a C-like language. It allows you to see the program's logic without needing to interpret assembly manually.
- The decompiler works by attempting to reverse the assembly back into C code. While the output is not always perfect, it provides a much clearer view of the program's structure and flow than raw assembly.

Function and Data Navigation:

- The CodeBrowser makes it easy to navigate through functions, variables, and data structures in a binary. You can access functions from the Function Tree in the Symbol Tree and jump directly to their disassembly or decompiled code.
- Ghidra also offers a search functionality that enables you to locate specific symbols, functions, or addresses quickly.

Control Flow Graph (CFG):

- Ghidra can generate a Control Flow Graph (CFG), which visually represents the flow of execution in a function. The graph helps you identify the paths the program might take, making it easier to understand complex functions or reverse engineer code.
- The CFG can also help identify unreachable code, loops, and branches, which are important when determining the functionality of a binary.

Code Comments and Annotations:

- As you analyze the code, you can add comments and annotations to document your findings or provide context for your analysis. Comments can be added at any instruction, function, or data location and are saved with the project.
- Annotations can help you keep track of insights such as identified bugs, vulnerabilities, or areas that need further analysis.

3.1.4 Navigating CodeBrowser Efficiently

Navigating the CodeBrowser efficiently is key to speeding up your reverse engineering process. Here are some tips to help you navigate quickly and effectively:

Use the Go To Functionality:

Ghidra's Go To feature allows you to quickly navigate to specific functions, addresses, or labels in the Listing Window or Decompiler View. You can invoke the Go To functionality by pressing Ctrl + G and entering the address or symbol name you want to jump to.

Use the Symbol Tree for Quick Access:

The Symbol Tree provides an organized view of all the functions, variables, and symbols in the binary. Expanding nodes in the Symbol Tree lets you quickly locate functions or variables and jump directly to their location in the code.

Bookmark Important Locations:

If you encounter important sections of code during your analysis, you can use bookmarks to mark them for easy reference later. Bookmarks are persistent across sessions and can be used to quickly jump back to areas of interest.

Take Advantage of Search Functions:

Use Ghidra's built-in search functions to locate specific patterns, strings, or instructions within the binary. You can search for functions, variables, strings, or even specific assembly instructions.

Customize the CodeBrowser Layout:

The CodeBrowser interface can be customized to suit your needs. You can arrange different panels, such as the Decompiler, Listing Window, and Function Graph, in a way that optimizes your workflow.

Ghidra's CodeBrowser is an indispensable tool for reverse engineers, offering both a low-level disassembly view and a high-level decompiled view of the analyzed binary. With its flexible interface, rich feature set, and powerful navigation tools, the CodeBrowser helps you efficiently understand, annotate, and document the functionality of any binary. Whether you're debugging, analyzing malware, or conducting a vulnerability assessment, mastering the CodeBrowser is essential to becoming proficient in Ghidra. By utilizing its various views and features, you can streamline your reverse engineering process and gain deep insights into the inner workings of software.

3.2 An Introduction to Ghidra's Tool Suite (Decompiler, Debugger, etc.)

Ghidra is a comprehensive reverse engineering framework that includes a suite of powerful tools designed to facilitate the analysis of software binaries. Developed by the National Security Agency (NSA), Ghidra offers a variety of tools for static and dynamic analysis, providing a rich feature set that allows reverse engineers, security researchers, and software analysts to dissect and understand executable files, libraries, and firmware images. These tools help in tasks ranging from vulnerability assessment to malware analysis, and even software debugging.

In this section, we will introduce the key components of Ghidra's tool suite, including the Decompiler, Debugger, and other integral tools that can enhance your reverse engineering workflow. By understanding the role of these tools and how they interact within the Ghidra ecosystem, you'll be able to leverage Ghidra more effectively for various reverse engineering tasks.

3.2.1 The Decompiler: Translating Assembly to High-Level Code

One of Ghidra's most valuable tools is its Decompiler, which provides an automatic, high-level translation of the disassembled assembly code into a C-like representation. The Decompiler's purpose is to provide a more understandable version of the machine-level code, making it easier for reverse engineers to analyze and understand the logic of a program.

Key Features of the Decompiler:

High-Level Code Representation:

The Decompiler attempts to recreate the logic of the binary in a format that resembles C programming language code. While not perfect, it offers a significant improvement over raw assembly for understanding the high-level structure of a program. This representation can be invaluable when trying to reverse engineer functions, data structures, and logic.

Dynamic Decompilation:

As the analysis of the binary progresses, the Decompiler dynamically updates the decompiled output based on changes made to the disassembly or analysis results. This allows for real-time feedback and adjustments while working on the analysis.

Integration with the Listing View:

The Decompiler is fully integrated with the Listing View. This means that you can quickly toggle between assembly instructions and high-level code to get a better understanding of the underlying functionality. It enables an easy cross-reference between what the processor is executing at the assembly level and what the program logic looks like at a higher abstraction.

Control Flow Simplification:

The Decompiler makes attempts to simplify complex control flow structures into a more understandable format. For example, loops, if/else statements, and function calls are represented more intuitively, helping you trace the program's flow of execution.

Usage:

The Decompiler in Ghidra is particularly helpful when analyzing complex functions or when trying to understand a binary's core logic. By providing a higher-level view of the code, the Decompiler reduces the cognitive load of translating assembly language, making it a key tool for reversing compiled software.

3.2.2 The Debugger: Analyzing Code at Runtime

Ghidra's Debugger is a powerful tool for dynamic analysis. Unlike static analysis tools (such as the Decompiler and Disassembler), which examine the binary code without executing it, the Debugger allows you to run the program and observe its behavior in real time. This is critical when analyzing malware, vulnerabilities, or the behavior of software under certain conditions.

Key Features of the Debugger:

Debugging with Breakpoints:

The Debugger enables you to set breakpoints in the code. A breakpoint causes the program to pause execution at a certain point, allowing you to inspect variables, memory, and the call stack at that moment. This helps identify specific sections of code that are critical to understanding how the program operates.

Step-by-Step Execution:

With the Debugger, you can step through the execution of the binary, either line by line or instruction by instruction. This granular control over program execution allows you to trace exactly how a program proceeds through different functions, conditions, and loops.

Variable and Memory Inspection:

During debugging sessions, you can inspect the values of variables, the contents of memory locations, and other runtime data structures. This is essential for understanding how specific functions or inputs are processed during execution.

Attach to Running Process:

The Debugger can be used to attach to a running process, which allows you to analyze live programs that are already executing in the system. This is often crucial in malware analysis and debugging scenarios, where you need to observe how a program behaves when interacting with external resources, such as files or network connections.

Usage:

The Debugger is particularly useful when working with malware analysis or reverse engineering dynamic behavior. It allows you to monitor the program's execution and determine how inputs and conditions affect its actions, making it an indispensable tool for understanding runtime behavior and identifying security vulnerabilities.

3.2.3 The Listing View: Disassembly and Code Navigation

The Listing View is Ghidra's disassembly window, which displays the raw assembly instructions corresponding to the binary code. The Listing View is where reverse engineers can perform static analysis and manually inspect how the program works at the lowest level. Ghidra automatically disassembles the binary into assembly code, allowing you to view and navigate the program's machine-level instructions.

Key Features of the Listing View:

Disassembly:

The Listing View shows the assembly instructions, each mapped to the corresponding memory address and opcode. This provides insight into the low-level operation of the program, including function calls, conditionals, loops, and system calls.

Code Navigation:

You can navigate through the Listing View easily using the Symbol Tree, search functions, or the Go To command. You can also jump between functions, memory addresses, and references, which is crucial when dealing with large or complex binaries.

Function and Data Flow Analysis:

The Listing View allows you to analyze the control flow of functions in the program. You can also view references to variables and data structures, which helps in understanding how the program accesses and manipulates data.

Usage:

The Listing View is critical for detailed examination of the binary at the assembly level. It helps you to explore the program's machine-level operations and is often the starting point for deep analysis. When combined with other tools in Ghidra's suite, the Listing View provides a comprehensive picture of how a program functions.

3.2.4 Other Useful Tools in Ghidra's Suite

In addition to the Decompiler, Debugger, and Listing View, Ghidra includes other valuable tools that enhance the reverse engineering workflow.

Symbol Tree:

The Symbol Tree is an organized view of all the symbols (functions, variables, and other entities) in the binary. It allows you to quickly jump to different parts of the program without having to scroll through the disassembly. This is useful when you are looking for specific functions or variables in large codebases.

Function Graph:

The Function Graph visualizes the control flow within a specific function. It allows you to see the branches and paths of execution, which is useful for understanding complex functions. The graph shows how the program flows between different blocks, which can help you identify issues like infinite loops, unreachable code, or security vulnerabilities.

Memory Map:

The Memory Map provides a visual representation of the binary's memory layout, showing where different sections (code, data, heap, stack) are located in memory. It can help you understand the memory organization of the binary and is useful for identifying areas that need more in-depth analysis.

Scripts and Automation:

Ghidra also supports the use of scripts written in languages like Java, Python, or JavaScript to automate repetitive tasks. Scripts can be used to analyze specific patterns, rename functions or variables, and perform batch operations on large numbers of files.

Ghidra's tool suite is an incredibly powerful collection of reverse engineering resources that allow you to analyze binaries at different levels of abstraction. The Decompiler simplifies the translation of assembly code into C-like high-level code, while the Debugger enables real-time inspection of program execution. The Listing View provides essential insights into the machine-level operations of the binary, and additional tools like the Symbol Tree, Function Graph, and Memory Map further augment your analysis capabilities.

By mastering these tools, you'll be well-equipped to tackle a wide range of reverse engineering tasks, from malware analysis to vulnerability discovery. Ghidra's modular tool suite empowers reverse engineers to approach binary analysis systematically and efficiently, making it an indispensable tool for cybersecurity professionals, researchers, and software developers.

3.3 Collaboration with Multi-User Ghidra Projects

One of the standout features of Ghidra, especially in team-based environments, is its ability to facilitate multi-user collaboration through Ghidra Projects. Whether you're part of a security team, a research group, or collaborating on open-source reverse engineering efforts, Ghidra's multi-user project functionality allows multiple analysts to work together on the same project, sharing insights, findings, and analysis without stepping on each other's toes.

In this section, we will explore how multi-user Ghidra Projects work, how they enhance team collaboration, and the practical aspects of using this feature for reverse engineering tasks. Understanding how to set up and manage multi-user projects will allow you to take full advantage of Ghidra's collaborative capabilities, especially when working on large or complex binaries that require input from different team members.

3.3.1 Setting Up Multi-User Projects in Ghidra

The foundation for collaboration in Ghidra is the concept of Projects. A Ghidra Project contains all the files, analysis data, and configurations related to the reverse engineering process. In a multi-user Ghidra Project, this project can be shared across multiple users, allowing them to access and work on the same analysis simultaneously. To enable collaboration, the project needs to be hosted in a shared directory, which can be a networked location, a version control repository, or a Ghidra server. Ghidra supports two types of projects:

Local Projects:

These are individual, personal projects stored locally on a single machine. While local projects are useful for personal use, they are not suited for collaboration.

Shared Projects:

Shared Projects enable multiple users to access and work on the same project. They are stored in a shared repository (usually a networked location or Ghidra Server) that all users can access simultaneously. A shared project allows for concurrent analysis, where changes made by one user are visible to others in real time.

Key Steps to Set Up a Multi-User Project:

Create a Shared Project:

In Ghidra, when creating a new project, select the option to create a shared project. Choose a location on a shared network or a centralized server where all users can access the project files.

Select a Repository Type:

- Ghidra supports multiple types of repositories for shared projects:
- File-based repositories store the project data in a shared directory on a file server.
- **Ghidra Server repositories**: If you have a Ghidra Server configured, you can use it to host the project, providing a more robust and scalable solution for multi-user collaboration.

Add Users:

Once the project is created, users can be added to the shared repository. Each user gets their own workspace, and changes are tracked by the Ghidra system to ensure that data conflicts are minimized.

3.3.2 Managing Concurrent Analysis

With multiple analysts working on a shared project, it's important to ensure that users don't interfere with each other's work. Ghidra uses a system of locks and permissions to control access to project resources. The primary goal is to allow users to collaborate seamlessly while preventing conflicts from occurring when multiple users try to modify the same data.

Key Concepts in Managing Concurrent Analysis:

Locking:

- Ghidra employs a locking mechanism to prevent users from modifying the same item simultaneously. When an analyst opens a function, a file, or a portion of the binary for analysis, the system automatically locks that item to prevent other users from making conflicting changes.
- For example, if one user is analyzing a function's decompiled code, the function will be locked to that user, preventing another user from making edits to it at the same time. However, other users can still view the function's analysis and collaborate in other areas of the project.

Changes and Version Control:

- All changes made within a multi-user project are tracked by Ghidra. Each user's modifications are saved as part of the project history, ensuring that the contributions of each team member are preserved.
- Ghidra also supports check-in/check-out functionality, where users can check out a portion of the project (such as a function or a piece of code) to work on it, and later check it back in once they are done. This ensures that work is organized and doesn't interfere with others' analyses.

Project Synchronization:

- When multiple users are working in a shared project, Ghidra automatically synchronizes their changes. When one user commits their work (such as new analysis results or annotations), those changes are immediately available to other users working on the same project.
- Synchronization minimizes the risk of data loss, ensuring that all users are working with the most up-to-date information.

3.3.3 Tools for Collaboration in Ghidra Projects

Ghidra provides several built-in tools to enhance collaboration and ensure that team members can efficiently share insights, findings, and analysis data.

Commenting and Annotations:

- Analysts can add comments and annotations directly in the code within the Listing View or the Decompiler. This makes it easy for team members to share their thoughts, explain certain findings, or leave notes for other users working on the same project.
- Comments are visible to all project members and are a critical part of collaboration. For instance, when one team member identifies a suspicious function or a possible vulnerability, they can annotate it, ensuring that others are aware of it.

Sharing Functions and Variables:

Shared projects allow users to create global variables and shared functions that all team members can access. These functions and variables can be used across different parts of the project, ensuring consistency and reducing the chances of errors.

Bookmarks and To-Do Lists:

- Ghidra allows users to create bookmarks that can be shared across the project. A bookmark might represent an important location, such as a function of interest or a potential vulnerability, and allows multiple team members to quickly return to critical areas in the code.
- To-do lists can also be created within the project to track tasks that need to be completed. These lists are useful for dividing the analysis workload among team members, making sure that everyone knows which tasks need attention.

Function and Code Review:

When one team member completes the analysis of a function or code segment, they can review their findings with other analysts. Ghidra's collaborative features allow team members to provide feedback or suggestions, ensuring that no analysis detail is overlooked and that the overall work is aligned with the team's goals.

3.3.4 Managing Project Data and User Permissions

When collaborating on a reverse engineering project, especially when multiple users are involved, managing permissions and ensuring data integrity is critical.

Key Features for Managing Project Data:

User Permissions:

Ghidra allows the project administrator to assign different user roles and permissions. For example, some users might have read-only access, while others can modify and annotate data. Administrators can also grant certain users the ability to check in and check out data, controlling who can make significant changes.

Audit Trails:

Ghidra maintains a detailed audit trail of all changes made within a multi-user project. This includes information about who made the changes, when they were made, and what was modified. Audit trails help ensure accountability and make it easy to track the progress of the project and resolve any issues that arise.

Conflict Resolution:

Ghidra provides mechanisms for resolving conflicts that may arise when multiple users attempt to modify the same item. In cases where a conflict occurs, the system alerts the users and allows them to manually resolve the issue by reviewing the differences in the modifications made by different users.

Ghidra's multi-user project capabilities significantly enhance collaboration, making it possible for reverse engineering teams to work together efficiently on complex software analysis tasks. Whether you're working with colleagues on malware analysis, debugging a program, or analyzing a binary for vulnerabilities, Ghidra provides a suite of tools that allow multiple users to contribute to the project without interfering with each other's work. By leveraging features like real-time synchronization, commenting, version control, and user permissions, teams can streamline their workflows and ensure that all analysis is documented and accessible to everyone involved.

With Ghidra's powerful multi-user collaboration features, teams can collaborate seamlessly and efficiently, leading to more thorough, accurate, and productive reverse engineering efforts.

3.4 Comparing Ghidra with IDA Pro and Other Tools

When it comes to reverse engineering, particularly analyzing binaries, there are a number of specialized tools that reverse engineers rely on to dissect compiled software. Among the most popular and widely used tools are Ghidra and IDA Pro (Interactive DisAssembler), two heavyweights in the reverse engineering space. While both are excellent tools, they have different features, workflows, and strengths. In this section, we will compare Ghidra with IDA Pro, as well as discuss other notable reverse engineering tools, to help you understand how Ghidra stands out and where it might fit into your reverse engineering toolkit.

3.4.1 Ghidra vs. IDA Pro: A Direct Comparison

IDA Pro, developed by Hex-Rays, is one of the oldest and most widely recognized disassemblers and decompilers in the reverse engineering community. Ghidra, developed by the National Security Agency (NSA), is a newer entrant, but it has quickly gained popularity due to its comprehensive features, extensibility, and, importantly, its open-source nature.

Let's break down the key aspects of both tools:

1. Cost and Licensing

Ghidra:

Open-source and free to use under the Apache 2.0 license. This means that Ghidra can be freely downloaded, modified, and redistributed, making it an attractive option for individuals and organizations looking for a cost-effective tool without licensing restrictions.

IDA Pro:

Commercial software with a hefty price tag, which can range from hundreds to thousands of dollars depending on the version and features. The pricing structure can be a limiting factor for hobbyists or smaller teams. While IDA Pro also offers a free version, it comes with significant limitations in terms of functionality.

2. User Interface and Usability

Ghidra:

Modern GUI that is intuitive and customizable. While there is a learning curve, especially for those new to reverse engineering, Ghidra's interface is designed to be straightforward, with most features accessible from the main interface. It also offers a powerful scripting environment for automating tasks and extending functionality.

IDA Pro:

IDA Pro's GUI is somewhat more mature and polished but can feel outdated by modern standards. While it is incredibly powerful, the user interface can be more difficult to navigate for beginners, especially compared to Ghidra's more intuitive layout. Advanced users often rely on hotkeys and custom scripts to speed up their workflow.

3. Decompilation

Ghidra:

Ghidra includes a Decompiler as part of the core toolset, which is capable of converting disassembled machine code into C-like high-level code. While not as mature as IDA Pro's decompiler, Ghidra's decompiler performs admirably for most use cases, and it's continuously improving.

IDA Pro:

IDA Pro has an advanced Hex-Rays Decompiler plugin, which is one of the most powerful decompilers available. Hex-Rays' decompiler produces highly readable C-like code, even for complex binaries. However, this plugin is commercial and not included in the base version of IDA Pro, requiring a separate purchase.

4. Disassembly and Analysis

Ghidra:

Ghidra has robust disassembly features that allow users to explore binaries at the assembly level. It provides good support for many architectures, and users can also perform static analysis and trace function calls through the Listing View and Function Graph. However, its performance can slow down when dealing with particularly large binaries.

IDA Pro:

IDA Pro is renowned for its disassembly capabilities. It supports a wide variety of processor architectures and has the best-in-class disassembler for analyzing machine code. IDA Pro's analysis tools are highly advanced and can handle large, complex binaries with speed and precision. The tool also offers enhanced graphical views of disassembled code to track function flows and program logic.

5. Scripting and Automation

Ghidra:

Ghidra provides built-in scripting support via Java, Python, and JavaScript. This allows users to automate repetitive tasks, enhance functionality, and create custom analysis scripts. The extensive scripting capabilities make Ghidra very customizable, and its scripting environment is user-friendly.

IDA Pro:

IDA Pro also supports scripting, but it uses IDC (IDA Scripting Language) or Python (in the more recent versions). Python support is robust, and many users write Python scripts for tasks like automated analysis, plugin development, and enhancing disassembly. IDA Pro also has a large library of community-developed plugins.

6. Multi-User Collaboration

Ghidra:

Ghidra supports multi-user collaboration through shared projects, allowing multiple users to work on the same project simultaneously. Changes made by one user are instantly reflected for others, enabling efficient teamwork, especially for large teams working on complex analyses.

IDA Pro:

IDA Pro does not natively support multi-user collaboration in the same way Ghidra does. While it is possible to use version control systems to collaborate in a team, IDA Pro does not have built-in multi-user project functionality like Ghidra's shared repository system.

3.4.2 Other Notable Reverse Engineering Tools

While Ghidra and IDA Pro are the most widely used tools, there are other reverse engineering tools worth mentioning, each with their own strengths and use cases.

1. Binary Ninja

Binary Ninja is another commercial reverse engineering tool that provides an intuitive user interface and powerful disassembly and analysis features. It offers a built-in decompiler, and its low cost compared to IDA Pro makes it an attractive option for many reverse engineers. It supports scripting via Python and has advanced analysis capabilities, but its architecture support and decompiler aren't as extensive as IDA Pro's or Ghidra's.

2. Radare2

Radare2 is an open-source reverse engineering tool that can be used for disassembly, debugging, and analysis. Unlike Ghidra and IDA Pro, Radare2 is command-line-driven, which can be intimidating for newcomers, but it offers scripting, automation, and a modular architecture that makes it highly extensible. It's a solid choice for those comfortable with command-line tools and who require a flexible, open-source solution.

3. OllyDbg

OllyDbg is a 32-bit Windows debugger that is often used for dynamic analysis of executables. While it lacks many of the advanced disassembly and decompilation features of Ghidra and IDA Pro, it is a useful tool for debugging and examining running binaries, especially when analyzing malware or reverse engineering software to identify vulnerabilities.

3.4.3 Summary: Which Tool Should You Choose?

When deciding between Ghidra, IDA Pro, and other reverse engineering tools, it largely depends on your specific needs and preferences:

Ghidra:

Ideal for users who need an open-source tool with a modern interface and strong multi-user collaboration capabilities. It offers a powerful Decompiler, a suite of tools for disassembly and analysis, and is highly extensible via scripting.

IDA Pro:

Best suited for professional reverse engineers who require the most robust and mature tool with support for a wide variety of architectures. Its advanced Hex-Rays Decompiler and disassembly capabilities make it a top choice for complex analysis tasks, though the high cost may be prohibitive for some users.

Other Tools:

- **Binary Ninja** is a cost-effective option for those who prefer a graphical interface and a strong decompiler without breaking the bank.
- **Radare2** offers a powerful, open-source alternative for users who prefer command-line tools and require deep customization and scripting.
- **OllyDbg** is great for dynamic analysis of Windows binaries but lacks the static analysis features of Ghidra and IDA Pro.

Ultimately, the choice of tool depends on the task at hand, your budget, and your comfort with the tool's interface and features. Each of these tools has its place in a reverse engineer's toolkit, and many analysts find themselves using a combination of tools to get the best results.

3.5 Practical Tips for First-Time Users

If you're just getting started with Ghidra, the powerful open-source reverse engineering tool developed by the NSA, it's natural to feel overwhelmed by its feature set and capabilities. While Ghidra provides a rich environment for analyzing binaries, it has a steep learning curve, especially for newcomers to reverse engineering. This section aims to provide practical tips for first-time users to help them get started on the right foot and make the most out of their experience with Ghidra.

3.5.1 Start with Simple Binaries

As a first-time user, it's tempting to dive straight into complex and large binaries, but this can lead to frustration. Start with simple, small programs to get a feel for Ghidra's interface and features. Focus on basic tasks like disassembly and function analysis. For example, you might start with small programs written in C or simple challenges like Hello World or basic CrackMe binaries. This allows you to familiarize yourself with the various views and tools without being bogged down by complexity.

Why it's helpful:

Simple binaries allow you to focus on learning the core functionality of Ghidra, such as importing binaries, navigating the Listing View, identifying functions, and using the Decompiler, all without being distracted by complex code or heavy analysis.

3.5.2 Familiarize Yourself with the Ghidra Interface

Ghidra's user interface (UI) can seem daunting at first, but once you understand the core components, navigating the tool becomes much easier. Spend time getting acquainted with the different views and menus, such as:

- **Listing View**: Displays the disassembled code.
- **Decompiler View**: Converts assembly code back into C-like pseudocode, which is easier to understand.
- **Program Tree**: Allows you to explore and manage the structure of the analyzed binary.
- **Symbol Tree**: Displays functions, variables, and other symbols in the binary.
- **Memory Map**: Shows the loaded memory areas of the binary and helps you understand the memory layout.

Tip: Use Windows > Toolbars to customize your UI for faster access to tools and functions you use frequently.

Why it's helpful:

Familiarity with the layout and organization of Ghidra's interface makes navigation more efficient. Once you understand how to access key components, you'll be able to analyze binaries more effectively.

3.5.3 Learn to Use Ghidra's Built-in Help System

Ghidra has a robust built-in Help system that provides documentation on its features and usage. This can be a valuable resource when you encounter specific tasks or need clarification on a tool's functionality. You can access the Help system through:

- **Help > Help Contents**: Gives access to Ghidra's user manual and documentation.
- **Help > Ghidra Glossary**: A reference for terms and concepts used throughout Ghidra.
- **Help > Online Resources**: Provides links to official Ghidra tutorials, FAQs, and the user community.

Tip: Keep the Help window open in the background while you explore, so you can quickly look up terms or features that you're unfamiliar with.

Why it's helpful:

When you're just starting out, the documentation can be a lifesaver. It helps clarify the purpose of features you might not yet fully understand and can point you toward helpful resources.

3.5.4 Leverage Ghidra's Scripting Capabilities Early

One of Ghidra's most powerful features is its scripting functionality, allowing users to automate repetitive tasks and extend the tool's capabilities. Even as a beginner, you can benefit from learning basic scripts, such as:

- Running a simple Python script to perform basic analysis or find functions in a binary.
- Using Ghidra's built-in analysis scripts: Ghidra comes with several pre-written scripts for common tasks like identifying functions, performing control flow analysis, or locating vulnerabilities.

Tip: Start by experimenting with the provided scripts in Ghidra's script manager and modify them for your own needs. Ghidra supports Python, Java, and JavaScript, so you can choose the scripting language you're most comfortable with.

Why it's helpful:

Scripts allow you to automate repetitive tasks like renaming functions, identifying certain patterns, or analyzing large codebases. This can speed up your workflow and reduce the manual effort required for analysis.

3.5.5 Get Comfortable with the Decompiler

Ghidra's Decompiler is one of its most powerful features, converting assembly code back into a more human-readable form. It simplifies complex code analysis, but understanding how to use it effectively requires some practice.

Tip:

- Use the Decompiler View to see high-level pseudocode while navigating the disassembled instructions in the Listing View. This allows you to confirm the accuracy of the decompiled code and make changes as necessary.
- Don't just rely on the Decompiler to understand the binary—use it in conjunction with the Listing View, which displays the assembly code and provides more precise control over the analysis process.
- Take advantage of Decompiler comments: You can annotate the decompiled output with your own notes, which will help you keep track of what you've learned during your analysis.

Why it's helpful:

The Decompiler is a great tool for making sense of complex assembly code. Using it alongside disassembly allows you to improve your understanding of the binary and can help you identify key functions and logic faster.

3.5.6 Practice Static and Dynamic Analysis Together

While static analysis (analyzing the code without executing it) is the main approach in Ghidra, it's often beneficial to combine static and dynamic analysis to get a deeper understanding of the binary. Ghidra supports integration with debuggers and external tools, which can help you observe how the binary behaves when executed.

Tip: While Ghidra is primarily focused on static analysis, consider using tools like OllyDbg, x64dbg, or GDB for dynamic analysis in conjunction with Ghidra. You can analyze a binary in a debugger and correlate the dynamic behavior with the static information you've gathered in Ghidra.

Why it's helpful:

Static analysis in Ghidra allows you to understand the structure and logic of the code, while dynamic analysis shows how the binary operates at runtime. Combining both methods helps uncover hidden functionality and vulnerabilities that might not be obvious through static analysis alone.

3.5.7 Learn to Use Comments and Annotations

As you work through reverse engineering tasks, keeping detailed notes is crucial for tracking your progress and insights. Ghidra allows you to add comments and annotations to functions, variables, and instructions.

Tip: Use comments to explain what each part of the code does, especially when you're unsure about its functionality. For example, if you find a function that appears to be performing an encryption task, you can annotate the function to remind yourself of its role.

Why it's helpful:

Comments and annotations provide valuable context as you continue analyzing the binary. If you come back to the project later or share your findings with others, these notes will help you remember key details and collaborate more effectively.

3.5.8 Join the Ghidra Community

Ghidra has a growing community of reverse engineers, security researchers, and developers. Participating in the community is a great way to learn, share knowledge, and stay up to date on new developments.

Tip:

Join online forums like the Ghidra Users Google Group or visit Reddit's r/ghidra to ask questions, share your experiences, and learn from others.
Explore the Ghidra Wiki and YouTube tutorials to find helpful guides and example projects.

Why it's helpful:

The Ghidra community is filled with experienced users who can provide helpful tips, scripts, and guidance. Engaging with the community can fast-track your learning and help you solve problems faster.

Starting with Ghidra may feel overwhelming, but with the right approach, you can quickly get up to speed and unlock its full potential. By starting with simple binaries, familiarizing yourself with the interface, learning to script, and combining static and dynamic analysis, you can improve your reverse engineering workflow significantly. Additionally, don't hesitate to leverage Ghidra's Decompiler, community resources, and collaborative features to speed up your analysis process. As you gain more experience with Ghidra, you'll find that it becomes an indispensable tool for tackling increasingly complex reverse engineering challenges.

Part II: Core Ghidra Functionality

Part II focuses on the heart of reverse engineering with Ghidra, where you'll get hands-on with its most essential functionality. This section will guide you through analyzing binaries, disassembling code, and using the decompiler to transform complex assembly into more readable high-level languages. You'll gain a deeper understanding of how Ghidra works under the hood, including navigating its disassembly views and mapping control flow. As you progress, you'll develop the skills needed to dissect and manipulate binaries with confidence, setting the stage for more advanced techniques in later chapters. With these core functions in your toolkit, you'll be well-equipped to tackle real-world reverse engineering challenges.

Chapter 4: Analyzing Binaries

In this chapter, we explore the foundational process of analyzing binaries in Ghidra. You'll start by learning how to import various binary file formats, such as ELF, PE, and Mach-O, and how to manage and organize them within a Ghidra project. We'll walk through the process of performing initial analysis on a binary, focusing on key elements like headers, sections, and symbols. You'll also gain a deeper understanding of how Ghidra automatically identifies functions and data structures within the binary. We'll cover common issues you may encounter during binary analysis, such as missing or incorrect symbols, and how to resolve them effectively. By the end of this chapter, you'll be ready to dive deeper into disassembly and decompilation, having established a solid foundation for analyzing binaries in Ghidra.

4.1 Importing Binary Files: Supported Formats and Common Issues

One of the first steps in reverse engineering a binary with Ghidra is importing the binary file into a Ghidra project. The process of importing a binary is fairly straightforward, but there are a few key details to keep in mind, especially when it comes to supported formats and common issues that may arise during the import process. This section will cover the basics of importing binary files, outline the file formats that Ghidra supports, and provide tips on how to address common problems that you may encounter.

4.1.1 Supported Binary Formats

Ghidra supports a wide variety of file formats, ensuring that you can analyze a broad range of binaries regardless of their platform or architecture. Below are some of the most common formats that Ghidra can handle:

1. Executable and Linkable Format (ELF)

- **Platform**: Linux and Unix-like systems.
- **Use**: Common format for executables, object files, and shared libraries on Linux.
- **Details**: Ghidra provides full support for ELF files, which includes recognizing and parsing ELF headers, sections, and segments. You can analyze the binary as well as its associated symbols, debugging information, and relocation data.

2. Portable Executable (PE)

- **Platform**: Windows.
- **Use**: Standard format for executables, dynamic link libraries (DLLs), and other Windows-based binaries.
- **Details**: Ghidra handles PE files well, including support for Windows EXE and DLL formats. Ghidra can extract useful information from the PE headers, and the disassembler will help identify Windows API calls, imported functions, and other key components.

3. Mach-O

- **Platform**: macOS.
- **Use**: Format for executables, object files, and shared libraries on macOS.
- **Details**: Ghidra supports Mach-O files for macOS, including 32-bit and 64-bit binaries. Similar to ELF and PE formats, Ghidra parses the Mach-O header to extract important sections, symbols, and relocation data.

4. Raw Binary Files (Raw)

- **Platform**: Cross-platform (generic).
- **Use**: Unstructured binary data or firmware images.
- **Details**: Ghidra can also handle raw binary files, which do not include a structured header or metadata. These are common when dealing with firmware or non-executable data like custom file formats. When importing raw binaries, users must manually specify the memory layout, including the base address and segment sizes, since Ghidra won't have this information readily available.

5. Other Formats

- **Firmware Images (e.g., Intel HEX files, Bin, etc.):** Ghidra can also handle various firmware and embedded system formats, including custom binary formats that you may encounter while analyzing embedded software.
- **Android APK/DEX files**: Though Ghidra doesn't natively support Android APK or DEX files directly, you can still reverse-engineer them using third-party plugins or by extracting the native libraries from APKs, which are typically in ELF format.

4.1.2 The Import Process

The process of importing a binary file into Ghidra is fairly simple. Here's a step-by-step guide for importing a supported binary:

Step 1: Open Ghidra

Start Ghidra and open or create a new project.

Step 2: Create or Open a Project

If you haven't already, create a new project by selecting File > New Project and choosing between a non-shared or shared project. Choose the non-shared option for local analysis or shared for collaborative efforts.

Step 3: Import the Binary

- Once you have a project open, select File > Import File from the main menu.
- Navigate to the location of your binary file and select it for import.

Step 4: Choose the Binary Format

Ghidra will automatically try to detect the file format of the binary based on its content. If it cannot detect the format, you may be prompted to manually specify the binary format (e.g., PE, ELF, Mach-O, etc.).

Step 5: Configure Import Settings

- During the import process, you will be asked to specify several options related to the binary, such as:
- Language: Choose the correct processor architecture (e.g., x86, ARM, MIPS, etc.).
- Loader Options: You may need to select additional options, such as whether the file is stripped (lacking debug symbols) or if there are any special sections.
- Base Address: For raw binaries, this is critical. You'll need to specify the address where the binary will be loaded in memory.

Step 6: Analyze the Binary

Once the binary is imported, Ghidra will initiate automatic analysis. You can customize the analysis options to tailor the analysis process, including what features or functions to focus on (e.g., function identification, data types, symbols).

4.1.3 Common Issues When Importing Binaries

While Ghidra is quite powerful and supports a wide array of binary formats, there are a few issues you might encounter during the import process. Below are some common challenges and tips on how to handle them:

1. File Format Detection Failures

- **Problem**: Ghidra may fail to automatically detect the correct format of the binary. This can happen if the binary is in a non-standard format, or if it has been obfuscated or corrupted.
- **Solution**: If Ghidra cannot detect the format, you can manually select the appropriate format from the import options (e.g., ELF, PE, Mach-O). In cases of custom or unknown formats, you can use external tools (like file on Linux) to identify the file type before importing into Ghidra.

2. Missing or Incorrect Architecture

- **Problem**: Ghidra may not automatically detect the correct processor architecture, especially with raw binaries or custom firmware images.
- **Solution**: If Ghidra misidentifies the architecture, you can manually set the processor type (e.g., ARM, x86, MIPS) in the import configuration options. Ensure that you're importing the binary with the right architecture to avoid mismatched disassembly.

3. Raw Binary Imports (No Header)

- **Problem**: Raw binaries (without headers) don't come with metadata (such as entry points, memory layout, or segment information), making them difficult to import.
- **Solution**: When importing raw binaries, you'll need to manually configure the memory layout. You'll have to specify the base address, segment sizes, and any entry points if applicable. Without this, Ghidra will not be able to properly analyze the binary.

4. Corrupted or Stripped Binaries

- **Problem**: Stripped binaries, which lack debug symbols and metadata, can be challenging to analyze since you won't have function names, variable names, or other helpful metadata.

- **Solution**: Even though stripped binaries are harder to analyze, Ghidra can still perform disassembly and decompilation. You'll need to rely on manual analysis and techniques like function identification through control flow graphs and pattern recognition.

5. Unsupported or Custom File Formats

- **Problem**: Ghidra's support for certain file formats may be limited or unavailable, especially for proprietary or less common formats.
- **Solution**: For unsupported formats, you can check the Ghidra community for plugins or extensions that might add support for additional file formats. Ghidra's plugin architecture allows users to create or import custom file format loaders.

4.1.4 Best Practices for Importing Binaries

To avoid common pitfalls during the import process and ensure that your analysis proceeds smoothly, consider the following best practices:

1. Check File Integrity

Before importing, verify that the binary is intact and has not been corrupted. If the file is corrupted or truncated, the import process will likely fail or result in inaccurate analysis.

2. Understand the Binary's Context

Whenever possible, try to gather contextual information about the binary before importing it into Ghidra. Knowing the target platform, architecture, and binary type (e.g., firmware, executable) will help you configure the import process more effectively.

3. Review Import Settings

Always double-check the import settings for correctness. If you're importing a raw binary, ensure that the base address and segment sizes are accurate. A misconfiguration can lead to incorrect disassembly or analysis results.

4. Use the Latest Version of Ghidra

Ensure you are using the latest version of Ghidra, as new versions include bug fixes and improvements that may address issues related to binary imports or analysis.

Importing binaries into Ghidra is a crucial first step in the reverse engineering process. By understanding the supported formats, following the correct import procedure, and being aware of common issues, you can set yourself up for a successful analysis. Whether you're working with PE, ELF, Mach-O, or raw binary files, Ghidra provides the tools needed to import and analyze a wide range of binaries. Just be mindful of potential challenges and take advantage of Ghidra's customization options to handle them effectively.

4.2 Understanding Executable Formats (ELF, PE, Mach-O)

When reverse engineering software, one of the first challenges is understanding the structure of the executable file you are analyzing. Executable files are typically stored in well-defined formats, each designed to support different operating systems and architectures. These formats contain important metadata and structural components that allow the operating system to load and run the program. Ghidra supports several executable formats, with the most common being ELF (Executable and Linkable Format), PE (Portable Executable), and Mach-O (Mach Object). Understanding these formats is crucial when working with Ghidra to analyze binaries. This section will explain the key features and structures of each of these formats, providing insights into how Ghidra interprets them during reverse engineering.

4.2.1 Executable and Linkable Format (ELF)

ELF (Executable and Linkable Format) is the standard binary format used on Unix-based systems, including Linux and some versions of BSD. ELF files are used for executables, object code, shared libraries, and core dumps. This format is designed to be flexible, allowing the operating system to load executables and shared libraries at runtime, and it is structured to allow for easy linking during program compilation.

Key Components of ELF:

- **ELF Header**: The ELF header provides essential information about the file, such as the file type (e.g., executable, shared object), the machine architecture (e.g., x86, ARM), and the entry point (where execution starts).
- **Program Header Table**: This table tells the operating system how to load the file into memory. It includes information about the segments of the binary, such as code, data, and other segments needed for execution.

- **Section Header Table**: This table provides details on various sections within the ELF file, such as .text (code), .data (data), .bss (uninitialized data), .rodata (read-only data), and others.

Sections: These are the individual segments within the ELF file. Common sections include:

- **.text**: Contains executable code.
- **.data**: Contains initialized global and static variables.
- **.bss**: Holds uninitialized variables.
- **.symtab**: Stores symbol information (function names, variable names, etc.).

Dynamic Section: In shared libraries or dynamically linked executables, this section contains information about dynamic linking, including shared library dependencies and relocation tables.

Analysis in Ghidra:

- Ghidra provides strong support for ELF files and can automatically parse the ELF header, sections, and program headers. It uses the Program Header Table to identify the segments that should be loaded into memory during analysis, and it utilizes the Section Header Table to break down the structure of the binary.
- Ghidra's Disassembler works seamlessly with ELF files, recognizing standard ELF sections and identifying functions, variables, and imports.
- The Decompiler can convert the raw machine code into high-level pseudocode, aiding the analyst in understanding the flow of the program.

4.2.2 Portable Executable (PE)

PE (Portable Executable) is the format used by Windows operating systems for executables, object files, and dynamic link libraries (DLLs). The PE format is derived from the older COFF (Common Object File Format) and is designed to support both 32-bit and 64-bit Windows systems. It is the standard format for all Windows applications and system binaries.

Key Components of PE:

- **DOS Header**: The PE format starts with a legacy DOS header to maintain compatibility with older systems. It contains a simple "magic number" and a pointer to the PE header.

- **PE Header**: The PE header follows the DOS header and contains crucial information about the binary, including the type of the file (e.g., executable, DLL), the target machine architecture, and the entry point.
- **Section Table**: The Section Table contains metadata about the individual sections of the binary, such as .text, .data, .rdata, .bss, and .idata (import data). This table provides the offset and size of each section.
- **Import Table**: The import table lists the external functions and libraries that the binary relies on. This includes dynamic links to system libraries such as kernel32.dll or user32.dll.
- **Export Table**: If the binary is a DLL, the export table contains a list of the functions that the DLL exposes for use by other applications.
- **Resource Section**: This section holds resources like icons, bitmaps, version information, strings, and other application data.
- **Relocation Table**: This table contains information needed to adjust addresses for position-independent code or when the binary is loaded at a different address in memory.

Analysis in Ghidra:

- When analyzing PE files in Ghidra, the tool can automatically read the PE Header and Section Table to identify executable code and data. Ghidra also automatically identifies the import and export tables, which help in understanding external dependencies.
- Ghidra can identify Windows API calls through the import table, making it easier to trace how the binary interacts with the underlying operating system.
- Ghidra can disassemble and decompile PE binaries just like ELF, breaking down machine code into functions, loops, and high-level structures.

4.2.3 Mach-O (Mach Object)

Mach-O (Mach Object) is the executable format used by macOS and iOS. It is based on the Mach kernel and is primarily used for executables, shared libraries, and object code on Apple's platforms. Like ELF and PE, Mach-O files are designed to provide the operating system with the necessary information to load, link, and execute the binary.

Key Components of Mach-O:

- **Mach-O Header**: The Mach-O header contains metadata that describes the architecture, load commands, and the entry point of the binary. This header is similar to the ELF header in that it describes how the binary should be loaded into memory.

- **Load Commands**: Mach-O files contain a series of load commands that tell the operating system how to load the executable into memory. These commands include information about segment sizes, the binary's entry point, and sections.

Sections: Similar to ELF, Mach-O files contain multiple sections. Common sections include:

- **__text**: Contains executable code.
- **__data**: Holds initialized data.
- **__bss**: Contains uninitialized data.
- **__symbol_stub**: Used for lazy symbol resolution.

- **Symbol Table**: The symbol table stores function and variable names used in the binary. This is especially important for debugging or reverse engineering.
- **Dynamic Symbol Table**: This table includes symbols for dynamically linked libraries. It helps the operating system resolve symbols at runtime.
- **UUID**: The Universally Unique Identifier (UUID) in the Mach-O file identifies the binary. This is useful for version control and identifying the source of the binary.

Analysis in Ghidra:

- Ghidra can parse the Mach-O header and load commands, which allows it to correctly identify segments of the binary and how they should be loaded into memory.
- Ghidra's disassembly and decompilation tools work effectively with Mach-O binaries, converting assembly code back into high-level pseudocode and identifying key functions.
- The symbol table and dynamic symbol table are automatically parsed, allowing Ghidra to display function names and variable names, if available.

4.2.4 Commonalities Between ELF, PE, and Mach-O

While ELF, PE, and Mach-O each have distinct features tailored to their respective operating systems, there are several common characteristics they share:

- **Headers**: All three formats have a header section that contains metadata about the file's structure, the machine architecture, the entry point, and other key information required for loading and executing the binary.

- **Sections**: These formats use sections to organize different parts of the binary, such as code, data, and symbols. Common sections include .text, .data, and .bss.
- **Symbol Information**: These formats often include symbol tables that store information about functions, variables, and imported/external dependencies. This is essential for reverse engineers when analyzing binaries.
- **Support for Dynamic Linking**: All three formats allow dynamic linking, meaning they contain sections or tables for resolving symbols at runtime, making them highly flexible and extensible.

Understanding the structure and key components of ELF, PE, and Mach-O formats is fundamental to effective reverse engineering with Ghidra. Each format has its own nuances, but Ghidra's powerful tools can automatically parse and process these formats, allowing analysts to focus on higher-level tasks like code analysis, vulnerability identification, and debugging. Whether you are working on Linux, Windows, or macOS, understanding how Ghidra interprets and handles these formats will significantly enhance your reverse engineering workflow.

4.3 Running Initial Analysis on Binaries

Once a binary is successfully imported into Ghidra, the next step is to perform an initial analysis. This is a crucial part of the reverse engineering process, as it allows you to gather valuable insights about the binary's structure and behavior. During the initial analysis, Ghidra automatically processes the binary, identifies functions, strings, and references, and presents an overview of the program's flow. Running initial analysis is essential for providing a baseline from which you can explore more detailed reverse engineering tasks, such as function analysis, control flow analysis, or data manipulation.

This section will guide you through the process of running initial analysis on a binary in Ghidra, explain the different types of analysis that can be performed, and provide tips for maximizing the effectiveness of the initial analysis process.

4.3.1 Starting the Analysis

To begin the analysis in Ghidra, follow these steps:

Load the Binary: After importing the binary file into your Ghidra project, double-click on the binary file in the Project Tree to open it in the main workspace.

Initial Analysis Prompt: Upon opening the file, Ghidra will often prompt you to start the analysis. This prompt appears in the form of a dialog box, asking you if you want to perform the analysis and allowing you to customize the analysis options before proceeding.

If this prompt does not appear, you can manually start the analysis by selecting Analysis > Auto Analyze from the main menu or right-clicking the program in the Project Tree and choosing Analyze.

Analysis Options:

When you initiate the analysis, Ghidra offers several configuration options to tailor the analysis. These options are divided into different categories, such as:

- **Function Identification**: Ghidra will automatically identify known functions (such as library functions) based on the binary's structure.
- **Instruction Analysis**: The tool will disassemble the code and attempt to recognize instruction patterns.
- **Data Flow Analysis**: This will attempt to detect how data flows through various variables and functions, providing insight into the program's behavior.
- **Symbol and String Identification**: Ghidra will search for identifiable strings, symbols, and references, which can be helpful when trying to identify known patterns or pieces of functionality.
- **Stack Frame Analysis**: Ghidra will attempt to detect function prologues and epilogues, enabling stack frames to be recognized for function calls.
- **Start the Analysis**: Once you've selected the appropriate options, click OK to begin the analysis process. Ghidra will analyze the binary and, depending on the complexity of the file, this may take a few seconds to several minutes.

4.3.2 What Happens During Initial Analysis?

Ghidra performs a comprehensive set of analysis tasks automatically when it runs the initial analysis. These tasks help to build the foundation for deeper reverse engineering work. Here are some key things that Ghidra does during the initial analysis:

Disassembly:

- Ghidra identifies machine instructions and disassembles the binary code into assembly language. The disassembler will attempt to determine the boundaries of functions and loops, providing an organized view of the program's control flow.

- It also identifies entry points such as the program's main() function or other starting points for execution.

Function Identification:

- Ghidra attempts to identify functions within the binary. This involves analyzing the binary's flow of control, identifying known patterns of function prologues, and recognizing calls to standard library functions.
- Functions are tagged and displayed in the Function Tree, allowing you to quickly jump to any function of interest for further analysis.

String Identification:

- During analysis, Ghidra looks for string references in the binary. These may include hardcoded strings, error messages, file paths, or other textual data embedded within the binary. Identifying these strings is critical for understanding the binary's behavior, as they often provide clues about its functionality.
- These strings are displayed in the String Table for easy access and may be linked to relevant code sections for further investigation.

Symbol Identification:

- Ghidra identifies symbols, such as function names, variable names, and external symbols. For stripped binaries, this may be limited, but Ghidra's heuristic analysis can still detect and label many symbols.
- These symbols can be found in the Symbol Tree and used to trace function calls and data references throughout the binary.

Data and Pointer Analysis:

- Ghidra analyzes the binary's data structures, identifying data references and pointers that indicate how memory is being accessed and modified.
- This analysis helps in understanding how the program handles internal data, which is essential for tasks like malware analysis or exploit development.

Control Flow Graphs (CFG):

- The Control Flow Graph provides a high-level overview of how execution flows through the program. It helps in visualizing the branching structure of the code, making it easier to understand complex routines.

- Ghidra generates CFGs for functions, allowing reverse engineers to identify loops, conditionals, and function calls.

4.3.3 Customizing Initial Analysis

While the default settings for initial analysis are generally sufficient for most binaries, Ghidra allows you to customize the analysis process to focus on specific aspects of the binary. You can adjust the settings based on your goals or the particular challenges of the binary being analyzed.

Customization Options Include:

- **Function Signature Matching**: By enabling this option, Ghidra will attempt to match functions against known signatures, which can help identify common library functions or patterns in the code.
- **Data Types**: You can enable Ghidra to perform automatic type inference, which will attempt to determine the data types of variables, structures, and arrays.
- **Stack and Call Analysis**: Enabling advanced stack analysis allows Ghidra to more accurately model function calls, stack frames, and local variables, improving the understanding of function behavior.
- **Code Reordering and Bytecode Patterns**: For certain types of binaries, Ghidra can also attempt to reorder instructions or identify bytecode patterns to improve disassembly and analysis.

To configure these options, go to Analysis > Auto Analyze in the main menu and customize the settings according to your needs.

4.3.4 Understanding the Results of Initial Analysis

Once the initial analysis has completed, Ghidra provides a comprehensive overview of the binary, organized into several key areas that will guide you through further analysis. Here are the most important results and features that Ghidra generates after an initial analysis:

Function List:

The Function List displays all identified functions within the binary. Functions are typically named (if symbols are available) or automatically labeled by Ghidra. You can navigate through the list to explore specific functions.

Disassembly View:

The Disassembly View shows the raw machine instructions of the binary, with each instruction annotated with its corresponding address. This view will display the results of the disassembly, showing which areas of the binary contain executable code and highlighting any potential issues or unusual sections of code.

Symbol Table:

The Symbol Table will list all the identified symbols in the binary, including function names, variables, and imported functions from dynamic libraries. This table can be particularly useful when attempting to map the flow of the program and understand its interaction with external libraries.

Strings:

The String Table will list all the recognized strings from the binary. This includes both human-readable strings and potential indicators of functionality. Strings can give important context for understanding the program's purpose.

References and Cross-References:

Ghidra generates a list of references to functions, variables, and data structures. This allows you to trace how different parts of the binary interact with each other and identify critical areas of code that require further investigation.

4.3.5 Best Practices for Initial Analysis

Here are some tips for getting the most out of your initial analysis in Ghidra:

Allow Ghidra to Complete Full Analysis:

Be patient and allow Ghidra to complete the full analysis. While Ghidra can still be useful with partial analysis, completing the full analysis will provide a more comprehensive overview of the binary.

Verify Results:

After the initial analysis, verify the identified functions and symbols. Sometimes, Ghidra might incorrectly identify a function or misinterpret the flow of control. Manually checking for consistency and accuracy is a good practice.

Look for Key Indicators:

Pay close attention to any identified strings, imports, or unusual code sections. These can provide valuable insights into the binary's behavior and potential vulnerabilities.

Leverage Ghidra's Visualizations:

Use Ghidra's visualizations, such as Control Flow Graphs (CFGs) and Function Graphs, to understand the structure of the binary. These can help clarify how the program operates and where the most important areas of interest lie.

Running initial analysis on binaries in Ghidra is a foundational step in the reverse engineering process. The analysis uncovers key structural elements of the binary, including functions, data references, strings, and control flow, that provide critical insights into the program's behavior. By understanding how to configure and interpret the results of initial analysis, reverse engineers can lay a solid foundation for deeper analysis, vulnerability identification, and further exploration of the binary.

4.4 Identifying and Resolving Import Errors

When working with binary files in Ghidra, one of the most common challenges that reverse engineers face is dealing with import errors during the binary import process. Import errors typically arise when Ghidra is unable to correctly interpret or analyze certain portions of the binary file due to issues with the file format, missing dependencies, or incorrect settings. Identifying and resolving these errors is crucial to ensuring that the analysis proceeds smoothly and the data is processed correctly.

This section will guide you through the process of identifying common import errors in Ghidra, understanding their causes, and providing steps for resolving them effectively.

4.4.1 Common Import Errors in Ghidra

When importing a binary into Ghidra, the tool attempts to automatically detect the file type and begin analysis. However, several errors can occur during this process, often due to issues with the binary itself or the import settings. Some common import errors include:

Unsupported File Format:

- Ghidra supports a wide range of file formats, including ELF, PE, and Mach-O. However, if the binary is in an unsupported format, or if it is a custom or non-standard format, Ghidra may fail to recognize the file, resulting in an import error.
- **Error Message**: "Unsupported file format" or "Unable to recognize the binary format."

Corrupted or Incomplete Binaries:

- A binary that is corrupted or incomplete can result in a failed import. This could happen if the binary was truncated, had issues during download or transfer, or was improperly compiled.
- **Error Message**: "File corruption detected" or "Invalid binary structure."

Missing Symbols or Missing Dependencies:

- Ghidra may also encounter issues if the binary is missing symbols (function names, variable names) that are required for analysis. In cases where the binary depends on shared libraries or external components that Ghidra cannot access, it may struggle to perform a complete analysis.
- **Error Message**: "Missing symbol information" or "Failed to resolve external dependencies."

Incorrect Architecture Detection:

- Ghidra relies on the binary's header to determine the target architecture (e.g., x86, ARM, MIPS). If the architecture is incorrectly identified or unsupported, it can prevent the binary from being properly disassembled and analyzed.
- **Error Message**: "Architecture detection failed" or "Unsupported architecture."

Byte Order Issues:

- Ghidra may fail to correctly interpret the byte order of a binary, especially when dealing with big-endian or little-endian architectures. Incorrect byte order can result in the incorrect interpretation of data, instructions, and structures.
- **Error Message**: "Byte order mismatch" or "Data misalignment detected."

4.4.2 Identifying Import Errors

When Ghidra encounters an import error, it typically provides an error message in the Ghidra Console or in the Log Window. These messages can give you a general idea of what went wrong. To identify and troubleshoot import errors effectively:

Check Ghidra's Log Output:

- When importing a binary, Ghidra logs messages that can be accessed via the Log tab in the main interface. These logs provide detailed information about any issues encountered during the import process.
- Look for any error messages or warnings in the log output. Errors related to unsupported formats, missing dependencies, or architecture mismatches will often be reported here.

Examine File Metadata:

Before importing the file, you can examine its metadata to verify its format and architecture. Tools like file (Linux) or PEiD (Windows) can give you insight into the structure and format of the binary, which can help you diagnose any compatibility issues with Ghidra.

Verify Architecture and File Type:

- Double-check that the file is indeed in a supported format (PE, ELF, Mach-O, etc.) and that the target architecture matches the binary's actual architecture. Mismatches can lead to analysis failures.
- You can also open the binary in a hex editor to check the file signature, magic number, or header information, which can give you clues about the file's structure.

4.4.3 Resolving Import Errors

Once you've identified the root cause of the import error, it's time to resolve it. Below are some strategies for resolving common import issues in Ghidra:

Unsupported File Format:

- If the binary is in a format that Ghidra does not support, you may need to convert the file to a supported format. Tools like objcopy, hex2bin, or elf2bin (on Linux) can help convert certain binary formats into something Ghidra can read.

- Alternatively, you may need to use a different disassembly tool that supports the file format in question, or analyze the binary manually by bypassing Ghidra's automated features.

Corrupted or Incomplete Binary:

- If the binary is corrupted, you'll need to obtain a clean version of the file. Incomplete binaries may need to be recompiled, re-downloaded, or restored from a backup.
- If a binary appears to be missing parts, but you still want to analyze the available sections, you can choose to import just the relevant sections of the file (using Ghidra's Import File options) or attempt to repair the file using specialized tools.

Missing Symbols or Dependencies:

- For missing symbols, check if the binary is stripped of symbol information. If it is, there may be little to no helpful metadata available for analysis. You can attempt to reconstruct the missing symbols manually by reverse engineering the binary, but it will require significant effort.
- For missing dependencies (e.g., dynamic libraries), you may need to provide Ghidra with additional information. You can manually import the library or try to link the binary to the required dependencies using Ghidra's External Program feature.
- Another option is to use dynamic analysis or debugging to run the program and trace the interactions with missing libraries or symbols.

Incorrect Architecture Detection:

- If Ghidra incorrectly detects the architecture of the binary, you can manually specify the correct architecture during the binary import process.
- In the Import Binary dialog box, you can change the architecture by selecting the Language setting and choosing the correct processor and endian type.
- If the architecture still cannot be detected or is unsupported, consider using a different disassembly tool or re-compiling the binary with proper architecture flags.

Byte Order Issues:

- Byte order issues can usually be resolved by manually specifying the correct endianness of the binary during the import process. Ghidra allows you to configure the endian type (big-endian or little-endian) based on the binary's architecture and the target system.

- In the Language settings of the binary import dialog, make sure to choose the correct endianness that matches the binary's native format.

4.4.4 Best Practices for Preventing Import Errors

Verify File Integrity:

Before importing a binary into Ghidra, ensure the file is not corrupted. Tools like md5sum (Linux) or certutil (Windows) can help verify the file's integrity by comparing checksums.

Check the Architecture:

Always verify the binary's architecture and file format before importing it into Ghidra. Having this information ahead of time can help you avoid issues related to incorrect architecture detection.

Use Compatible Formats:

Stick to commonly supported binary formats such as PE (Windows), ELF (Linux), or Mach-O (macOS). If you're working with a custom or proprietary format, you may need additional tools or manual analysis to handle the import.

Regularly Update Ghidra:

Ghidra is an actively developed tool, and new updates often include support for additional file formats and bug fixes. Make sure you are using the latest version of Ghidra to avoid running into known import issues.

Import errors are a common challenge when working with binary files in Ghidra, but they can usually be identified and resolved through careful investigation. By understanding the potential causes of import errors and applying the troubleshooting techniques discussed in this section, you can ensure that Ghidra successfully imports and analyzes your binaries, providing you with the insights needed for further reverse engineering tasks.

4.5 Exploring File Metadata and Headers

When analyzing a binary in Ghidra, understanding the file metadata and headers is a crucial step in deciphering how the program is structured and how it operates. The metadata and headers contain essential information about the binary, such as its format, architecture, entry points, and dependencies. These components are fundamental for accurate disassembly, analysis, and debugging. Exploring this information can provide you with a deeper understanding of the binary, reveal potential areas of interest for reverse engineering, and help guide the analysis process.

This section will focus on the key components of a binary's metadata and headers, how to explore them using Ghidra, and how this information can aid in the reverse engineering process.

4.5.1 What is File Metadata and Headers?

File metadata refers to the data that describes the structure, type, and other attributes of a file. In the context of binary files, metadata often includes the file format, target architecture, entry points, and dependencies. The header is a section at the beginning of the binary that contains essential information needed to load, execute, and interpret the file. The specific content and structure of the header depend on the file format (e.g., PE, ELF, Mach-O).

Here are some of the most important sections of file metadata and headers:

File Format Identification:

The header contains a magic number or identifier that indicates the file format (e.g., PE for Windows executables, ELF for Linux, Mach-O for macOS). This allows the operating system and analysis tools like Ghidra to recognize and interpret the file correctly.

Target Architecture:

The header often specifies the target architecture (e.g., x86, ARM, MIPS) and the endian type (big-endian or little-endian). This information is essential for correctly interpreting machine instructions and data structures.

Entry Point:

The entry point is the address in the binary where execution begins. In many cases, this corresponds to the start of the main() function or the program's initialization code.

Sections and Segments:

Binary files are typically divided into sections (e.g., .text for code, .data for data) and segments (e.g., code segment, data segment). The header provides information about these sections and how they are loaded into memory during execution.

Library and Dependency Information:

For dynamically linked binaries, the header contains information about external libraries or dynamic link libraries (DLLs) that the binary depends on. This includes the names and locations of shared libraries.

4.5.2 Understanding Binary File Headers

The most common binary file formats (PE, ELF, and Mach-O) have distinct header structures that contain critical information. Ghidra allows you to view and explore these headers, giving you insight into the file's internal structure.

PE (Portable Executable) - Windows Executables:

- **DOS Header**: The first part of a PE file is the DOS header, which includes the magic number MZ, signaling that it's a valid PE file. This section also contains a pointer to the PE header.
- **PE Header**: The PE header contains important details such as the target architecture (e.g., x86 or x64), timestamp, and section headers. It also provides a pointer to the Optional Header, which contains information like the entry point, base address, and image size.
- **Section Headers**: The PE file is divided into sections, and each section (e.g., .text, .data, .rdata) has a corresponding header that describes its size, location, and properties.

ELF (Executable and Linkable Format) - Linux and Unix Systems:

- **ELF Header**: The ELF header contains the magic number 7f 45 4c 46 (0x7F, ELF), which identifies the file as an ELF binary. It also includes information about the architecture, endianness, and version.
- **Program Header Table**: This table provides details about how the file should be loaded into memory. It specifies the memory locations for different segments (e.g., code, data).
- **Section Header Table**: ELF files are divided into sections, each of which is described in this table. It provides information about sections like .text, .data, and .bss.

Mach-O (Mach Object) - macOS Executables:

- **Mach-O Header**: Similar to ELF, the Mach-O header contains a magic number to identify the file and information about the architecture (e.g., x86, ARM) and byte order (little-endian or big-endian).
- **Load Commands**: These are commands that describe how to load the binary into memory. They contain information about the binary's segments and sections, such as where to load the executable code and where to find libraries.
- **Segment and Section Headers**: Mach-O files are divided into segments and sections, which are described in the corresponding headers. Sections typically include code, data, and symbol tables.

Each of these formats contains vital information in their headers that can be used to guide further reverse engineering efforts, such as identifying the architecture, understanding the entry point, and analyzing how the binary is structured in memory.

4.5.3 Exploring Binary Headers in Ghidra

Ghidra provides several ways to explore the headers and metadata of imported binaries. Here's how you can examine the file headers using Ghidra:

Opening the File:

After importing a binary into Ghidra, double-click on the file in the Project Tree to open it in the workspace. The CodeBrowser window will appear, showing the disassembly of the file.

Viewing the File Header:

To view the file's header, go to the File menu and select Properties. In the Properties window, you'll find information about the file, including the File Type, Entry Point, Target Architecture, and other metadata.

For more detailed information, you can also look at the Program Properties window, which provides insights into the segments, sections, and layout of the binary.

Viewing the PE Header (for PE files):

If you are analyzing a PE binary, Ghidra provides a specialized view of the PE header. Right-click in the CodeBrowser and select PE > Show Header to display detailed information about the PE header, including section information, imported libraries, and the entry point.

Examining ELF Header (for ELF files):

For ELF binaries, Ghidra provides an easy way to explore the ELF header and section headers. In the CodeBrowser, you can navigate to Window > ELF Header to view details about the ELF header, including program and section headers.

Exploring Mach-O Header (for Mach-O files):

Ghidra also allows you to inspect Mach-O headers by selecting Window > Mach-O Header. This view provides details about load commands, segments, and sections in a Mach-O binary.

Hex View for Raw Header Information:

Another method to explore binary headers is by opening the Hex View in Ghidra. In this view, you can directly examine the raw bytes of the binary file, including the header. This is particularly useful when trying to identify the magic number, architecture, or other key markers in the header.

4.5.4 Using File Metadata and Headers for Reverse Engineering

The information stored in the binary's metadata and headers can be incredibly useful for guiding your reverse engineering efforts. Here are several ways in which file metadata and headers aid in analysis:

Identifying Entry Points:

The entry point indicated in the header is the first place the program begins execution. By knowing the entry point, you can begin your analysis by focusing on the instructions executed at the start of the program.

Understanding the Target Architecture:

The target architecture specified in the header helps you understand the instruction set used by the binary. This allows you to properly interpret the disassembly and know which instructions are valid for the target CPU.

Finding Dependencies:

If the binary has dynamic dependencies (e.g., DLLs in Windows or shared libraries in Linux), the metadata will tell you which external libraries the binary requires. This is useful for setting up an environment where the binary can be properly analyzed or executed.

Optimizing Disassembly:

The section and segment information provided in the header can help guide the disassembly process. You can focus on the .text section for code or the .data section for data and variables. This can save time by allowing you to directly navigate to relevant areas of the binary.

Debugging and Emulation:

For debugging or emulation purposes, knowing the binary's format and architecture helps set up an appropriate emulator or debugger. You'll need to use the correct architecture settings to ensure that the instructions are correctly interpreted during dynamic analysis.

4.5.5 Best Practices for Analyzing Binary Headers

- **Always Check the Header First**: When you begin working with a new binary, always start by inspecting the header. This will give you valuable information about the binary's format, architecture, and sections.
- **Verify Architecture and Endianness**: If you encounter issues with disassembly or analysis, double-check the architecture and endianness specified in the header. Misinterpretation of the architecture can lead to errors in understanding the binary's behavior.
- **Use Ghidra's Header Views**: Ghidra provides dedicated views for each file format (PE, ELF, Mach-O), which makes it easier to examine the header without needing to manually parse raw bytes.
- **Document Key Header Information**: Keep notes or document key pieces of header information, such as the entry point, target architecture, and section details, as they can guide your analysis throughout the reverse engineering process.

Exploring the file metadata and headers is an essential step in understanding a binary file. Ghidra provides robust tools to easily inspect and interpret this information, helping reverse engineers gain insight into the structure, target architecture, and execution flow of the binary. By leveraging header information, you can optimize your analysis process, identify important areas for further exploration, and more efficiently tackle the challenges of reverse engineering.

Chapter 5: Disassembly in Ghidra

Disassembly is a crucial step in reverse engineering, and in this chapter, we'll guide you through the process of disassembling code in Ghidra. You'll learn how to navigate Ghidra's assembly view and interpret low-level instructions to understand how a program operates. We'll cover key concepts like disassembly syntax, addressing modes, and instruction semantics to help you make sense of the raw machine code. You'll also discover how to identify and resolve common issues, such as incorrect disassembly or missing functions. By understanding how Ghidra disassembles code and how to manipulate the assembly view, you'll be able to analyze and modify binary programs with greater precision. Additionally, you'll explore how to track cross-references between different functions and variables, helping you build a clear map of the program's structure. By the end of this chapter, you'll be proficient in disassembling and navigating assembly code in Ghidra, setting the stage for more advanced reverse engineering tasks.

5.1 The Role of Disassembly in Reverse Engineering

Disassembly is one of the most fundamental and powerful techniques in reverse engineering. It is the process of converting machine code—typically found in executable binary files—back into assembly code, which is human-readable. This step is crucial for reverse engineers, as it allows them to understand how a program works at a low level without having access to the original source code. In this chapter, we will explore the role of disassembly in reverse engineering, the benefits it provides, and how tools like Ghidra can facilitate the process.

The Importance of Disassembly in Reverse Engineering

Disassembly is a cornerstone of reverse engineering, particularly when dealing with compiled or obfuscated binaries. Reverse engineers use disassembly to bridge the gap between the raw, low-level machine code and the higher-level logic of a program. This process is invaluable for a wide range of tasks, including:

Malware Analysis:

In cybersecurity, disassembly is essential for analyzing malicious software (malware). By disassembling the binary code of a suspected malware file, reverse engineers can identify its behaviors, commands, and payloads. Disassembly helps uncover hidden functionality, like self-replicating code or code designed to evade detection.

Software Debugging and Patching:

Developers use disassembly to debug programs when source code is unavailable or corrupted. In reverse engineering scenarios, disassembling binaries can reveal bugs or vulnerabilities in software that attackers could exploit. Disassembly also enables the creation of patches for fixing flaws or modifying program behavior, without needing access to the original source code.

Understanding Legacy Code:

For legacy systems where source code may no longer be available, disassembly is one of the few options for understanding how the software operates. Reverse engineers can study the disassembled code to learn the program's logic, which is useful for maintaining or updating old systems.

Reversing Software Protections:

Disassembly plays a key role in bypassing or understanding anti-reverse engineering mechanisms and protections in software. Many programs include obfuscation, code packing, or encryption techniques designed to make analysis difficult. Disassembly can help reverse engineers unpack these protections and understand the underlying code.

Intellectual Property (IP) Investigations:

Disassembly can also be used to investigate potential copyright infringements or violations of software patents. Reverse engineers might need to disassemble a binary to verify whether its code or algorithms infringe on another company's intellectual property.

The Disassembly Process

The disassembly process involves taking a binary file—whether it's a Windows PE file, a Linux ELF file, or a macOS Mach-O file—and translating its machine code into assembly instructions. Each processor architecture (x86, ARM, MIPS, etc.) has its own set of assembly instructions and formats, and disassembling a binary requires knowledge of the architecture it was compiled for.

Here's an outline of the key stages involved in disassembly:

Loading the Binary:

The first step in the disassembly process is loading the binary file into a reverse engineering tool like Ghidra. Ghidra automatically detects the architecture of the binary and initializes the disassembly process based on that architecture.

Identification of Sections:

The disassembly process begins with identifying the sections in the binary, such as the .text section (which contains code), .data section (for data), and .bss section (uninitialized data). Each section has its own role in the binary's execution, and disassembling each of them helps in understanding how the program is structured.

Machine Code to Assembly:

In this phase, the tool translates the raw machine code into assembly code. This code is often in low-level instructions that the processor executes. For example, in an x86 architecture, machine code might be converted into assembly instructions like MOV, ADD, or JMP.

Control Flow Analysis:

Disassembly tools like Ghidra attempt to identify the program's control flow—what functions are called, what paths are taken, and how the program interacts with memory. This phase is crucial for identifying key parts of the binary and for understanding the program's logical flow.

Identifying Functions and Variables:

During disassembly, Ghidra will try to identify functions and variables by analyzing the code structure, labels, and patterns. Tools like Ghidra help automate this process to a large extent, allowing reverse engineers to quickly identify where functions start and end, and how data is manipulated.

Commenting and Annotating:

After disassembling the code, reverse engineers can annotate and comment on the assembly code. This step is essential for making the disassembly more understandable, especially when working with complex or obfuscated code. It helps create documentation for future analysis and makes it easier to understand the logic of the binary.

Disassembly Challenges

While disassembly is a powerful technique, it comes with challenges that reverse engineers must overcome. Some common difficulties include:

Code Obfuscation:

Many developers use obfuscation techniques to make the disassembly process harder. This could include techniques such as control flow flattening, string encryption, or packing (compressing) the code. These techniques can obscure the original intent of the program and complicate disassembly.

Function Boundaries:

In some cases, Ghidra or other disassembly tools may fail to correctly identify function boundaries, especially if the binary is obfuscated or compiled with optimizations. Manually identifying function start and end points can be time-consuming and requires a deep understanding of the binary's logic.

Incomplete or Corrupted Binaries:

When dealing with incomplete or corrupted binaries, disassembly may be partial or misleading. Missing data or broken function calls can lead to incorrect interpretations, requiring additional effort to fill in the gaps.

Data Interpretation:

Disassembled code often involves a combination of instructions and data. Differentiating between code and data, especially in areas where the binary contains self-modifying code or embedded strings, can be difficult. Reverse engineers need to be cautious in interpreting what is truly code and what is data.

Memory Protections and Anti-Reverse Engineering:

Modern software often includes protections to thwart reverse engineering efforts. These protections can include techniques like encryption of code at runtime, self-modifying code, and anti-debugging measures. Disassembling these types of binaries requires additional tools or advanced techniques to bypass the protections.

Disassembly with Ghidra

Ghidra is a powerful and flexible tool that automates much of the disassembly process, helping reverse engineers overcome many of the challenges mentioned above. It provides several features to make disassembly more manageable:

Automatic Function Recognition:

Ghidra automatically recognizes functions and labels them in the disassembly view. It tries to identify the boundaries of each function, making it easier to follow the program's flow.

Control Flow Graph (CFG):

The tool automatically generates a control flow graph (CFG) that visually represents the program's execution paths. This graph is crucial for understanding how different parts of the program interact and for identifying critical code regions.

Decompiler Integration:

Ghidra includes an integrated decompiler that can translate assembly code back into high-level pseudo-C code. While this is not always perfect, it can significantly aid in understanding the logic behind disassembled functions and algorithms.

Custom Scripts and Extensions:

Ghidra supports scripting (via Python and Java), which allows reverse engineers to automate repetitive tasks during disassembly. Custom scripts can help identify patterns, extract specific information, or automate the recognition of common function types.

Interactive Debugging:

In combination with disassembly, Ghidra supports debugging and allows reverse engineers to step through code execution interactively, making it easier to track down bugs or verify how specific sections of code operate.

Disassembly is a critical component of reverse engineering and provides insight into how a program operates at the machine code level. Whether it's for malware analysis, debugging, patching, or understanding legacy systems, disassembly allows reverse engineers to unlock the secrets hidden in binary files. Tools like Ghidra automate and streamline the disassembly process, helping reverse engineers navigate the complexities of binary code more efficiently. However, disassembly remains a challenging task, especially in the face of obfuscation, protections, and incomplete binaries. By mastering the disassembly process, reverse engineers gain the ability to thoroughly analyze and manipulate software at its most fundamental level.

5.2 Navigating the Assembly View

In reverse engineering, understanding the flow of a program at the machine level is essential. The assembly view is where reverse engineers interact with the disassembled code, interpreting low-level instructions in human-readable format. Navigating the assembly view in tools like Ghidra is a critical skill for effective reverse engineering, as it allows users to explore and analyze the behavior of binaries in great detail. In this section, we'll discuss how to navigate the assembly view within Ghidra, and how to make the most of the provided tools and features to gain insights into the binary's execution flow.

The Basics of Ghidra's Assembly View

Ghidra's assembly view presents the disassembled machine code in a readable format, displaying the instructions the processor will execute. Each instruction corresponds to a specific operation that the CPU performs, such as moving data, arithmetic operations, or conditional jumps. Ghidra automatically organizes and labels these instructions, making it easier for users to follow along with the program's flow.

In the assembly view, Ghidra organizes instructions into blocks of code, often labeled with function names or memory addresses. Each instruction is accompanied by a mnemonic (like MOV, ADD, JMP) and its corresponding operands (such as memory locations, registers, or constants).

Here are the key elements you'll see in Ghidra's assembly view:

- **Mnemonic**: The textual representation of the instruction that corresponds to an operation the CPU executes (e.g., MOV, ADD, CMP).
- **Operands**: The arguments for the instruction, such as registers (e.g., eax, ebx), memory addresses, or immediate values.
- **Labels**: Memory addresses or symbolic names that represent locations in the program. Functions, loops, and jump destinations are often labeled for easier navigation.
- **Instruction Address**: A memory address is displayed next to each instruction, showing where it resides in the binary.

- **Comments**: Annotations that explain what the code does, often added by reverse engineers to make the analysis clearer. Ghidra allows users to add comments directly in the assembly view.

Understanding these components is crucial for following the program's execution and interpreting its purpose.

Key Features of Ghidra's Assembly View

Ghidra's assembly view offers a range of features to make the reverse engineering process more efficient and user-friendly. Let's explore some of the most useful features you'll encounter:

Navigation Panel:

- On the left side of the Ghidra interface, you'll find the navigation panel. This panel provides an overview of the functions and code blocks within the loaded binary. It allows you to quickly jump to specific functions, code segments, or memory regions.
- You can click on function names, addresses, or labels in the navigation panel to instantly navigate to the corresponding code in the assembly view.

Code Browser:

- The main area where you interact with the assembly view is the Code Browser. This is where the disassembled instructions are presented. In Ghidra, the Code Browser is interactive, allowing you to click on instructions, jump to related functions, and explore the flow of the program.
- Ghidra automatically highlights control flow paths, like conditional jumps and function calls, to help you identify how the program operates.

Control Flow Graph (CFG):

- Ghidra automatically generates a control flow graph (CFG), which visually represents the program's execution paths. This graph helps to navigate the assembly code by showing how different parts of the program are connected. The CFG is especially useful when dealing with complex binaries with multiple functions and branches.
- The graph allows reverse engineers to trace the program's execution and identify critical parts of the binary that warrant further analysis.

Instruction Highlighting:

- Ghidra highlights instructions based on their functionality. For example, data manipulation instructions are often colored differently from control flow instructions like jumps or function calls. This color-coding makes it easier to understand the behavior of the program at a glance.
- In the assembly view, you may see highlighted instructions that indicate specific conditions, such as conditional branches or functions. This can help reverse engineers quickly spot important areas of the code.

Function and Variable Identification:

- Ghidra automatically identifies and labels functions and global variables as part of the disassembly process. These labels make it easier to track how functions interact with each other and with memory. You can also see the function's entry point, its calls, and its return points.
- Ghidra's ability to identify and annotate functions automatically reduces the amount of manual work required to navigate complex binaries.

Decompiler Integration:

- One of Ghidra's most powerful features is the integrated decompiler. The decompiler takes assembly code and attempts to generate a higher-level pseudo-C representation of the code. This is useful when trying to understand complex assembly logic, as the pseudo-C code can often be more readable than raw assembly.
- By switching between the assembly view and the decompiler view, you can gain a higher-level understanding of how a function works, which is critical for more in-depth analysis.

Instruction Details and Information:

- Ghidra provides additional information about each instruction. When you click on an instruction in the assembly view, Ghidra provides a detailed breakdown of the instruction's operands, registers, and associated memory locations. This detailed information helps reverse engineers interpret the exact operation being performed by the binary.

Techniques for Efficiently Navigating the Assembly View

Use of Shortcuts:

- Ghidra provides a wide range of keyboard shortcuts to navigate the assembly view more efficiently. Learning these shortcuts can significantly speed up your workflow. For example, you can use shortcuts to quickly jump to functions, instructions, or addresses, or to toggle between the assembly and decompiler views.
- Familiarize yourself with basic navigation commands like jumping to a specific address (Ctrl+G), moving to the previous/next instruction, or scrolling through the disassembled code.

Follow the Control Flow:

- Reverse engineers should follow the control flow of the program to understand how different code blocks are executed. In Ghidra, you can quickly follow control flow by examining jump instructions (e.g., JMP, CALL) and their targets. The assembly view allows you to trace these control flows step by step, either manually or with the help of the control flow graph.

Annotate and Comment:

- As you analyze the assembly code, it is essential to add comments to the code to document your findings. This helps to track your analysis and aids future readers of the disassembly. In Ghidra, comments can be added directly in the assembly view by right-clicking on instructions and selecting the comment option.
- Documenting function names, variables, and specific operations will make it easier to understand and communicate your analysis.

Use the "Function Calls" and "Cross References":

- Ghidra allows you to right-click on function calls or variables and view their cross-references. This feature enables you to quickly see where and how a particular function is used in the binary, giving you more context for your analysis.
- By following these cross-references, you can gain a better understanding of how different functions interact and identify key areas that may need further analysis.

Navigating the assembly view in Ghidra is a vital skill for any reverse engineer. It allows you to dive deep into the inner workings of a binary, understanding how it operates at the lowest level. Ghidra's interactive assembly view, along with features like automatic function recognition, control flow graphs, and the integrated decompiler, makes the process of analyzing assembly code much more manageable. By mastering these navigation techniques and leveraging Ghidra's robust tools, reverse engineers can effectively explore and analyze complex binaries, whether for malware analysis, software debugging, or other reverse engineering tasks.

5.3 Recognizing and Understanding Assembly Instructions

Assembly instructions are the fundamental operations that a CPU performs during program execution. For reverse engineers, recognizing and understanding these instructions is a crucial skill. When a binary is disassembled into assembly code, each instruction represents a low-level operation that manipulates data, controls program flow, or interacts with memory. By decoding these instructions, reverse engineers can understand how a program behaves, locate vulnerabilities, and gain insights into the program's inner workings. In this section, we'll explore how to recognize and understand common assembly instructions, and how tools like Ghidra help simplify this process.

The Basics of Assembly Instructions

Assembly instructions vary depending on the processor architecture (e.g., x86, ARM, MIPS). However, all assembly instructions have common elements:

Opcode (Operation Code):

The opcode is the part of the instruction that specifies the operation the CPU should perform (e.g., add, subtract, load, store, jump). Each processor has its own set of opcodes, and the specific syntax and set of instructions vary between architectures. For example, MOV (move), ADD (addition), and JMP (jump) are common opcodes.

Operands:

The operands specify the values or addresses the operation will work with. These can include registers, memory addresses, or immediate values (constants). Operands can be thought of as the "data" that the instruction manipulates. For example, in the instruction MOV AX, 10, AX is a register operand, and 10 is an immediate value.

Addressing Modes:

Assembly instructions use different addressing modes to specify the location of operands. Some common modes include:

- **Immediate Addressing**: The operand is a constant value. Example: MOV AX, 10.
- **Direct Addressing**: The operand is a memory address. Example: MOV AX, [0x1234].
- **Register Addressing**: The operand is a CPU register. Example: MOV AX, BX.
- **Indirect Addressing**: The operand is a memory address stored in a register. Example: MOV AX, [BX].

Understanding the basic structure of an assembly instruction is essential for interpreting its function in the program.

Common Assembly Instructions

Here, we'll go through some of the most commonly encountered assembly instructions and their meanings. These instructions are present across many processor architectures, though the syntax may differ slightly.

MOV (Move):

- The MOV instruction is used to transfer data from one location to another. It's one of the most frequently used instructions in assembly language.
- **Example (x86): MOV AX, 10** – Moves the value 10 into the AX register.
- **Example (x86): MOV [0x1000], AX** – Moves the value in the AX register to the memory address 0x1000.

ADD (Addition):

- The ADD instruction adds the contents of two operands together.
- **Example (x86): ADD AX, BX** – Adds the value in BX to AX and stores the result in AX.
- **Example (ARM): ADD R0, R1, R2** – Adds the values in registers R1 and R2 and stores the result in R0.

SUB (Subtraction):

- The SUB instruction subtracts one operand from another.
- **Example (x86): SUB AX, BX** – Subtracts the value in BX from AX and stores the result in AX.

CMP (Compare):

- The CMP instruction compares two operands by subtracting one from the other, but it does not store the result. Instead, it sets the processor's flags, which can then be used for conditional branching.
- **Example (x86): CMP AX, BX** – Compares the values in AX and BX by performing AX - BX.

JMP (Jump):

- The JMP instruction causes an unconditional jump to a different part of the code, changing the flow of execution.
- **Example (x86): JMP 0x2000** – Jumps to the instruction located at address 0x2000.

CALL (Function Call):

- The CALL instruction is used to invoke a function. It pushes the return address onto the stack and then jumps to the function's entry point.
- **Example (x86): CALL 0x3000** – Calls the function located at address 0x3000.

RET (Return):

- The RET instruction is used to return from a function. It pops the return address from the stack and jumps back to the calling function.
- **Example (x86): RET** – Pops the return address from the stack and returns to the caller.

NOP (No Operation):

- The NOP instruction does nothing. It is often used for padding or as a placeholder during debugging or code analysis.
- **Example (x86): NOP** – Does nothing but occupies space in the instruction stream.

PUSH and POP:

- These instructions are used to manipulate the stack. PUSH saves a value onto the stack, while POP retrieves a value from the stack.
- **Example (x86): PUSH AX** – Pushes the value in AX onto the stack.
- **Example (x86): POP BX** – Pops the top value from the stack into the BX register.

TEST (Bitwise Test):

- The TEST instruction performs a bitwise AND operation between two operands but does not store the result. Instead, it updates the processor flags, which can be used for conditional branching.
- **Example (x86): TEST AX, AX** – Performs a bitwise AND of AX with itself, essentially checking if AX is zero.

AND, OR, XOR:

- These logical instructions perform bitwise operations on the operands.
- **Example (x86): AND AX, BX** – Performs a bitwise AND between AX and BX, storing the result in AX.
- **Example (x86): OR AX, BX** – Performs a bitwise OR between AX and BX, storing the result in AX.
- **Example (x86): XOR AX, BX** – Performs a bitwise XOR between AX and BX, storing the result in AX.

Interpreting Assembly Instructions with Ghidra

Ghidra simplifies the process of recognizing and understanding assembly instructions by automatically disassembling binaries and providing a readable and navigable format for reverse engineers. Here's how Ghidra can help:

Disassembly View:

Ghidra displays disassembled instructions in a clean, human-readable format. Each line of code represents a single instruction, making it easy to follow the program's flow.

Instruction Highlighting:

Ghidra highlights certain types of instructions, such as control flow instructions (JMP, CALL) or arithmetic operations (ADD, SUB), to help reverse engineers quickly identify key instructions in the binary.

Decompiler Integration:

The decompiler in Ghidra converts assembly instructions into pseudo-C code, which makes understanding complex assembly operations easier. By switching between the assembly view and the decompiler, you can gain a higher-level perspective on how specific functions operate.

Comments and Annotations:

Reverse engineers can add comments and annotations directly to instructions in the assembly view. This feature allows you to document what each instruction does, making it easier to track your progress and explain your findings to others.

Cross-references and Functions:

Ghidra automatically identifies function calls and cross-references between different parts of the binary. By following these cross-references, you can see how instructions interact with each other and trace the program's behavior through multiple layers of execution.

Instruction Details:

Ghidra provides detailed information about each instruction when you click on it. This includes the operation being performed, the operands involved, and their values or addresses, helping you gain a deeper understanding of each operation.

Recognizing and understanding assembly instructions is a vital skill for reverse engineers. Assembly instructions provide a direct view into how a program manipulates data, controls flow, and interacts with memory. By learning the basic opcodes, operands, and addressing modes, you can begin to decode the meaning behind each instruction in the disassembled code. Ghidra aids this process by providing an interactive and user-friendly environment for viewing and analyzing assembly instructions. With practice, you'll be able to navigate the complexities of assembly code, uncover hidden functionality, and gain deeper insights into the behavior of software at the machine level.

5.4 Resolving Cross-References in Assembly Code

In reverse engineering, cross-references refer to instances where a specific instruction, function, variable, or address is referenced or used multiple times throughout the binary. Understanding and resolving these cross-references is a critical task for reverse engineers because they help map out the relationships between different parts of a program. Cross-references can reveal how functions are interconnected, how data flows through the program, and where critical pieces of code or data are accessed. In this section, we'll discuss how to recognize and resolve cross-references in assembly code, and how Ghidra assists in this process to streamline analysis.

What are Cross-References?

A cross-reference (XREF) is a reference from one part of the program to another. This could be:

- Function calls where one function calls another.
- Data references where a function accesses global variables or other data structures.
- Control flow instructions like jumps or branches that direct execution to another section of code.
- Memory access where a certain memory address is accessed by various instructions.

Cross-references are essential for understanding how different parts of the program interact. Without recognizing and analyzing these references, reverse engineers would struggle to follow the flow of execution or fully comprehend the purpose of various code segments.

The Importance of Resolving Cross-References

By resolving cross-references, reverse engineers can:

- **Map Function Interactions**: Cross-references often indicate how functions interact with each other. By tracking calls and returns, you can identify the program's overall structure and dependencies.
- **Identify Data Flow**: Data is often passed between functions or accessed in different places throughout the program. Recognizing cross-references helps you understand where and how data is manipulated.
- **Track Program Execution**: Control flow instructions like JMP or CALL can lead you to different parts of the program. Understanding where code branches and how it flows is essential for a complete analysis.
- **Locate Important Functions or Code Segments**: Cross-references can help identify key functions or areas of interest, such as security-critical sections or hidden functionalities, like anti-debugging mechanisms or malware behavior.

Types of Cross-References

Function Cross-References:

A function cross-reference occurs when one function calls another. This is one of the most common types of cross-references encountered in reverse engineering.

- **Example**: If function A calls function B, you will see a reference in function A to the memory address or label of function B.
- **Identifying Function Calls**: Instructions like CALL (in x86) or BL (in ARM) are used for function calls. These instructions push the return address onto the stack and jump to the called function. When reverse engineering, these calls form essential links between different parts of the program.
- **Resolving Function Xrefs**: By navigating to the address or label associated with the call, you can follow the execution flow to the destination function. Once there, you can examine the instructions, variables, and return points to understand the function's role in the program.

Data Cross-References:

Data cross-references involve instances where functions or instructions read from or write to data (variables, buffers, memory locations). These cross-references are particularly useful when analyzing how data is passed between functions or manipulated in various parts of the code.

- **Example**: A function might read a global variable or input buffer, perform an operation, and then store the result elsewhere in memory. The data cross-references help track this flow.
- **Resolving Data Xrefs**: In Ghidra, you can easily identify data references by examining the disassembled code. When you see memory accesses such as MOV [0x1000], AX or ADD [EBX], 4, these represent references to memory locations. By resolving these references, you can trace how data is being used or modified.

Control Flow Cross-References:

Control flow cross-references occur when instructions like jumps (JMP, CALL, RET) and conditional branches (JZ, JNZ, JG, JL) reference other parts of the code.

- **Example**: A JMP instruction will unconditionally jump to a different section of the code, while a conditional jump (JZ) will only jump if the Zero Flag (ZF) is set. These cross-references indicate how the program's execution flow moves between different segments.

- **Resolving Control Flow Xrefs**: In Ghidra, you can follow these jump instructions to see where the program will go next. This can help you understand the program's logic, conditional execution paths, and important branching decisions.

Indirect Cross-References:

Indirect cross-references occur when the target of a jump or call is stored in a register or memory location, rather than being hardcoded. These types of references are harder to analyze because the target address isn't explicitly known until runtime.

- **Example**: In the instruction MOV EAX, [EBX], the value in the EBX register (which might contain a function pointer or memory address) is moved into the EAX register. If EAX is later used in a jump instruction (JMP EAX), the jump is to the address stored in EBX at the time of execution.
- **Resolving Indirect Xrefs**: Identifying indirect references often involves deeper analysis, as the target address isn't immediately visible in the disassembly. Reverse engineers may need to trace the value of the register or memory location to identify the target.

How Ghidra Helps Resolve Cross-References

- Ghidra provides several tools and features to help reverse engineers quickly recognize and resolve cross-references within assembly code. Let's look at some of the ways Ghidra simplifies this process:

Cross-Reference Viewing:

- In Ghidra, you can view cross-references for specific instructions, functions, or variables. When you right-click on a function or memory address in the disassembly view, Ghidra provides an option to "Show Xrefs" (cross-references).
- This feature allows you to see all places in the binary where that function, variable, or memory address is referenced, giving you a comprehensive view of how different parts of the program interact with it.

Function Call Graph:

- Ghidra automatically generates a call graph, which visualizes how functions within the binary call each other. This graph helps reverse engineers trace the relationships between functions and follow the program's execution flow.

- By clicking on a function in the call graph, you can quickly jump to its location in the disassembly and analyze how it operates, as well as where it is called from.

Automatic Function Recognition:

- Ghidra automatically detects functions and labels them in the disassembly, making it easier to spot cross-references to and from specific functions. When you view the disassembly, function calls and returns are clearly marked, which simplifies understanding how control flows between functions.
- Ghidra can even identify library functions and system calls, which are often used in malware analysis and vulnerability research.

Decompiler Integration:

- Ghidra's Decompiler converts assembly code into pseudo-C code, which can make it easier to understand complex cross-references and function interactions. By examining the decompiled code, reverse engineers can get a higher-level view of how functions and data are used in the program.
- This high-level perspective can make it much easier to identify the overall flow of execution and how various sections of code are interrelated.

Control Flow Graph (CFG):

- The Control Flow Graph in Ghidra helps visualize the execution paths that the program might take. This graphical representation of the program's flow allows reverse engineers to see how control is passed between different parts of the code, making it easier to follow cross-references related to jumps and branches.

Comments and Annotations:

- Adding comments and annotations is essential for resolving and tracking cross-references. Ghidra allows you to add comments directly to disassembled instructions. By annotating key cross-references, you can better document your findings, which is especially useful for understanding complex binaries or when working in a team.

Resolving cross-references in assembly code is an essential task in reverse engineering. Cross-references connect different parts of the binary and provide insights into how functions interact, how data is passed around, and how control flows through the program. Recognizing these references and following them can help reverse engineers uncover hidden logic, locate vulnerabilities, and better understand the program's behavior. Ghidra's powerful tools, such as cross-reference viewing, the function call graph, and decompiler integration, make this process significantly easier, providing a comprehensive and efficient way to trace cross-references and gain deeper insights into complex binaries.

5.5 Using Assembly to Locate Key Functions

Locating key functions in a binary is one of the most important tasks in reverse engineering. These functions could be critical to the operation of the program, potentially revealing vulnerabilities, sensitive data, or hidden functionality. Whether you're analyzing malware, debugging an application, or conducting a security audit, understanding how to efficiently find and analyze key functions using assembly code is crucial. In this section, we'll explore the techniques and strategies used to locate important functions in assembly code and how Ghidra can assist in this process.

What Are Key Functions?

Key functions are parts of a program that play a central role in its operation. These could include:

- **Core Logic**: Functions that contain the main business logic or algorithms of the program.
- **System Calls**: Functions that interact with the operating system, such as file handling, network communication, or memory management.
- **Security Functions**: Functions that implement authentication, encryption, or other security mechanisms.
- **Vulnerabilities**: Functions with flaws that could be exploited, such as buffer overflows, improper memory handling, or access control weaknesses.
- **Malicious Code**: In malware analysis, key functions could include the parts of the code that implement malicious payloads, exploit techniques, or persistence mechanisms.

Identifying these functions in assembly code requires understanding the program's flow, analyzing control structures, and recognizing patterns that indicate the presence of important functionality.

Key Strategies for Locating Functions in Assembly Code

Recognizing Function Prologues and Epilogues

In most programs, functions follow a predictable structure. This structure typically consists of a prologue (beginning of the function) and an epilogue (end of the function). Recognizing these patterns is one of the simplest ways to identify functions in assembly code.

Prologue: The prologue sets up the function environment by saving registers and preparing the stack for local variables and return addresses. In many architectures (e.g., x86, ARM), common instructions in the prologue include:

- PUSH or MOV instructions to save registers.
- SUB to allocate space for local variables on the stack.
- LEA to load addresses for accessing local variables or parameters.

Epilogue: The epilogue restores the function's environment and prepares for the return. Typical instructions in the epilogue include:

- MOV to restore saved registers.
- ADD to clean up the stack.
- RET to return to the calling function.

In x86 architecture, a simple prologue might look like:

```
push ebp
mov ebp, esp
sub esp, 0x10
```

And the epilogue would look like:

```
mov esp, ebp
pop ebp
ret
```

By recognizing these patterns, you can identify the boundaries of functions in assembly code, even if the function addresses are not explicitly labeled in the binary.

Identifying Function Calls

One of the most straightforward ways to find key functions is to look for function calls. A function call in assembly is typically represented by an instruction like CALL in x86 or BL in ARM. When a function is called, control is transferred to the target function, and the program execution returns to the next instruction after the CALL when the function finishes executing.

To identify key functions, search for function call instructions (CALL, BL, JMP) in the disassembly. These calls may target functions with important logic or system calls. Additionally, indirect function calls (where a function pointer or register is used to jump to the target function) are common in complex applications and can indicate dynamically loaded or conditionally executed functions.

Example: Identifying System Calls

In system-level programs or malware analysis, you might be looking for system calls or APIs that interact with the operating system, such as file I/O operations, network sockets, or memory management functions. These often involve a call to a kernel function or an API in a shared library (e.g., kernel32.dll on Windows, libc.so on Linux).

- In x86, system calls are typically performed using an interrupt (e.g., INT 0x80), or through the SYSCALL instruction in 64-bit systems.
- In ARM, system calls often involve the SVC (Supervisor Call) instruction.

By searching for these call instructions, you can pinpoint functions that are interacting with the OS or handling critical operations.

Using String References to Identify Key Functions

Often, strings in a program can provide useful hints about the functionality of specific functions. For example, you may encounter strings like "Error", "Success", or "Welcome" that are associated with specific functions in the program. Similarly, system error messages or library names can also point to key functions.

In assembly, strings are typically stored in data sections or read-only memory. A function may reference these strings during its execution. By identifying string references in the disassembly (often by looking for memory accesses like MOV EAX, [0x1234] where the address 0x1234 contains a string), you can locate functions that handle specific actions related to those strings.

For example, if you find the string "Enter password" in the binary, you may trace the function that handles password input or validation.

Control Flow Analysis

Program control flow is a critical aspect of understanding how functions are executed and how they interact with each other. In assembly code, jump instructions (such as JMP, JE, JNE, JG, etc.) and conditional branches (JZ, JNZ, CALL, RET) indicate how execution flows between different sections of the program.

In malware analysis, reverse engineers often focus on control flow to detect malicious payload execution, hidden functions, or obfuscated logic. A malicious function may be obfuscated through complex jumps and conditional checks, making it harder to spot. By analyzing the program's control flow—using tools like Ghidra's Control Flow Graph (CFG)—you can visualize how execution is directed across different parts of the binary, making it easier to spot hidden or key functions.

How Ghidra Aids in Locating Key Functions

Ghidra's robust features help reverse engineers efficiently locate key functions in assembly code. Here's how Ghidra can assist:

Function Identification:

Ghidra automatically detects and labels functions during the disassembly process. It marks each function's start and end, making it easier to navigate the code and find key functions.

If Ghidra does not automatically label a function, you can manually define function boundaries by analyzing prologues and epilogues, or by recognizing common function call patterns.

Function Call Graph:

Ghidra generates a call graph, which visually represents the relationships between functions. This graph allows you to quickly see how functions interact with one another, making it easy to identify which functions are central to the program's operation.

Cross-References:

Ghidra allows you to view cross-references (Xrefs) to a specific function. This helps you understand how a function is used and by which other functions. By following the Xrefs, you can uncover hidden or critical functions based on how they are accessed by other parts of the code.

Decompiler:

Ghidra's Decompiler can help you understand assembly code by translating it into pseudo-C code. The decompiled code is often more readable, making it easier to recognize key functions that might be obfuscated in raw assembly. The decompiler also allows you to examine how variables, functions, and data structures interact.

Search and Navigation:

Ghidra provides powerful search functionality that allows you to locate specific instructions, strings, or references to functions. This search capability is invaluable when you are looking for specific functions or patterns across large binaries.

Program Analysis Tools:

Ghidra's analysis tools, such as the Control Flow Graph (CFG) and Function Graph, enable you to visualize the flow of execution and understand how different functions are connected. These tools are especially useful when analyzing complex or obfuscated binaries.

Locating key functions in assembly code is essential for understanding how a program works, identifying vulnerabilities, and uncovering hidden functionality. By analyzing function prologues, function calls, control flow instructions, and string references, reverse engineers can find important functions in the binary. Ghidra simplifies this process by automating many of these tasks, offering powerful features like function identification, cross-referencing, decompilation, and visualizations like the call graph and control flow graph. By leveraging these tools, reverse engineers can efficiently navigate assembly code and locate the functions that are crucial to the program's operation, allowing for more effective analysis and security assessments.

Chapter 6: Decompilation Techniques

Decompilation is the process of converting low-level assembly code back into a higher-level programming language that is easier to understand, and in this chapter, we'll delve into Ghidra's powerful decompiler. You'll start by exploring the basics of how Ghidra's decompiler works and the types of code it generates, typically in C-like syntax, to make reverse engineering more accessible. We'll cover the various options and settings in the decompiler, including how to configure it for optimal output and what factors influence the decompilation quality. You'll learn how to identify and interpret common patterns in the decompiled code, such as function calls, loops, and conditional structures. Additionally, we'll examine the limitations of decompilation, such as incomplete type information or obfuscation techniques, and provide strategies to overcome these challenges. Finally, we'll explore ways to clean up and simplify decompiled code to make it more readable and analyzable. By the end of this chapter, you'll be equipped to use Ghidra's decompiler effectively, giving you a higher-level view of the program and enabling deeper analysis.

6.1 Introduction to Ghidra's Decompiler

The process of reverse engineering often involves analyzing machine code to understand the high-level behavior of a program. While disassembly provides a detailed view of the raw instructions executed by a CPU, it can be difficult to understand at a glance, especially when dealing with large, complex binaries. This is where decompilation comes into play.

Ghidra's Decompiler is one of its most powerful tools, allowing reverse engineers to convert low-level assembly code back into a higher-level representation—typically resembling C-like pseudocode. This high-level representation makes it easier to comprehend the logic of a program, track down specific functionality, and identify potential vulnerabilities. In this chapter, we will explore Ghidra's Decompiler, its features, and how it can be used to facilitate reverse engineering.

What is a Decompiler?

A decompiler is a tool that takes machine code or assembly instructions and attempts to convert them into a higher-level representation that is more understandable to human analysts. In practice, decompilers do not create perfect high-level code, as they must infer logical structures and operations from a set of low-level instructions. However, they can generate a significant amount of code that is closer to what a developer might write in a high-level language like C.

Decompilers perform the opposite task of compilers: where a compiler translates high-level code into machine code, a decompiler attempts to reverse this process. However, because some information is lost during compilation (such as variable names, types, and certain optimizations), a decompiler can only reconstruct an approximation of the original code.

How Ghidra's Decompiler Works

Ghidra's Decompiler is designed to take the raw assembly instructions from disassembled binaries and attempt to generate high-level pseudocode that closely resembles C. It provides reverse engineers with several advantages over manually inspecting assembly code:

Readable Output:

The primary benefit of the decompiler is its ability to convert raw assembly code into more readable pseudocode. This output often looks much closer to the high-level logic of the original program, making it easier to understand the function of the code.

Handling Complex Control Flow:

When dealing with intricate code structures such as loops, function calls, and conditionals, the decompiler identifies these patterns and structures them in a more readable manner. For example, a loop in assembly code (using jump instructions) might be translated into a for or while loop in the decompiled code, making it far easier to follow the logic.

Function Identification:

The decompiler not only translates assembly instructions into high-level code but also works in conjunction with Ghidra's function identification system. If Ghidra has already identified and labeled functions, the decompiler uses this information to group related instructions into function definitions.

Variable Renaming and Types:

While the decompiler cannot fully recover variable names or data types (as this information is lost during the compilation process), it can still identify local variables and function parameters based on the program's stack operations. It attempts to assign meaningful names, like arg1, var1, or local_0x10, and infers the likely types based on the function's behavior and use of data.

Data Structures:

The decompiler also attempts to recognize and recreate high-level data structures (such as arrays, structs, and linked lists) based on the code's memory accesses. For example, it can recognize when a series of memory accesses represents an array or a structure, and it will reflect that structure in the decompiled code.

Key Features of Ghidra's Decompiler

Pseudocode Generation:

Ghidra's Decompiler generates pseudocode that resembles C, including function definitions, conditional branches, loops, and variable assignments. While it doesn't fully restore the original source code, the generated pseudocode can be a huge help for reverse engineers, as it gives a more abstract view of the program's behavior.

Flow and Control Structures:

The Decompiler analyzes the control flow of the program and creates corresponding control structures in the pseudocode. For instance, if statements, loops, and switch-case structures are typically detected and represented appropriately. This helps reverse engineers understand how the program makes decisions and iterates over data.

Handling Obfuscation:

While decompilers cannot perfectly handle all types of obfuscation, Ghidra's Decompiler is designed to handle common obfuscation techniques like function inlining and complex jump patterns. It will try to represent obfuscated code in a clearer form, even if the original developer employed tricks to make the code harder to understand.

Type Inference:

The Decompiler infers variable and function types where possible, using analysis of memory addresses, function signatures, and other programmatic clues. It does this by examining the code that operates on variables and attempting to deduce the likely types.

Call Graph Integration:

Ghidra's Decompiler integrates seamlessly with the call graph, allowing users to see the relationship between functions. As you examine the decompiled code of one function, Ghidra makes it easy to navigate to other functions called by it, enhancing your understanding of the program's flow.

Support for Multiple Architectures:

Ghidra supports a wide range of processor architectures, including x86, ARM, MIPS, PowerPC, and more. The Decompiler works for many of these architectures, making it a versatile tool for reverse engineers working on different types of binaries.

Using Ghidra's Decompiler

Accessing the Decompiler:

To access Ghidra's Decompiler, you first need to load a binary into a project and perform an analysis. Once Ghidra completes the analysis, you can navigate to a function in the CodeBrowser window. Right-click on the function or highlight the code section you want to decompile, and select "Decompiler" from the context menu. The Decompiler will open in a separate pane displaying the high-level pseudocode.

Navigating Decompiled Code:

In the Decompiler pane, Ghidra will display the pseudocode for the selected function. You can scroll through this code just like any other text document. The decompiled code provides an immediate understanding of what the function does, along with control structures like loops, if conditions, and function calls. It can also show the flow of data through the program, such as variable assignments or memory accesses.

Interpreting Decompiled Output:

While the decompiled output is often highly readable, it's important to remember that Ghidra's Decompiler is still an approximation of the original source code. The variable names and types may be generic or incorrect, and complex code optimizations (such as inlining or loop unrolling) may not always be accurately reconstructed. Reverse engineers often need to combine decompiled output with manual inspection of the assembly code to fully understand the program's behavior.

Cross-Referencing Decompiled Functions:

Ghidra allows you to cross-reference between the decompiled pseudocode and the disassembled assembly code. By selecting a function in the decompiled view, Ghidra will highlight the corresponding part of the disassembly in the CodeBrowser, allowing you to see how Ghidra arrived at the pseudocode. This cross-referencing is crucial for verifying the correctness of the decompiled code and diving deeper into specific parts of the binary.

Advantages of Ghidra's Decompiler

- **Increased Efficiency**: Decompilation saves time by presenting a higher-level view of the code, allowing reverse engineers to focus on the logic of the program rather than wrestling with complex assembly instructions.
- **Better Understanding**: The decompiled code provides an abstraction that simplifies recognizing patterns, understanding function behavior, and identifying potential security issues or bugs.
- **Improved Analysis**: The ability to work with pseudocode rather than raw assembly is particularly useful for identifying high-level vulnerabilities such as buffer overflows, incorrect memory handling, and logic flaws that might be obscured in assembly.

Limitations of Ghidra's Decompiler

- **Inaccuracy in Complex Cases**: The decompiler cannot always perfectly reconstruct the original source code, particularly in cases of heavy optimization, obfuscation, or encryption. In such cases, the decompiled code may require significant interpretation.
- **Loss of Original Identifiers**: The decompiler cannot restore original variable names, function names, or comments, which means that the pseudocode is often not as clear as the original source code.
- **Complex Control Flow**: While Ghidra does an excellent job handling common control flow patterns, it may struggle with extremely complex or obfuscated control structures.

Ghidra's Decompiler is a powerful tool that helps reverse engineers bridge the gap between raw assembly code and high-level program logic. By converting disassembled machine code into readable pseudocode, Ghidra makes it significantly easier to understand program behavior, identify key functions, and track data flow. While it's not perfect and can't restore all aspects of the original source code, it is an invaluable tool in a reverse engineer's toolkit, especially when paired with other Ghidra features like cross-referencing and the call graph. Understanding how to leverage the Decompiler can dramatically improve the efficiency and effectiveness of reverse engineering tasks.

6.2 Understanding High-Level Decompilation Output

When reverse engineering a binary, understanding the decompiled output is crucial for efficiently analyzing the program. Ghidra's decompiler generates high-level pseudocode that is designed to resemble a C-like language, which makes it far more readable than raw assembly code. However, while the decompiled code is more accessible, it still requires interpretation and understanding of how it maps back to the original assembly instructions. In this chapter, we will dive deeper into how Ghidra's decompiled output works and how you can read and understand it effectively.

1. Overview of Decompiled Code

Ghidra's decompiler takes low-level assembly instructions from the binary and attempts to reconstruct them into a higher-level pseudocode, usually resembling C code. This allows reverse engineers to more easily grasp the program's flow, logic, and data manipulation without needing to manually trace each instruction.

The decompiled output is organized in a way that mirrors the structure of a high-level language:

- **Functions**: Each function in the program is reconstructed into a block of pseudocode. This includes the function's name, arguments, and local variables (if identifiable).
- **Control Flow**: Loops (for, while), conditionals (if, else), and switches are all expressed in familiar high-level structures.
- **Variable Types**: Ghidra makes educated guesses about variable types (such as int, char, or float) based on its analysis of the program's memory usage and operations.
- **Data Structures**: The decompiler attempts to identify arrays, structs, and other data structures, reflecting these in the pseudocode as they would appear in a high-level language.

Understanding these components is the first step to interpreting the output and using it effectively in your reverse engineering work.

2. Function Definitions

In the decompiled code, each function will appear with a function header, typically displaying the return type, function name, and parameters. For example:

int foo(int a, char b) {
*   // Function body*
}

This representation allows you to quickly identify the function's purpose and arguments. However, it's important to remember that the function name and the types may be inferred by Ghidra based on the analysis of the program. If the original program had obfuscated or stripped symbols, the names might not be meaningful. For instance, a function might be named sub_0043d2c0, which doesn't give much information, but the decompiler may assign it a name like foo() based on its logic.

The arguments of the function will be represented with generic names like int arg1, char arg2, and so on, based on the function's signature. In many cases, the function parameters' types are inferred from how they are used within the function. However, certain optimizations or obfuscation techniques might make it more difficult to determine the exact type of each parameter, leading to less accurate decompiled output.

3. Control Flow Structures

One of the key advantages of using Ghidra's decompiler is its ability to translate low-level assembly operations into recognizable control flow structures. Here's a breakdown of common control flow elements you'll encounter:

If-Else Statements: These are expressed clearly in the decompiled code as conditional blocks. For example:

if (a > b) {
*   return a;*
} else {
*   return b;*
}

The decompiler uses analysis of jump instructions (e.g., jmp, jne) to identify conditional branches and then represents them as if-else statements, making the program flow easier to follow.

Switch Statements: The decompiler will represent cases with a switch statement when multiple jump instructions correspond to a single comparison. This is more compact and readable than manually tracing each jump.

```
switch (a) {
    case 1:
        return 100;
    case 2:
        return 200;
    default:
        return 0;
}
```

Loops: Loops are identified based on repeated jump instructions or the use of loop counters. Ghidra attempts to reconstruct them into the familiar for or while loop syntax, depending on the pattern of instructions it identifies.

For example, a simple while loop in assembly might look like this:

```
while (i < 10) {
    sum += i;
    i++;
}
```

The decompiler traces back the loops to figure out the iteration pattern and converts it into a high-level equivalent.

Goto Statements: In certain low-level code, goto statements may be used instead of traditional control flow. Ghidra can identify such situations and turn them into more structured constructs like loops or switch statements when possible.

4. Variables and Data Types

The decompiler assigns types to variables where possible, based on how they are used throughout the program. However, because the decompiler is working with binary code, it can't always determine the precise data type used in the original program. For example, an integer might be identified as int, but if the program uses it in a way that suggests it could be a pointer or an array, the decompiler might adjust its output accordingly.

Ghidra will label the variables in a consistent way, often using names like arg1, local_0x4, or var_0x8 for parameters and local variables, respectively. If Ghidra can infer a more appropriate type (e.g., int, float, char*), it will adjust its decompiled code to reflect that. This makes it easier for reverse engineers to understand the data structures and values in use, even if the original source code has been obfuscated or stripped of symbols.

However, due to optimization or obfuscation, Ghidra might not always determine the correct type. For example, it may assign an incorrect type (such as assigning an integer type to a pointer) or leave a variable untyped.

5. Memory Access and Pointers

In decompiled code, memory accesses such as pointers or arrays are shown with an appropriate high-level representation. For example, a pointer dereference in assembly might be converted to something like:

ptr = &array[5];

The decompiler uses the patterns of memory accesses to identify such data structures. When memory addresses are used in a loop or function, Ghidra often infers that the data being accessed represents an array or other structured data.

However, interpreting pointers in decompiled code requires care, as Ghidra may misinterpret certain memory accesses, especially when dealing with complex heap structures or dynamically allocated memory. It's important to cross-reference with the disassembly and data section in such cases.

6. Inaccuracies and Limitations

While Ghidra's decompiler generates highly readable pseudocode, it's important to understand that the output is an approximation of the original high-level code. The decompiled output is limited by several factors, such as:

Optimizations: Compilers optimize code in ways that are difficult to reverse. Inline functions, loop unrolling, and aggressive optimization can make it challenging for the decompiler to recover the original logic accurately.

Obfuscation: Obfuscation techniques like control flow flattening, junk code insertion, and string encryption can confuse the decompiler, resulting in incorrect or incomplete pseudocode.

Missing Information: Data about variable names, types, and structures are often lost during compilation. The decompiler can only guess the types and names based on its analysis of the code flow, which may not always be correct.

Because of these factors, decompiled code is often just the starting point for reverse engineering. Analysts will need to manually inspect both the decompiled pseudocode and the raw assembly to make sure they fully understand the program's functionality.

Ghidra's decompiler provides an invaluable tool for transforming low-level assembly code into high-level pseudocode that is easier to read and understand. The decompiled output is typically organized into functions, control flow structures, variables, and data types, making it easier to trace the program's logic. However, while Ghidra does an excellent job of generating readable pseudocode, it is not perfect. Analysts must be prepared to interpret the output, validate assumptions, and cross-reference with the raw disassembly to achieve a complete understanding of the program. By mastering the reading and interpretation of high-level decompilation output, you can greatly improve the efficiency and effectiveness of your reverse engineering efforts.

6.3 Recognizing Common Patterns in Decompiled Code

When working with Ghidra's decompiler, one of the most valuable skills a reverse engineer can develop is the ability to recognize common patterns in the decompiled code. Identifying these recurring patterns can significantly speed up the analysis process and help you understand the structure and intent of the program more quickly. In this chapter, we will explore some of the most common patterns you may encounter in decompiled code and how to recognize and interpret them effectively.

1. Control Flow Structures

Control flow structures are fundamental to understanding how a program behaves. These structures represent how a program makes decisions and repeats actions, which is key to reverse engineering. Ghidra's decompiler attempts to reconstruct these control flow elements from low-level assembly instructions, often translating them into their more recognizable high-level equivalents.

If-Else Statements: One of the most common control flow structures in decompiled code is the if-else statement. It's often used to represent conditional branching based on some comparison or logical condition. The pattern for this is straightforward: an expression is evaluated, and based on the result, the program either executes one block of code or another.

Example:

if (a > b) {
    return a;
} else {
    return b;
}

How to Recognize: If you see a conditional jump (e.g., jne, je, jmp in assembly), you can often map it to an if-else condition in the decompiled code. The test will typically compare two values and direct the flow of execution based on the comparison.

Switch-Case Statements: A switch or case structure is often used in programs where multiple possible values of a variable lead to different branches. The decompiler will represent this pattern by converting a series of conditional jumps based on a single value into a switch statement.

Example:

switch (a) {
    case 1:
        return 100;
    case 2:
        return 200;
    default:
        return 0;
}

How to Recognize: If you notice a series of comparisons to a single variable or register followed by jumps, it's likely that these jumps represent a switch-case structure. The decompiler will often convert these patterns into a switch statement.

Loops: Loops, including for, while, and do-while loops, are another common pattern in decompiled code. These structures allow the program to repeat a certain block of code multiple times until a condition is met. The decompiler reconstructs loops by analyzing repeated code and jump instructions.

Example (While Loop):

while (i < 10) {
   sum += i;
   i++;
}

How to Recognize: If you see repeated jump instructions in the disassembly where one condition is checked (such as checking whether a counter is greater than or less than a limit), the decompiler may convert this into a while or for loop.

2. Function Calls and Recursion

Functions are the building blocks of any program, and reverse engineers often need to identify how a program organizes its code into functions. When decompiled, function calls and recursion are often expressed in the form of function_name() in C-like pseudocode.

Function Calls: A function call in decompiled code represents a jump in the flow of execution. The decompiler identifies a jump to a specific address in the program, infers that it is the start of a function, and then converts that call into a high-level function call.

Example:

int result = add(a, b);

How to Recognize: If you see an instruction like call or jmp in assembly code, the decompiler will often generate a function call in the pseudocode. The name of the function may be inferred, or if symbols are available, it may use the original function name.

Recursion: Recursion occurs when a function calls itself. In the decompiled code, this can often be recognized by the function calling its own name within its body.

Example:

int factorial(int n) {
   if (n <= 1) return 1;
   return n * factorial(n - 1);

```
}
```

How to Recognize: In assembly, a recursive function call will typically involve a jump to the same function address with modified parameters (often involving stack manipulation). The decompiler may convert this into a recursive function call in the pseudocode.

3. Memory and Pointer Access

Memory manipulation and pointer dereferencing are common in low-level code, and they can often be identified in decompiled output. The decompiler attempts to map raw memory accesses, such as loading data from or writing to memory locations, into high-level operations like array or pointer accesses.

Pointer Dereferencing: When a pointer is dereferenced, the value it points to is accessed. In the decompiled code, this is typically represented as an array or pointer access.

Example:

int value = ptr[5]; // Dereferencing pointer to access 5th element

How to Recognize: In assembly, pointer dereferencing will often involve memory accesses like mov or lea, followed by a memory address calculation. The decompiler will map this into array indexing or pointer dereferencing in the high-level code.

Array Access: Arrays are often used in C-like languages to store sequential data. In assembly, accessing an array element typically involves calculating an index and loading the value from that address.

Example:

int arr[10];
arr[5] = 20;

How to Recognize: When you see memory operations involving indexed addresses (e.g., array[index] or [base + offset]), these will be converted to array accesses in the decompiled code.

Buffer Overflows: A buffer overflow occurs when data exceeds the boundaries of a buffer, potentially leading to memory corruption or crashes. In decompiled code, this can sometimes be identified by excessive use of pointers or unsafe memory operations.

Example:

char buffer[10];
strcpy(buffer, "This string is too long!");

How to Recognize: In assembly, this often manifests as memory accesses that appear to overwrite adjacent buffers or stack variables. The decompiler may not directly detect the overflow, but suspicious memory writes to arrays or buffers can be a strong indicator.

4. String Handling and Constant Data

Programs frequently deal with strings and constants, which are often stored in the binary as immutable data. The decompiler will typically convert these constants into string literals or constant definitions in the pseudocode.

String Manipulation: String handling functions like strcmp, strcpy, or strlen are common patterns that Ghidra's decompiler will recognize and convert into high-level C function calls.

Example:

if (strcmp(str1, str2) == 0) {
*   printf("Strings are equal");*
}

How to Recognize: If you see calls to functions like strlen, strcmp, or memcpy in the assembly, these will often map to string manipulation functions in the decompiled code.

Constant Values: Constants, including numeric values, are often embedded in the binary as part of the program's initialization or static data. The decompiler will present these values in the pseudocode.

Example:

int max = 100;

How to Recognize: Constants in the binary are typically initialized with immediate values or loaded from a data section. The decompiler will replace these with readable variable assignments in the pseudocode.

5. Identifying Obfuscated Code Patterns

Obfuscation techniques are used to make the reverse engineering process more difficult. While decompilers are often successful in recovering high-level patterns, they may struggle with obfuscated code.

Control Flow Obfuscation: This technique involves scrambling the control flow, making it harder to detect the true logic. The decompiler will try to group these instructions into recognizable structures, but in some cases, the output may appear as a jumble of nested conditions or misleading control flow.

How to Recognize: Obfuscated code often features odd jumps, seemingly unrelated blocks of code, or long sequences of arithmetic or logic operations. Cross-referencing the assembly with the decompiled output and manually simplifying these constructs can help uncover the true logic.

String Obfuscation: This involves encoding or encrypting string values within the program, often making them hard to recognize in the binary.

How to Recognize: If you see strange sequences of characters or non-printable values, the decompiler may have decoded the strings, but there could be further encoding involved. Recognizing these obfuscated patterns and using Ghidra's built-in tools to trace them back to their original form is essential.

Recognizing common patterns in decompiled code is a key skill for reverse engineers. Understanding how the decompiler reconstructs control flow, function calls, memory access, string manipulation, and even obfuscated code allows you to make better use of the decompiled output. By becoming familiar with these patterns, you can more quickly interpret the pseudocode and identify important structures, enabling you to efficiently analyze and reverse engineer binaries. This knowledge helps you understand the logic behind the program and identify potential vulnerabilities, security risks, or other areas of interest during the reverse engineering process.

6.4 Decompiler Limitations and How to Overcome Them

While Ghidra's decompiler is a powerful tool that simplifies the process of reverse engineering by translating low-level assembly code into higher-level pseudocode, it is not without its limitations. Understanding these limitations is crucial for any reverse engineer, as it allows you to adapt and apply additional techniques to overcome challenges. In this section, we will explore the common limitations of Ghidra's decompiler and strategies for overcoming them.

1. Loss of High-Level Constructs

One of the primary challenges when decompiling a binary is the loss of high-level information during compilation. Compilers often optimize code and remove certain constructs that are present in the source code. This means that information such as variable names, data types, and original comments are not present in the binary, leaving only the raw machine code. As a result, the decompiled output can sometimes be difficult to interpret without context.

Limitation: Missing variable names and comments can make understanding the original intent of the program challenging.

How to Overcome:

- **Symbol Recovery**: If the binary contains debug symbols or is partially stripped, Ghidra can sometimes recover these symbols and provide more meaningful names for functions and variables. If you are working with a stripped binary, you can look for patterns in the assembly or try to use external symbol databases.
- **Manual Reconstruction**: In cases where the decompiler struggles to recover meaningful names or data types, reverse engineers often resort to manual annotation. By analyzing the code and recognizing patterns (like common string functions or arithmetic operations), you can manually infer the purpose of certain variables or functions and add comments or rename variables to make the code more understandable.

2. Handling Complex Control Flow

The decompiler in Ghidra is generally effective at recognizing simple control structures such as loops and conditionals. However, when dealing with complex control flow or unusual patterns, the decompiler may struggle to properly reconstruct the program's logic. This can happen when the code involves deeply nested conditions, indirect function calls, or dynamically determined control flow.

Limitation: Complex control flow, especially when there are indirect jumps or function pointers, may not be accurately decompiled. The decompiler might present this as a jumble of nested conditions or loops, making it difficult to understand the program's behavior.

How to Overcome:

- **Manual Reconstructing of Control Flow**: In cases of complex or obfuscated control flow, you can attempt to manually trace the flow of execution by examining the assembly code directly. Identifying key jump instructions and tracing them back to their origin can help clarify the underlying control flow.
- **Code Graph Analysis**: Ghidra allows users to explore the function graph and call graph to visualize how the program is structured. Using these tools, you can often get a better sense of how control flows between different sections of the code and help you manually map out complex structures.

3. Incomplete or Incorrect Type Inference

The decompiler attempts to infer variable types based on the usage patterns and the assembly code, but in many cases, this inference can be inaccurate or incomplete. The absence of explicit type information in the binary means that the decompiler has to make educated guesses, which can result in incorrect or vague type assignments.

Limitation: The decompiler may assign incorrect types to variables, resulting in a misleading or confusing decompiled code. For example, a variable may be incorrectly recognized as an integer when it should be a pointer, leading to incorrect decompiled logic.

How to Overcome:

- **Type Reconstruction**: Reverse engineers often need to manually adjust types in the decompiled code. By inspecting how variables are used in the program (e.g., looking for pointer arithmetic or specific function calls), you can determine the correct data types and change them within the decompiled output.
- **Use Ghidra's Data Types Repository**: Ghidra has a built-in data type manager that allows users to define custom data types. If the decompiler does not infer types correctly, you can create and apply your own data types, especially for complex structures or user-defined types like structs or enums.

4. Handling Inline Assembly or Custom Calling Conventions

Many programs make use of inline assembly or employ custom calling conventions that deviate from standard conventions. This can present a significant challenge for the decompiler, as the control flow and function prologues/epilogues may not follow standard patterns.

Limitation: Inline assembly can bypass the high-level abstractions that the decompiler typically relies on. Additionally, custom calling conventions may not be recognized correctly by the decompiler, leading to incorrect function signatures and call analysis.

How to Overcome:

- **Manually Handle Inline Assembly**: When the decompiler encounters inline assembly, it typically leaves it as-is or translates it to raw assembly instructions. You may need to manually interpret these instructions and re-integrate them into the decompiled code.
- **Custom Function Signatures**: For functions using custom calling conventions, Ghidra allows you to define custom function signatures and calling conventions. By analyzing the function prologue and the way parameters are passed, you can adjust the decompiled function signatures to correctly represent the custom convention.

5. Dealing with Obfuscated Code

Code obfuscation is often used to make reverse engineering more difficult. Obfuscators manipulate the binary to make the program's logic harder to understand by renaming variables, altering control flow, or inserting junk instructions. This can significantly impact the accuracy and quality of the decompiled output.

Limitation: Obfuscated code can result in decompiled pseudocode that appears nonsensical or convoluted. This might include apparent random jumps, unnecessary operations, or confusing patterns that obscure the original program logic.

How to Overcome:

- **Manual Code Simplification**: To deal with obfuscation, reverse engineers must often simplify the decompiled code manually. This could involve eliminating redundant operations, refactoring complex control flow, or reordering instructions to expose the true logic of the program.

- **Dynamic Analysis**: Dynamic analysis (i.e., running the program in a debugger or emulator) can be invaluable in dealing with obfuscated code. By analyzing how the program behaves at runtime, you can get a clearer understanding of the program's true functionality and reverse-engineer the obfuscated parts more effectively.

6. Dealing with High-Level Constructs in Low-Level Code

The decompiler strives to reverse-engineer high-level constructs such as classes, structures, and objects, but this can be difficult when the original program uses low-level representations or unusual memory layouts. Object-oriented programs, for example, often require the decompiler to recognize classes and virtual functions.

Limitation: The decompiler might fail to correctly reconstruct high-level constructs like classes, structs, or object-oriented code, especially in programs that use complex memory layouts or non-standard object representations.

How to Overcome:

- **Manual Reconstruction of High-Level Constructs**: If the decompiler cannot correctly recognize classes or structures, you can manually infer these from the program's behavior. For example, by identifying how memory is allocated and used, you can reverse-engineer the class structures and manually define them in Ghidra.
- **Use Ghidra's Structure Definitions**: Ghidra allows users to define and apply structure definitions to memory regions. This is especially useful for reconstructing complex data structures from memory dumps or program analysis.

Despite its many strengths, Ghidra's decompiler is not flawless. By understanding its limitations, you can better approach the reverse engineering process. Whether it's handling complex control flow, dealing with obfuscated code, or reconstructing high-level data types, there are strategies you can use to overcome these challenges. By combining manual analysis, dynamic analysis, and the use of Ghidra's advanced features, you can often bridge the gaps in the decompiled output and gain a deeper understanding of the program you are analyzing.

6.5 Tips for Cleaning and Simplifying Decompiled Code

Decompiled code is often raw and difficult to understand. While Ghidra's decompiler does a good job of translating assembly into high-level pseudocode, the output can still be cluttered with extraneous details, incorrect type assignments, or complex control flow that makes it hard to follow. To improve readability and simplify the code, reverse engineers often need to apply a series of techniques and best practices. In this section, we will explore several tips and strategies to clean and simplify decompiled code, making it easier to analyze and understand.

1. Renaming Functions, Variables, and Labels

One of the first things you should do when working with decompiled code is to rename functions, variables, and labels. Decompiled code often contains generic or meaningless names like sub_12345678, var_4, or loc_9876543. These names are usually the result of the decompiler trying to infer the role of a piece of code without having access to the original variable names or function signatures.

Tip: Rename functions and variables based on their context in the program. For example, if a function appears to calculate the sum of two numbers, rename it calculate_sum(). Similarly, variables should be renamed to reflect their role in the code, like user_input or counter.

In Ghidra, you can right-click on a function or variable and select Rename to assign it a meaningful name. By gradually renaming key elements in the decompiled code, you will improve your understanding of the program and make the code easier to follow.

2. Simplifying Complex Control Flow

Decompilers sometimes struggle with complex control flow, resulting in convoluted and difficult-to-read structures in the output. This could manifest as deeply nested if statements, overly complicated loops, or unnatural branching. Simplifying these control flow constructs will make the decompiled code more readable and help you quickly understand the program's logic.

Tip: Identify and simplify deeply nested conditionals or loops. For example, nested if statements can often be flattened into simpler logical conditions, and complex while or for loops can be restructured into more straightforward forms. This can be done by manually rewriting the decompiled output to reduce nesting or splitting complicated expressions into intermediate steps.

Example:

if (a > b) {

```
    if (c > d) {
        return true;
    }
}
return false;
```

Can be simplified to:

```
return (a > b) && (c > d);
```

3. Removing Redundant Code

Decompilers sometimes generate redundant or unnecessary code, particularly when analyzing optimized or obfuscated binaries. For example, the decompiler may produce extra variables or assignments that don't contribute to the program's behavior. Cleaning up this redundant code can greatly improve readability.

Tip: Carefully examine the decompiled code for variables or functions that are initialized but never used, or functions that don't affect the program's state. Remove or refactor these parts to eliminate unnecessary complexity. Additionally, check for loops or conditions that always evaluate to the same result, and simplify or eliminate them.

Example:

```
int x = 5;
int y = x + 2;
int z = y + 1;
return z;
```

This can be simplified to:

```
return 8;
```

4. Converting Complex Expressions into Intermediate Variables

When the decompiler encounters complex expressions, it may present them in an unoptimized or overly complicated form. Breaking these expressions down into simpler components using intermediate variables can help clarify their intent and make the code easier to follow.

Tip: Look for complex expressions, especially those involving multiple arithmetic or logical operations, and break them down into simpler parts by introducing temporary variables. This improves both readability and maintainability of the code.

Example:

*return (a * b) + (c * d) - (e / f);*

Can be simplified to:

*int temp1 = a * b;*
*int temp2 = c * d;*
int temp3 = e / f;
return temp1 + temp2 - temp3;

5. Refactoring Obfuscated Code

Obfuscated code is deliberately designed to be difficult to understand. It may involve random variable names, unnecessary code insertions, or confusing control flow. Ghidra's decompiler may struggle to recognize these patterns and present them in a convoluted way. Refactoring obfuscated code is a critical skill for reverse engineers.

Tip: Look for common obfuscation techniques, such as redundant operations, unusual jumps, or unnecessary function calls. Simplify the code by removing or rewriting these obfuscated sections. In some cases, you may need to revert to static or dynamic analysis to better understand the code's intent and remove the obfuscation.

For example, obfuscated code may look like this:

int obf_func(int a) {
*   int temp = a ^ 0xabcdef;*
*   temp = temp + 12345;*
*   return temp;*
}

You can refactor it to a simpler form:

int obf_func(int a) {
*   return (a ^ 0xabcdef) + 12345;*
}

6. Fixing Incorrect Type Inference

Decompilers attempt to infer data types based on the operations they observe in the binary, but this can result in incorrect or incomplete type assignments, especially when working with custom types, pointers, or structures. Incorrect type inference can make the code harder to understand and lead to bugs if not addressed.

Tip: Manually adjust variable types when necessary. If you spot variables that have been incorrectly identified as integers but are actually pointers or structures, update the decompiled code with the correct types. Use Ghidra's Data Types window to define and apply proper types to variables and functions.

Example:

```
// Decompiler might infer a pointer as an integer
int* ptr = (int*)0x12345678;
```

Can be corrected to:

```
int* ptr = (int*)0x12345678;
```

7. Using Ghidra's Data Structures and Functions

Ghidra has powerful features that can help clean and simplify decompiled code. For instance, the Data Type Manager allows you to define custom data types, structures, and functions. By using these features, you can replace raw memory accesses with meaningful variable names and structures, and simplify your analysis significantly.

Tip: Use the Data Type Manager to define custom structs, enums, or other complex types that the decompiler may have missed or misinterpreted. This allows you to better understand complex data structures and reduces the noise in the decompiled code.

8. Simplifying Unnecessary Memory Access

Sometimes the decompiler will generate code that accesses memory in a complicated or redundant manner. For instance, it may create complex pointers when simple array access or direct variable manipulation would suffice. These unnecessary memory accesses can complicate the code and make it harder to analyze.

Tip: If you recognize that certain memory accesses are redundant or convoluted, try to simplify them by replacing them with direct variable manipulation or array access. You can refactor the code to use simpler expressions or data structures.

Example:

```
// Decompiled code with redundant memory access
int* ptr = (int*)malloc(sizeof(int));
*ptr = 10;
return *ptr;
```

Can be simplified to:

```
int x = 10;
return x;
```

9. Use Function and Control Flow Graphs

When the decompiled code is overly complex or difficult to understand, leveraging Ghidra's Function Graph and Control Flow Graph (CFG) can be invaluable. These graphical representations can help you see how functions and program flow are structured, which can guide you in simplifying and cleaning the code.

Tip: Use the Function Graph to see how functions are interconnected and identify areas where control flow could be simplified. Similarly, use the Control Flow Graph (CFG) to identify redundant or unnecessary paths in the code that can be eliminated.

Cleaning and simplifying decompiled code is a crucial part of reverse engineering. By following these tips, you can improve the readability of the decompiled output, making it easier to understand and analyze. Renaming variables, simplifying control flow, eliminating redundancy, and correcting type inference are all key steps in making the decompiled code more manageable. By combining these techniques with Ghidra's powerful features, you can streamline your reverse engineering workflow and gain deeper insights into the program you are analyzing.

Part III: Advanced Analysis and Techniques

Part III takes you beyond the basics, diving into the more sophisticated aspects of reverse engineering with Ghidra. In this section, you'll learn advanced techniques to analyze and manipulate binaries, with a focus on the in-depth analysis of control flow, data flow, and complex function structures. We'll explore debugging and emulation methods, giving you the tools to analyze runtime behavior and interact with running binaries. Additionally, you'll gain insights into patching and modifying binaries, a vital skill for software modification, malware analysis, and exploit development. By mastering these advanced techniques, you'll be prepared to tackle more challenging reverse engineering tasks and fully leverage Ghidra's capabilities to analyze, debug, and manipulate software.

Chapter 7: Function and Data Flow Analysis

In this chapter, we focus on the critical techniques of function and data flow analysis, which are essential for understanding how a binary operates at a deeper level. You'll learn how to identify and analyze functions within a binary, whether they're automatically detected by Ghidra or require manual identification. We'll guide you through the process of mapping control flow graphs (CFGs) to visualize the logic and flow of execution, helping you understand how different functions interact within the program. You'll also explore data flow analysis, which helps track the movement of data through the program, uncovering dependencies, variable usage, and memory access patterns. By mastering function and data flow analysis, you'll be able to navigate complex binaries more effectively, pinpointing key areas of interest for further analysis, modification, or exploitation. This chapter provides the foundational skills for understanding how software behaves internally, empowering you to reverse engineer programs with confidence and precision.

7.1 Identifying Functions Automatically vs. Manually

When reverse engineering a binary, one of the most fundamental tasks is identifying and understanding the functions that make up the program. Functions are crucial building blocks of a program, and understanding their purpose and interrelationships can provide insights into the overall behavior of the program. Ghidra, a powerful reverse engineering tool, offers both automatic and manual methods for identifying functions within a binary. Understanding when and how to use these different approaches is essential for an effective analysis.

This section will explore both automatic and manual methods for identifying functions, highlighting the strengths, weaknesses, and when to use each approach.

1. Automatic Function Identification

Ghidra's automatic function identification capabilities are designed to streamline the process of discovering functions within a binary. The tool uses various heuristics to detect the start of functions and maps out the program's structure. This process is relatively fast and can provide an overview of the functions within the binary, making it a good starting point for reverse engineers.

How Automatic Identification Works:

- **Function Prologues**: Ghidra detects function prologues (the initial instructions that set up a function, such as stack setup, register saving, etc.). This is done by analyzing the binary's control flow and recognizing standard patterns that indicate the beginning of a function.
- **Cross-Referencing**: Ghidra also identifies functions by looking at cross-references, such as function calls or jump instructions. When a function is called, the tool can often infer the entry point for the function being called.
- **Symbol Information**: If the binary contains debug symbols or if the program has not been stripped of information, Ghidra can leverage this metadata to automatically identify function boundaries and provide more accurate results.

Benefits of Automatic Function Identification:

- **Speed**: Automatic identification is fast and can quickly map out a large number of functions in a binary.
- **Ease of Use**: Ghidra's built-in heuristics make automatic function identification simple and convenient for reverse engineers, especially when dealing with unfamiliar or large codebases.
- **Useful for Overview**: The automatic detection can give an immediate high-level overview of the structure of the binary and provide a good starting point for further analysis.

Limitations of Automatic Function Identification:

- **Inaccurate or Missed Functions**: Ghidra's heuristics are not perfect. In some cases, the tool may miss functions that have unusual prologues, such as those with non-standard calling conventions or functions that don't follow conventional patterns.
- **Over-identification**: In some cases, Ghidra may over-attribute code as a function, identifying blocks of code that aren't actual functions, such as library calls or obfuscated code sections.

How to Improve Automatic Function Detection:

- **Manual Inspection**: After the automatic identification, manually inspect the identified functions for accuracy. Ghidra provides features like the Function Graph and Call Graph, which can be useful for verifying that the identified functions are correct.

- **Adjust Function Boundaries**: If the automatic identification misidentifies a function or misses one, Ghidra allows you to manually adjust the function boundaries by marking function start and end points, correcting the automatic output.

2. Manual Function Identification

While automatic methods are useful for quickly identifying many functions, manual identification is sometimes necessary when dealing with complex or obfuscated binaries. Manual function identification involves analyzing the assembly code, looking for patterns that indicate the start of a function, and marking these as functions within Ghidra.

How Manual Identification Works:

- **Disassembly Analysis**: Reverse engineers look for specific assembly instructions that indicate the beginning of a function, such as push, mov, or sub instructions that set up the stack, save registers, or allocate space for local variables.
- **Control Flow**: Identifying function boundaries manually often involves tracing the control flow by following jump and call instructions. Functions are typically called through call instructions, and identifying these calls can help pinpoint the locations of the target functions.
- **Code Comments and Strings**: Sometimes reverse engineers use context clues, such as recognizable strings or code comments, to identify functions. For example, if you see a string like "User Login" in the disassembly, it might suggest the presence of a function related to user login functionality.

Benefits of Manual Function Identification:

- **Accuracy**: Manual identification allows for more accurate identification of functions, especially in cases where Ghidra's heuristics may miss functions or make errors.
- **Obfuscated Code Handling**: Manual identification is particularly useful when analyzing obfuscated or non-standard code, where automatic detection may fail to recognize legitimate functions due to the lack of recognizable prologues or irregular control flow.
- **Custom Function Boundaries**: When Ghidra's automatic analysis misidentifies the boundaries of a function, manual adjustments can be made to ensure that functions are accurately represented.

Limitations of Manual Function Identification:

- **Time-Consuming**: Manually identifying functions can be slow, especially for large or complex binaries. This process can require careful examination of assembly instructions, which can be tedious and error-prone.
- **Requires Expertise**: Effective manual function identification requires a deep understanding of assembly language, as well as knowledge of the binary's architecture and typical function prologues.

3. When to Use Automatic vs. Manual Identification

In practice, both automatic and manual function identification methods are often used in tandem to ensure a comprehensive understanding of a binary.

When to Rely on Automatic Identification:

- **Initial Overview**: When starting a reverse engineering project, automatic function identification provides a quick way to map out the program's structure and identify most of the functions.
- **Large Binaries**: For large binaries, automatic identification can save significant time by quickly identifying a broad range of functions that can then be manually refined.
- **Well-Standardized Code**: If the binary follows standard conventions and does not employ heavy obfuscation, automatic identification can be accurate and sufficient for most purposes.

When to Use Manual Identification:

- **Obfuscated or Irregular Code**: If you're dealing with a heavily obfuscated binary or one that employs custom calling conventions or non-standard function prologues, manual identification is often necessary.
- **Verification and Cleanup**: After automatic identification, manual inspection and adjustment are needed to ensure that functions are correctly identified and that boundaries are accurate.
- **Complex Control Flow**: In binaries with complex or non-linear control flow (such as virtual machines or dynamically generated code), manual function identification might be required to properly identify all relevant functions.

4. Combining Automatic and Manual Identification

In most cases, a hybrid approach that combines both automatic and manual identification is the most effective. Start with Ghidra's automatic function identification to quickly gather a list of potential functions. Then, review the list to ensure that all relevant functions are correctly identified, and manually adjust or add functions as needed. This approach ensures that you can quickly gain an overview of the binary while also addressing any complexities that automatic analysis might have missed.

Workflow Example:

- Run Ghidra's automatic analysis to detect functions.
- Review the identified functions using the Function Graph and Call Graph to check for accuracy.
- Manually add missing functions or adjust the boundaries of incorrectly identified functions.
- Use the Listing and Decompiled View to inspect the function bodies and ensure the program's structure is well understood.

Identifying functions is one of the most critical tasks in reverse engineering a binary. Ghidra provides both automatic and manual methods for identifying functions, each with its strengths and weaknesses. Automatic function identification is fast and can provide a general overview, while manual identification is more accurate and useful for handling obfuscated or complex code. By combining both methods, reverse engineers can quickly gain a comprehensive understanding of a binary's structure, improving their ability to analyze and manipulate the program effectively.

7.2 Mapping Control Flow Graphs (CFGs)

A Control Flow Graph (CFG) is an essential tool in reverse engineering, particularly for understanding how a program executes and how control flows between different parts of the code. By visualizing the execution paths that a program can take, CFGs help reverse engineers analyze, debug, and manipulate binary code more effectively. In Ghidra, mapping a Control Flow Graph (CFG) involves understanding how different functions or blocks of code are interconnected through control flow instructions such as jumps, calls, and returns.

This section will explore how to map and interpret Control Flow Graphs (CFGs) within Ghidra, how they are useful in reverse engineering, and how to apply this knowledge to improve your understanding of a binary's structure and behavior.

1. What is a Control Flow Graph (CFG)?

A Control Flow Graph (CFG) is a directed graph that represents the flow of control within a program. Each node in the graph represents a basic block (a sequence of instructions with no branches except at the end), and the edges between nodes represent the possible execution paths that the program might follow during execution.

In the context of reverse engineering, CFGs are crucial for:

- **Visualizing Execution Paths**: By seeing the possible paths of execution, reverse engineers can understand how the program behaves in different scenarios.
- **Identifying Loops and Branches**: CFGs help identify loops, conditional branches, and function calls within the program's control flow.
- **Analyzing Function Relationships**: By mapping how functions call each other, CFGs can reveal the overall structure of the program and its interdependencies.

2. Generating and Navigating the Control Flow Graph in Ghidra

Ghidra provides an interactive and visual way to generate and navigate the Control Flow Graph (CFG) of a binary. Once you've disassembled or decompiled a binary, Ghidra can automatically build the CFG based on its analysis of the control flow instructions.

Steps to Generate a CFG in Ghidra:

- **Open the Function**: Start by opening the function you wish to analyze in the Ghidra CodeBrowser.
- **Generate the Graph**: Right-click inside the function or the disassembly window and choose "Show Function Graph" or "Show Control Flow Graph". This will display the CFG for the selected function.
- **Explore the Graph**: The CFG will show a graphical representation of the function's control flow, with nodes representing basic blocks of instructions and edges representing the flow of execution between those blocks.
- **Navigation**: You can click on nodes and edges within the graph to zoom in on specific parts of the code, making it easier to navigate and understand complex control flow structures.

Understanding the Graph Elements:

- **Nodes**: Each node represents a basic block—a sequence of instructions that executes sequentially without branches. A basic block typically ends with a jump, call, return, or conditional branch instruction.
- **Edges**: The directed edges between nodes represent the flow of execution from one block to another. These can correspond to jumps, calls, returns, or conditional branches in the program.
- **Entry and Exit Points**: The graph will typically have an entry point (the first node that represents where the function starts) and one or more exit points (where the function ends or returns control to another part of the program).

3. Interpreting the Control Flow Graph

Interpreting a CFG requires a strong understanding of how control flow works in assembly and high-level programming languages. The goal of mapping the control flow is to identify key execution paths, such as loops, function calls, conditionals, and branches, within the program.

Key Features to Identify in the CFG:

Conditional Branches: These are edges that represent decisions in the program, such as if statements or switch cases. They usually have two outgoing edges—one for the "true" path and one for the "false" path.

Example:

```
if (x > 10) {
   // do something
} else {
   // do something else
}
```

In the CFG, this would appear as a node with two outgoing edges, one for each of the if and else blocks.

Loops: Loops are repeated sections of code that often have an edge pointing back to an earlier node. Identifying loops is crucial for understanding the program's logic, especially in cases like infinite loops or for-loop iterations.

Example:

```
while (x < 10) {
    x++;
}
```

In the CFG, you will see a cycle—an edge pointing from the end of the loop back to the beginning, indicating the repetition of the loop.

Function Calls: Function calls are edges that exit the current function and direct the program to another function. By following these edges, you can trace the program's execution flow across functions and explore interdependencies between different parts of the binary.

Example:

```
foo();
```

In the CFG, you will see an outgoing edge from the current function's node to the node representing the entry point of the foo() function.

Return Statements: These edges represent the exit points of a function. The return statements indicate where control will transfer back to the caller after the function has finished executing.

Example:

```
return 0;
```

In the CFG, the return statement will be a node that has no outgoing edges, indicating that the function is ending.

4. Using the CFG for Reverse Engineering

The primary benefit of mapping a Control Flow Graph is that it helps reverse engineers understand the program's control structure. By analyzing the CFG, reverse engineers can answer several key questions:

- **What functions are called, and in what order?**: The CFG helps identify which functions are being called and how control flows between them, giving insight into the program's structure.

- **What are the key decision points?:** By identifying conditional branches, reverse engineers can pinpoint areas where the program makes decisions based on user input or other data.
- **Are there loops or repeated code paths?:** The CFG helps spot loops and repeated paths, which are often areas of the program where bugs, vulnerabilities, or interesting behaviors occur.
- **How does the program return control to the caller?:** The return edges in the CFG help trace the program's exit points, showing where functions conclude and how the execution continues.

Example: Analyzing a CFG to Understand Program Flow

Imagine you are analyzing a binary and you generate the CFG for a specific function. By examining the graph, you notice that a particular node has two outgoing edges—one for a conditional branch and another for a function call. The conditional branch is based on a variable, which suggests that the program behaves differently depending on the value of that variable. The function call may represent a critical operation or decision point in the program, and by following the edges leading from it, you can identify other areas of interest.

By analyzing this CFG, you can infer the logic of the function and its interaction with other parts of the program, helping you understand the binary's behavior and identify potential vulnerabilities or points of interest.

5. Advanced CFG Techniques in Ghidra

Once you are comfortable with basic CFG generation and navigation, Ghidra offers several advanced techniques to enhance your analysis:

- **Function Graphs**: These are an extension of CFGs that show the interrelationships between functions in a program. The Function Graph visualizes how functions call one another, helping to trace execution paths across multiple functions.
- **Call Graphs**: Similar to Function Graphs, Call Graphs map the relationships between functions specifically in terms of calling each other. By navigating the Call Graph, you can see the flow of function calls, helping to understand the execution path better.
- **Flow Analysis**: In more complex binaries, manually navigating the CFG can be time-consuming. Ghidra provides flow analysis tools that automate some aspects

of navigating control flow, such as detecting unreachable code or redundant branches.

Control Flow Graphs (CFGs) are powerful visual representations of how a program executes, providing insights into how functions interact, where decisions are made, and where loops or branches occur. By mapping and analyzing the CFG in Ghidra, reverse engineers can gain a better understanding of the binary's structure and logic, making it easier to identify vulnerabilities, key functions, and areas of interest.

Using Ghidra's tools to generate and navigate CFGs enables reverse engineers to perform deeper, more effective analyses, facilitating tasks like vulnerability discovery, debugging, and malware analysis. Whether you are a beginner or an experienced reverse engineer, mastering the art of mapping and interpreting Control Flow Graphs is a fundamental skill that will enhance your ability to analyze complex binaries and understand their inner workings.

7.3 Tracking Variable Usage and Dependencies

In reverse engineering, understanding how variables are used and tracked throughout a program is crucial for analyzing its behavior, especially when dealing with complex binaries. Variables in a program, whether they are simple integers or complex data structures, often have interdependencies that are vital for understanding how a program operates. Tracking the usage and dependencies of variables allows reverse engineers to map out how different parts of a program interact with each other, reveal vulnerabilities, and identify critical program states that could be exploited.

In this section, we'll explore how Ghidra helps in tracking variable usage and dependencies, why it is important, and how to effectively map variables within the context of reverse engineering.

1. The Importance of Tracking Variables

In reverse engineering, variables are often the key to understanding how a program works. They represent inputs, outputs, and intermediate states within functions and across the entire program. Tracking the usage of these variables is essential for several reasons:

- **Understanding Program Logic**: By analyzing the values and dependencies of variables, reverse engineers can uncover the logic behind functions and the flow of execution.
- **Detecting Vulnerabilities**: Improper handling of variables can lead to vulnerabilities, such as buffer overflows, uninitialized variables, or incorrect memory access. Tracking variables helps identify such weaknesses.
- **Reversing Algorithms and Protocols**: Many programs implement specific algorithms or protocols that involve complex data structures. Tracking variables allows reverse engineers to reverse these algorithms and understand how they manipulate data.
- **Identifying Critical Data**: In malware analysis, tracking the usage of variables can help identify sensitive data such as passwords, encryption keys, or network packets, which can provide insights into the malicious intent of the program.

2. Types of Variables to Track

In a binary, variables are not always explicitly named or structured like they are in high-level languages. Instead, they can be represented by memory addresses, registers, or stack values, depending on the architecture and calling conventions used. Ghidra provides tools to help identify and track several types of variables:

a. Global Variables:

Global variables are accessible throughout the program, making them a critical focus for reverse engineers. These are typically stored in specific sections of the program, like the .data or .bss sections in an ELF binary.

Tracking Global Variables: In Ghidra, global variables can be found and analyzed in the Symbol Table or by examining the Data Type Manager. These variables often represent persistent states across function calls and can hold sensitive information, like configuration settings or data buffers.

b. Local Variables:

Local variables are used within functions and are often stored on the stack. They are vital for understanding the specific function's behavior, especially when dealing with recursive calls, function arguments, or return addresses.

Tracking Local Variables: Ghidra can automatically identify local variables during disassembly, especially if there are debugging symbols available. These variables are typically allocated space on the stack, and their use is usually confined to the scope of the function. Ghidra provides functionality to track these variables within the Decompiler view, where they are often represented by names or as memory addresses (e.g., [ebp+0x4]).

c. Registers:

In low-level programs, registers often hold intermediate results and variables, particularly in optimized code. Understanding how registers are used across functions is crucial for reverse engineering assembly language.

Tracking Register Usage: Ghidra's disassembler automatically tracks the usage of registers throughout the code and highlights their roles during function calls. Registers, such as the EAX, EBX, or RAX registers, are critical for understanding how the function's logic is implemented and can indicate data dependencies or states.

d. Heap and Stack Variables:

Dynamic memory allocations that occur during runtime (e.g., through functions like malloc in C or new in C++) create variables that are typically stored in the heap or stack.

Tracking Dynamic Variables: In Ghidra, variables allocated on the heap can be identified by tracing calls to dynamic memory allocation functions, such as malloc, calloc, or new. The stack variables can be tracked by observing the changes in stack frames and the way data is pushed and popped during function calls.

3. Tools and Techniques for Tracking Variables in Ghidra

Ghidra offers a variety of tools and techniques to help reverse engineers track the usage and dependencies of variables. Below are some of the key features and strategies for tracking variables in Ghidra:

a. Decompiler View:

The Decompiler in Ghidra is one of the most powerful tools for tracking variable usage and dependencies. It translates the low-level assembly code into a higher-level pseudo-C code, which makes understanding variables and their dependencies much easier.

- **Automatic Variable Mapping**: When analyzing a function, the Decompiler will attempt to map assembly instructions to high-level variables. This can help you see how variables are used and what data is passed between functions.
- **Variable Naming**: Ghidra provides the ability to assign names to variables within the Decompiler to better understand their roles. These names can be customized, helping reverse engineers track the function of variables throughout the code.

b. Listing View:

The Listing View in Ghidra provides a detailed assembly-level view of the code, where you can see all instructions and how they manipulate data in registers or memory.

Register and Stack Analysis: In the Listing View, you can track how registers and stack locations are used in each instruction. This is helpful when analyzing the flow of data through the program and how variables are passed or modified during execution.

c. Data Types and Structures:

In some cases, variables are not simple integers or characters, but more complex data structures. For example, arrays, structs, or classes in a C program represent collections of variables or objects.

Data Type Manager: Ghidra's Data Type Manager allows reverse engineers to define and track more complex data types. This feature can help identify how variables within structures are accessed or modified by various functions.

d. Cross-References:

Cross-references (Xrefs) in Ghidra help you track how variables are used across different parts of the program. When a variable is used in a function, Ghidra will generate cross-references to show all other locations in the program where the variable is referenced.

Viewing Xrefs: Right-click on a variable or address in the Ghidra Listing or Decompiler view, and select Show References to view all the places where that variable is used. This can help you trace how the variable affects the program's flow.

e. Stack and Heap Tracking:

Understanding the use of variables on the stack or heap is critical for identifying dynamic data and memory manipulation in the program.

- **Function Call Analysis**: Ghidra allows you to analyze function calls to track how data is passed in and out of functions, which can include both stack and heap variables.
- **Memory Map**: By analyzing the Memory Map in Ghidra, you can identify regions of memory that are allocated for heap or stack use, giving you insights into the location and use of dynamic variables.

4. Analyzing Variable Dependencies

Variable dependencies refer to how one variable's value depends on or influences the value of another variable. In reverse engineering, identifying these dependencies is critical for understanding the program's logic and potential vulnerabilities. Tracking variable dependencies helps reverse engineers follow data flow through the program and recognize how different parts of the program impact each other.

a. Data Flow Analysis:

Tracking data flow is a key aspect of understanding variable dependencies. In Ghidra, you can follow the flow of data through instructions to see how variables interact. This is especially useful for:

- **Identifying Input/Output Variables**: By analyzing the data flow, you can identify which variables represent user inputs or control inputs, and how these variables influence the execution of the program.
- **Discovering Obfuscated Code**: Obfuscated code often hides the true dependencies between variables, making it difficult to understand the program's logic. By following data flow paths, reverse engineers can often untangle complex, obfuscated logic and reveal hidden dependencies.

b. Tracing Variable Interactions:

In addition to data flow analysis, tracking how variables interact during function calls or across different parts of the code is key. For example, variables passed to functions as arguments may depend on the return values of other functions. Understanding these interactions helps build a full picture of how data flows and changes throughout the program.

Tracking variable usage and dependencies is a critical part of reverse engineering that enables a deep understanding of how a program works. Ghidra provides a robust set of tools for tracking and analyzing variables, including the Decompiler, Listing View, Data Type Manager, and cross-referencing features. By using these tools effectively, reverse engineers can track both simple and complex variables, understand their dependencies, and identify key areas of interest, such as potential vulnerabilities, data manipulation routines, and critical program states.

7.4 Using Data Flow Tools to Understand Memory Access

Memory access plays a critical role in the execution of any program. It defines how data is read from and written to memory during the program's runtime. Understanding memory access is essential for reverse engineers to gain insight into a program's functionality, identify vulnerabilities, and dissect the data structures that underlie its behavior. Data flow tools in Ghidra are invaluable for tracking how memory is accessed, manipulated, and affected by different program functions. These tools allow reverse engineers to visualize the flow of data within memory, enabling them to uncover patterns of memory usage, detect potential issues such as buffer overflows, and identify security vulnerabilities.

In this section, we will explore how to use Ghidra's data flow tools to understand memory access, the importance of memory tracking in reverse engineering, and how these tools assist in analyzing complex programs.

1. The Role of Data Flow in Memory Access

At the heart of reverse engineering is understanding how data is accessed and modified throughout the program's execution. Memory access refers to the interaction between a program and its memory, including both stack and heap allocations. Programs often read data from memory to perform operations, and write data back to memory after modifying it. By understanding the data flow, reverse engineers can see how variables, arrays, buffers, and other memory structures are being used within the program.

Data flow analysis can help identify the following key memory access issues:

- **Buffer Overflows**: These occur when data exceeds the boundaries of a buffer, overwriting adjacent memory. By tracking data flow, reverse engineers can spot where a buffer overflow could lead to unexpected behavior or security vulnerabilities.
- **Memory Leaks**: When a program allocates memory but fails to release it, it causes memory leaks. Data flow tools can help identify places in the code where memory is allocated but not properly freed.

- **Uninitialized Memory**: Using uninitialized memory can cause undefined behavior. Tracking data flow can help identify areas where memory is being accessed without proper initialization, leading to potential bugs or vulnerabilities.
- **Data Structure Manipulation**: Complex data structures such as linked lists, arrays, or structures are often accessed in non-trivial ways. Understanding how memory is accessed and manipulated is crucial for reverse engineers to interpret the program's logic.

2. Understanding Ghidra's Data Flow Tools

Ghidra provides several tools and views that help reverse engineers track and visualize data flow within the program. These tools make it easier to see how memory is accessed and manipulated by different parts of the program. Below are some of the key features in Ghidra for analyzing data flow and memory access.

a. Data Flow Analysis in the Decompiler

The Decompiler in Ghidra provides an abstracted view of the program's code, transforming low-level assembly code into high-level pseudo-C code. This view helps reverse engineers track data flow in a more understandable manner, making it easier to see how data moves through memory.

- **Data Flow Tracking**: The Decompiler automatically tracks the flow of data between registers, memory, and stack locations. This helps reverse engineers identify how values are passed around and how memory is accessed.
- **Variables and Memory Access**: Variables, arrays, and pointers are represented in the Decompiler, allowing reverse engineers to observe how different memory locations are accessed and modified within the program.
- **Identifying Memory Access Patterns**: By reading through the decompiled output, reverse engineers can spot patterns where memory is repeatedly accessed, possibly indicating potential problems such as buffer overflows or memory corruption.

b. Program Tree and Data Structures

Ghidra's Program Tree view provides an organized structure of the program's components, including functions, variables, and memory addresses. This view allows reverse engineers to quickly navigate and locate memory regions that are being accessed by different parts of the program.

- **Memory Regions**: The Program Tree allows users to explore sections of the program's memory and identify areas where memory is allocated. It can display both static and dynamic memory regions, such as global variables, heap, stack, and memory-mapped files.
- **Identifying Potential Memory Access Locations**: By using the Program Tree, reverse engineers can locate key variables and data structures that are accessed during runtime. This is particularly useful when analyzing the way functions interact with specific parts of memory.

c. Tracking Data Flow with Control Flow Graphs (CFG)

Control Flow Graphs (CFG) are graphical representations of a program's control flow, showing the paths that the program can take during execution. They are essential for understanding how the program's control structure dictates the flow of data.

- **Data Flow in CFG**: In Ghidra, the CFG can be used to trace the paths that data takes through different blocks of code. Each block in the CFG represents a set of instructions that manipulate memory, and edges between blocks represent how data moves from one instruction to another.
- **Understanding Conditional Data Flow**: Conditional branches in the CFG can represent different ways in which memory is accessed depending on the program's logic. By following these branches, reverse engineers can track how different data paths are taken and how memory is accessed under various conditions.

d. Cross-References and Variable Tracking

Cross-references (Xrefs) are references to a variable, function, or memory address from other parts of the program. Ghidra allows users to view Xrefs for variables and memory addresses, making it easier to track how memory is accessed in different parts of the program.

- **Tracking Memory Access Across Functions**: Xrefs can be used to trace how memory is passed between functions or how memory locations are accessed by different code blocks. This helps reverse engineers identify patterns of memory manipulation across the program.
- **Memory Write and Read Operations**: By using Xrefs, reverse engineers can pinpoint locations where memory is being read from or written to, providing insight into how data is accessed and modified in various parts of the program.

e. Memory Access Visualization with Ghidra's Listing View

The Listing View in Ghidra displays the disassembled code, showing each instruction and how it manipulates memory. This view can be used to track memory access at a low level, revealing how registers and memory addresses are used.

- **Memory Access Instructions**: Instructions such as mov, push, pop, call, and lea directly manipulate memory or move data between registers and memory. By closely examining these instructions in the Listing View, reverse engineers can gain a deeper understanding of how data flows through memory.
- **Tracking Stack and Heap**: Memory access instructions can be traced to see how memory is allocated on the stack or heap. By following these instructions, reverse engineers can understand how data is passed into functions, allocated in memory, and freed afterward.

3. Advanced Techniques for Understanding Memory Access

While Ghidra provides powerful tools for tracking memory access, reverse engineers may need to employ advanced techniques to fully understand memory access patterns and uncover hidden issues. Some advanced strategies include:

a. Analyzing Stack Frames and Function Calls

Stack frames are critical for understanding how local variables and function parameters are passed and accessed during function calls. Analyzing how data is pushed and popped from the stack during function calls provides insight into how memory is allocated and accessed in real-time.

Tracking Stack Usage: Reverse engineers can use Ghidra's Function Call Graph and Stack Frame Analysis features to track how function calls push data onto the stack and modify memory. This is useful for identifying memory access during runtime and understanding how functions interact with memory.

b. Heap Analysis and Dynamic Memory Allocation

Heap-based memory access involves dynamic memory allocation, often through calls to functions like malloc or free. Understanding how memory is dynamically allocated and accessed on the heap is essential for detecting memory corruption, memory leaks, or vulnerabilities in the code.

Heap Analysis: In Ghidra, reverse engineers can trace dynamic memory allocation and deallocation calls to uncover how heap memory is accessed and manipulated. Identifying which functions interact with the heap can help reverse engineers spot potential security risks.

c. Identifying Vulnerabilities Through Memory Analysis

Memory access patterns can often reveal security vulnerabilities in a program. Reverse engineers can use data flow analysis to detect issues such as buffer overflows, improper memory accesses, and uninitialized memory that could lead to exploits.

Vulnerability Detection: By carefully analyzing memory access and flow, reverse engineers can identify weaknesses in how a program handles memory. This includes spotting areas where user input may overwrite memory, where untrusted data is written to sensitive areas, or where memory is accessed out of bounds.

Understanding memory access is a fundamental part of reverse engineering. Ghidra's data flow tools, such as the Decompiler, Cross-Reference Viewer, Control Flow Graphs, and Listing View, provide invaluable resources for tracking how memory is accessed and manipulated throughout a program. By mastering these tools and techniques, reverse engineers can gain a deeper understanding of a program's functionality, uncover vulnerabilities, and analyze complex memory access patterns. Whether investigating security vulnerabilities, malware analysis, or general program behavior, tracking memory access is a key step in the reverse engineering process.

7.5 Case Study: Analyzing a Complex Function

In this case study, we will walk through the process of analyzing a complex function using Ghidra's tools and techniques for function and data flow analysis. This process demonstrates how reverse engineers can tackle challenging functions, gain insight into their behavior, and extract useful information for security assessments, malware analysis, or software debugging. We will focus on a real-world example, breaking down the steps involved in understanding how the function works and how memory is accessed and manipulated during execution.

Step 1: Initial Analysis and Understanding the Context

To start analyzing a complex function, it's important to understand the context in which it is located. The first step is to identify where the function resides in the program, what it interacts with, and what its role may be within the larger program.

For this case study, let's assume we have a binary executable that we are reverse-engineering using Ghidra. The function we are analyzing could be part of a cryptographic algorithm or a network communication protocol, both of which can be particularly complex.

Tasks for Step 1:

- **Identifying the Function**: Using Ghidra's CodeBrowser tool, we search for all the functions in the binary using the Function Window or Symbol Tree. This helps identify the location of the function in question.
- **Contextual Analysis**: Once located, we examine the function's name (if available), and review its immediate context—looking for function calls, local variables, and the data that is passed in or returned from the function. This helps us get an initial understanding of its purpose.
- **Start with a High-Level Decompilation**: We use Ghidra's Decompiler tool to generate a high-level view of the function. This will provide us with pseudo-C code, offering better readability and an understanding of what the function might be doing.

Step 2: Disassembling the Function

After obtaining an overview from the decompiled code, we shift our focus to the lower-level assembly to understand the underlying operations and identify how memory is accessed, modified, and used within the function. At this point, the disassembled code provides a more granular view of the function's behavior, which is essential for understanding complex logic.

Tasks for Step 2:

- **Disassembly**: Using Ghidra's Listing View, we explore the function's disassembly. This is especially helpful for identifying the exact assembly instructions that manipulate registers and memory locations.
- **Navigating through Instructions**: We carefully examine the instructions that are executed in the function, paying attention to memory operations like MOV, PUSH, POP, and arithmetic operations that modify registers. These instructions could

interact with memory regions, stack frames, or heap allocations, and it is crucial to understand the data flow at this level.

- **Identifying Key Memory Access**: For example, look for instructions that access or modify global variables, function parameters, or memory buffers. These are the points where memory access occurs and where the flow of data is controlled. Tracking the flow of data through registers and memory is critical for reverse engineering complex functions.

Step 3: Analyzing Control Flow and Data Flow

Once we have a better understanding of the individual instructions, the next step is to analyze the control flow and data flow within the function. This involves using Ghidra's tools to map out the function's control structure and understand how data moves between different memory locations, registers, and the stack.

Tasks for Step 3:

- **Control Flow Graph (CFG):** Use Ghidra's Control Flow Graph (CFG) feature to map the flow of execution through the function. The CFG shows how the program jumps from one block of instructions to another, and helps identify loops, conditionals, and branches. By following the CFG, you can track how data might be manipulated based on specific conditions or branches.
- **Data Flow Analysis**: In addition to control flow, it is equally important to analyze how data flows within the function. Ghidra allows us to track variable usage and memory access through Xrefs (cross-references) to identify where specific memory locations or variables are read from or written to.
- **Identifying Memory Access Patterns**: As we analyze the data flow, we identify patterns in memory access. For example, are there any memory buffers being overwritten? Are certain memory areas being accessed repeatedly? These patterns can reveal important details about the program's behavior or potential vulnerabilities.

Step 4: Tracking Stack and Heap Usage

Memory usage within a function typically involves both stack and heap allocations. In many complex functions, particularly those that deal with data structures like arrays, strings, or buffers, both types of memory are heavily utilized. In this step, we analyze how the stack and heap are used by the function to understand how data is stored and accessed during execution.

Tasks for Step 4:

- **Stack Analysis**: The stack is used for function arguments, local variables, and return addresses. In Ghidra, we can trace how memory is allocated on the stack by analyzing the Prolog and Epilog sections of the function. These are the parts of the function where the stack frame is set up and torn down, respectively. We also track how data is pushed and popped from the stack, and how stack-based variables are accessed throughout the function.
- **Heap Analysis**: If the function allocates memory dynamically (for example, using calls to malloc or calloc), we examine how this memory is allocated on the heap. We can use Ghidra's Function Call Graph and Cross-References to trace calls to memory allocation functions and understand how dynamically allocated memory is being accessed and manipulated.
- **Data in Memory**: Pay attention to how data on the stack or heap is used by the function. Are buffers being written to or read from in an unexpected manner? Are there any suspicious memory accesses that might indicate vulnerabilities like buffer overflows or memory corruption?

Step 5: Understanding Algorithm and Logic

After analyzing the function's memory and data flow, we focus on understanding the algorithm or logic behind the function's purpose. Many complex functions, especially those found in cryptography, compression, or networking code, involve intricate logic that may not be immediately apparent from just looking at the assembly code.

Tasks for Step 5:

- **High-Level Algorithm Identification**: Using the decompiled output, we try to identify the high-level algorithm that the function is implementing. For example, if the function is part of a cryptographic operation, we may recognize standard cryptographic functions like encryption, hashing, or key exchange.
- **Simplifying the Function's Logic**: If the function is still difficult to understand, we can simplify it by renaming variables, functions, or memory locations in Ghidra to make the decompiled output more readable. This process allows us to clarify how the function works and what data it is operating on.
- **Cross-Referencing with External Documentation**: If the function is part of a known algorithm or protocol, we may cross-reference it with external documentation or source code to better understand the function's purpose and behavior.

Step 6: Drawing Conclusions and Documenting Findings

Once we have fully analyzed the function, it's time to document our findings. We summarize the purpose of the function, how memory is accessed, and any notable patterns or vulnerabilities that we have discovered. If the function is part of a larger program, we also consider its interactions with other parts of the program and how it contributes to the program's overall behavior.

Tasks for Step 6:

- **Document the Function**: Create a detailed report describing the function's behavior, the memory areas it interacts with, and any potential issues (such as buffer overflows or memory leaks).
- **Vulnerability Identification**: If any security vulnerabilities were identified during the analysis, such as improper bounds checking, uninitialized memory access, or buffer overflows, we make note of these and recommend appropriate mitigations.
- **Conclusions and Further Steps**: Depending on the analysis goal (e.g., malware analysis, software debugging, or vulnerability discovery), we conclude the analysis and plan the next steps based on the findings.

By following the steps outlined in this case study, reverse engineers can effectively analyze complex functions in a program, gain insight into how memory is accessed and manipulated, and uncover critical information that might not be immediately apparent from high-level views alone. The ability to dissect complex functions, understand their data flow, and track their memory usage is an essential skill in reverse engineering, whether for security analysis, debugging, or general program analysis. Ghidra's powerful tools—such as the decompiler, control flow graphs, data flow analysis, and memory tracking features—play a pivotal role in uncovering these insights and ensuring that reverse engineers can perform comprehensive and accurate analyses.

Chapter 8: Debugging and Emulation

In this chapter, we explore dynamic analysis techniques, specifically debugging and emulation, to enhance your reverse engineering workflow. Debugging allows you to step through code execution in real-time, revealing how a program behaves under various conditions. You'll learn how to set up Ghidra to work with external debuggers, configure breakpoints, and analyze the program's runtime behavior by observing registers, memory, and stack changes. Additionally, we'll cover the use of emulation to simulate code execution, enabling you to test and analyze code without requiring a physical execution environment. We'll dive into Ghidra's built-in emulation tools, explaining how they can be used to analyze difficult-to-debug code, such as obfuscated or encrypted sections. This chapter will also address common challenges, such as debugging in protected or virtualized environments, and offer strategies to work around them. By the end of this chapter, you'll have the skills to debug and emulate code effectively, providing you with powerful tools for understanding complex binaries and uncovering hidden vulnerabilities.

8.1 Setting Up Ghidra with External Debuggers

Integrating external debuggers with Ghidra is an essential step for performing dynamic analysis and debugging, especially when you need to understand how a binary behaves during execution. Ghidra's static analysis capabilities are powerful, but pairing it with an external debugger allows you to step through the code in real time, inspect memory, and track runtime behavior. In this chapter, we will explore the process of setting up and configuring Ghidra to work with external debuggers, including the popular GDB (GNU Debugger) and other debuggers for different platforms.

Why Use an External Debugger with Ghidra?

Ghidra excels at static analysis, where you analyze the code without executing it. However, many times, you need to interact with the program as it runs, observing how the program's behavior aligns with the disassembled or decompiled output. An external debugger helps you:

- Set breakpoints to stop execution at specific code locations and inspect the state of the program.
- Step through execution one instruction at a time, allowing you to follow the flow of control.

- Inspect registers and memory to understand the real-time value of variables, function parameters, and return addresses.
- Analyze runtime data such as heap and stack memory, providing deeper insight into how data is manipulated.

By using Ghidra with an external debugger, you can improve your ability to reverse engineer complex binaries, perform malware analysis, or investigate potential vulnerabilities.

Setting Up Ghidra with GDB (GNU Debugger)

GDB is a widely used debugger for Linux-based systems, and it works well with Ghidra for dynamic analysis. Setting up Ghidra to communicate with GDB is straightforward, and it allows you to use Ghidra's analysis tools while having the ability to interact with the binary in real time.

Prerequisites:

- **Ghidra**: You need to have Ghidra installed and set up on your machine.
- **GDB**: Ensure that GDB is installed on your system. You can typically install GDB via package managers like apt for Ubuntu (sudo apt install gdb) or brew for macOS (brew install gdb).
- **A compatible binary**: You should be analyzing a binary for which debugging is supported (e.g., ELF for Linux, PE for Windows).

Step-by-Step Setup for Ghidra and GDB Integration:

Install Ghidra and GDB: Ensure both Ghidra and GDB are installed. You can download Ghidra from its official website, and GDB should be available through your system's package manager.

Start a New Project in Ghidra:

- Open Ghidra and create a new project. This is where you will import the binary that you want to analyze.
- Go to File > New Project and follow the prompts to set up your project.

Import the Binary into Ghidra:

- In Ghidra, click on File > Import File, and select the binary you wish to analyze. Ghidra will automatically detect the format (e.g., ELF, PE) and ask if you want to perform an initial analysis.

Configure the Debugger in Ghidra:

- Ghidra communicates with external debuggers via the Debugger Interface. To configure GDB, navigate to Debugger > Debugger Settings from the Ghidra main window.
- Select GDB as the external debugger and provide the path to the gdb executable on your system if it is not automatically detected.
- Configure any specific settings like architecture (e.g., x86, ARM) and operating system platform (e.g., Linux, Windows) based on the binary you are analyzing.

Connect to GDB:

Open a terminal on your system, and run GDB with the following command, where binary_name is the name of the executable you are analyzing:

gdb binary_name

Once GDB starts, set the appropriate architecture and any other settings needed to match the binary's platform (if applicable).

Start Debugging:

- Now that both Ghidra and GDB are set up, return to Ghidra's Debugger menu and click Connect to Debugger.
- In Ghidra, use the Debug menu options to start debugging the binary. You can set breakpoints, step through the code, and inspect memory and registers while Ghidra's static analysis features provide context to your dynamic analysis.
- You can control execution in GDB using commands like break, continue, and step, while Ghidra displays the results of each action and allows you to analyze the disassembly and decompiled code.

Debugging with Other External Debuggers

Although GDB is one of the most common debuggers used with Ghidra, you can also use other debuggers based on your target platform. For example, if you're working with

Windows-based binaries, you might use WinDbg, while on macOS, you might rely on LLDB. Below is a brief overview of configuring Ghidra with these debuggers.

WinDbg (Windows Debugger)

- **Install WinDbg**: WinDbg is part of the Windows SDK, so you can install it via the Microsoft website. It is useful for debugging Windows applications, including those in the PE format.
- **Connect WinDbg to Ghidra**: You can configure Ghidra to work with WinDbg via the Debugger Settings in the same way you configure GDB. WinDbg will allow you to set breakpoints, inspect the state of registers, and trace program execution on Windows platforms.

LLDB (LLVM Debugger for macOS)

- **Install LLDB**: LLDB is typically installed alongside Xcode on macOS. It is useful for debugging applications on macOS and iOS.
- **Connect LLDB to Ghidra**: As with GDB, you can set up LLDB as an external debugger in Ghidra's Debugger Settings. Once connected, you can use LLDB to step through the execution of a macOS or iOS binary while leveraging Ghidra's static analysis tools for additional context.

Using Ghidra's Debugger Interface Features

Once your debugger is configured and connected, Ghidra provides a set of powerful features to enhance the debugging experience:

Breakpoints: You can set breakpoints at specific instructions or function calls in Ghidra's CodeBrowser, and Ghidra will communicate with the debugger to pause execution at these points. This allows you to inspect variables, memory, and execution flow.

Step-by-Step Execution: After hitting a breakpoint, you can step through the program one instruction at a time, watching how memory, registers, and program state evolve. This is critical for understanding complex logic and behaviors that are difficult to analyze statically.

Memory Inspection: Ghidra's debugger interface allows you to inspect the state of memory during execution. You can view how memory is being accessed, what values are stored at specific memory locations, and whether there are any anomalies or unexpected behaviors.

Registers and Stack: Ghidra displays register values and stack frames during debugging, making it easier to understand the program's current state and track variable changes as execution progresses.

Call Graphs and Stack Tracing: Ghidra's Call Graph and Function Tracing features can be used in conjunction with external debuggers to better understand how functions are called and what the program's execution path looks like.

Troubleshooting Common Issues

While setting up an external debugger with Ghidra, you may encounter issues like:

- **Debugger Connection Issues**: If Ghidra is unable to connect to the external debugger, double-check the configuration in Ghidra's Debugger Settings. Make sure the correct path to the debugger executable is specified and that the correct platform and architecture are selected.
- **Compatibility Issues**: Some binaries might be compiled in a way that makes them difficult to debug (e.g., stripped binaries or anti-debugging techniques). In such cases, additional techniques like dynamic analysis or patching might be necessary.

Setting up an external debugger with Ghidra is a powerful way to enhance your reverse engineering workflow. It allows you to perform dynamic analysis on a binary, stepping through code execution, inspecting memory and registers, and identifying potential vulnerabilities or behaviors that may not be obvious from static analysis alone. By configuring Ghidra with popular debuggers like GDB, WinDbg, or LLDB, you can expand your reverse engineering capabilities, making it easier to understand and analyze complex binaries, especially in security assessments and malware analysis.

8.2 Basics of Using the Debugger Tool

Using a debugger effectively is one of the most critical skills in reverse engineering and cybersecurity. Debuggers allow you to monitor the execution of a program, observe how data and instructions evolve over time, and identify potential vulnerabilities, bugs, or malicious behaviors. Ghidra's integrated debugger tool enhances its static analysis capabilities by providing dynamic analysis features that let you interact with the program at runtime. In this section, we will cover the basics of using Ghidra's debugger tool, starting with fundamental concepts and progressing to hands-on techniques for debugging binaries.

Why Debugging Is Important in Reverse Engineering

In reverse engineering, the primary goal is often to understand how a binary behaves, both in terms of its functionality and its interaction with the system. Static analysis alone—where the binary is analyzed without execution—provides valuable insights into the structure and logic of the program. However, it often leaves out crucial details that are only visible when the program is running, such as:

- **Real-time variable values**: Some behaviors and logic depend on runtime data that is not captured in static analysis.
- **Memory manipulation**: Understanding how memory is allocated, accessed, and modified during execution is critical for understanding program flow.
- **Program flow**: Observing how control flow unfolds in real time can reveal subtle bugs, race conditions, or vulnerabilities like buffer overflows.
- **Malicious activity**: For malware analysis, tracking how the malware manipulates the system during execution is essential for understanding its payload and impact.

A debugger provides real-time insight into all of these aspects, making it an essential tool for advanced reverse engineering tasks.

Getting Started with Ghidra's Debugger Tool

Ghidra's debugger tool allows you to interact with a binary as it runs. To get started, we'll first walk through the basic components of Ghidra's debugger interface, then demonstrate common debugger actions.

1. Launching the Debugger in Ghidra

Before you can use the debugger, you need to ensure that Ghidra is configured to connect to an external debugger, such as GDB, WinDbg, or LLDB, depending on your operating system and target binary format. Follow the setup steps outlined in the previous section (8.1) to establish a debugger connection.

Once connected to a debugger, you can begin a debugging session directly in the Ghidra interface. Here's how to launch the debugger:

- **Start Your Ghidra Project**: Open your Ghidra project and ensure the binary has been loaded into the workspace.

- **Open the Debugger**: From the Ghidra main window, navigate to Debugger > Start Debugger. If your debugger is correctly configured, Ghidra will initiate the debugger connection and begin communicating with the target binary.
- **Select the Execution Mode**: You can choose between different execution modes like running the binary normally or using specific breakpoints.

2. Debugger Interface Overview

Once the debugger is running, you will be presented with several key features and panels within Ghidra's interface:

- **Debugger Console**: This is where you can enter debugger commands directly, similar to how you would interact with GDB or another debugger in a terminal.
- **Registers View**: This shows the values of the CPU registers (e.g., EAX, EBX for x86 or R0, R1 for ARM). Monitoring these values is critical for understanding how the program is manipulating data during execution.
- **Memory View**: This panel displays the memory layout of the program. You can inspect specific memory regions, track memory writes, and observe how the program manipulates memory during execution.
- **Stack View**: The stack view shows the call stack and the sequence of function calls, including the return addresses and arguments. This view is especially useful when stepping through functions or tracking program flow.
- **Breakpoints and Control Flow**: The Ghidra debugger tool lets you set breakpoints in your code, step through instructions, and control execution. These controls are available in the debugger toolbar and allow you to pause execution, step through code, or continue running.

3. Key Debugger Actions

Once the debugger is running and you've connected it to the binary, you can perform a variety of actions to interact with the program's execution. These actions include setting breakpoints, stepping through the code, inspecting memory, and modifying the execution flow. Below are some of the most common actions and how they can be performed in Ghidra.

3.1 Setting Breakpoints

Breakpoints are a fundamental tool for debugging. They allow you to halt the execution of the program at a specific point so that you can inspect the current state. Ghidra makes setting breakpoints simple:

- **Navigate to the Code**: In Ghidra's CodeBrowser window, find the location in the code where you want to set a breakpoint. This might be a function entry point, a specific instruction, or a suspected vulnerable area of the code.
- **Set the Breakpoint**: Right-click on the instruction or function where you want the breakpoint to occur, and select Set Breakpoint from the context menu.
- **Manage Breakpoints**: You can manage breakpoints from the Debugger menu by selecting Breakpoints. Here, you can enable, disable, or remove breakpoints as needed.

When the debugger hits a breakpoint, it will pause execution, allowing you to inspect the state of the program.

3.2 Stepping Through Code

Once a breakpoint is hit, you can step through the code line by line. Ghidra's debugger provides several stepping options:

- **Step Over**: This command allows you to move over a single instruction or function call without entering the called function. It's useful for skipping over code that doesn't require inspection.
- **Step Into**: This command steps into the function call, allowing you to observe how the function is executed.
- **Step Out**: This command allows you to step out of the current function and return to the calling function.
- **Continue**: This command resumes normal execution until the next breakpoint is encountered.

You can access these options via the toolbar or through keyboard shortcuts (e.g., F7 to step into, F8 to step over).

3.3 Inspecting Memory and Registers

As the program runs, you can observe how memory and registers are manipulated. This is critical for understanding program flow and identifying bugs or vulnerabilities.

- **Memory View**: Use the Memory window to inspect regions of memory that are relevant to the program. For example, you can check the values of buffers or heap allocations.

- **Registers View**: The Registers window shows the contents of CPU registers. Monitoring registers during execution helps you understand how data is being passed between functions or manipulated during computation.

Both the memory and registers can be updated in real-time as you step through code, allowing you to track how data changes during execution.

3.4 Manipulating Execution

Sometimes, you may want to alter the flow of the program or modify its state for testing purposes. Ghidra's debugger tool allows you to modify memory and register values on the fly.

- **Modify Memory**: If you suspect a memory-related bug, such as a buffer overflow or heap corruption, you can modify the contents of memory in real-time.
- **Modify Registers**: Similarly, you can change the value of specific registers, which may be useful for bypassing security checks or simulating specific inputs.

This is particularly useful in vulnerability research or when testing patches in a binary.

4. Debugger Shortcuts and Tips

To speed up the debugging process and increase productivity, it's important to be familiar with common keyboard shortcuts and tips for navigating the debugger tool:

- **F7**: Step into the current function.
- **F8**: Step over the current instruction.
- **Ctrl + F7**: Step out of the current function.
- **Ctrl + Shift + F7**: Continue execution until the next breakpoint.
- **Ctrl + B:** Toggle a breakpoint at the current instruction.

Ghidra's debugger tool provides an invaluable set of features for dynamic analysis. By integrating static analysis with real-time debugging, you can gain a deeper understanding of a binary's behavior, uncover vulnerabilities, and even track malware execution. The basic debugging actions covered here—setting breakpoints, stepping through code, inspecting memory and registers, and manipulating execution—form the foundation of effective debugging with Ghidra. With practice, you'll be able to apply these techniques to analyze complex binaries and develop your reverse engineering expertise.

8.3 Simulating Code Execution with Emulation

Emulation is a powerful technique used in reverse engineering to simulate the execution of a program without actually running it on a physical or virtual machine. Unlike debugging, which interacts with a program's live execution, emulation allows reverse engineers to observe the behavior of a binary in a controlled environment, enabling deeper analysis of how the program functions and how it interacts with the system. Ghidra's emulation features enhance its static analysis capabilities by providing a dynamic, but safer, way to execute code in a sandboxed manner.

In this section, we will explore the concept of emulation, its benefits, and how to use Ghidra's emulation features to simulate code execution. We will also highlight scenarios where emulation proves to be useful and provide guidance on how to configure and use emulation effectively within the Ghidra framework.

What is Emulation?

Emulation, in the context of reverse engineering, refers to the process of simulating the execution of a program's machine code on a different platform or within a virtual environment. The key difference between emulation and actual execution is that emulation does not require the program to run on the target system. Instead, it simulates the program's behavior, allowing the reverse engineer to observe its execution step by step, as though it were running on the actual hardware.

Emulators recreate the hardware or system behavior required for the code to run. They replicate the instruction set architecture (ISA), memory management, and the execution environment, but without executing the code on a physical machine. This makes emulation a particularly valuable tool in reverse engineering malware, embedded firmware, or when analyzing binaries for which the real execution environment is difficult to replicate or too risky to use.

Benefits of Emulation in Reverse Engineering

Safety and Containment: When analyzing potentially dangerous code—such as malware or unknown binaries—emulation offers a safer alternative to executing the code in a real environment. Since the code does not run on the actual machine, emulation reduces the risk of system compromise or unintended consequences.

Controlled Execution: Emulation allows you to simulate the execution of code with complete control. You can execute a program in a controlled, step-by-step manner, monitor its behavior, and track how it interacts with memory and registers at each step.

Recreating Real-World Scenarios: Emulation can be used to simulate different environments or hardware platforms. For example, if you are analyzing a binary intended to run on an embedded system, you can emulate the target system's architecture to observe how the binary interacts with that specific hardware configuration.

No Dependency on External Hardware: For binaries that rely on specific hardware or operating system configurations, emulation provides a way to simulate the environment without needing access to the physical machine.

Faster Analysis: By running code in an emulated environment, you can observe how the program functions without waiting for it to execute fully in real time. This can dramatically speed up the process of identifying bugs or malicious behaviors.

Ghidra's Emulation Features

Ghidra includes a set of emulation tools that can be used to simulate the execution of code. These features are designed to augment Ghidra's static analysis capabilities by allowing you to run code in a safe and controlled environment. Ghidra's emulation framework is integrated into the overall reverse engineering process, making it easy to use in conjunction with other features like disassembly, decompilation, and debugging.

The primary emulation tool in Ghidra is the Emulator plugin, which allows you to execute the binary's instructions within a virtualized environment that mimics the target architecture. The plugin supports various processor architectures, including x86, ARM, and MIPS, and can be used to simulate the execution of machine code on these platforms.

Setting Up Ghidra for Emulation

Before you begin simulating code execution in Ghidra, you need to configure the emulator to work with the binary you are analyzing. The setup process includes selecting the target architecture and ensuring that the necessary plugins and libraries are installed. Here's how you can set up Ghidra for emulation:

Open the Binary in Ghidra: Start by importing the binary you wish to analyze into your Ghidra project. Ghidra's disassembly and decompilation features will be used to process the binary, providing a detailed analysis of the program's structure and logic.

Install the Emulator Plugin: Depending on the platform and architecture you are analyzing, Ghidra may require the installation of additional emulator plugins. These plugins are typically available from the Ghidra official website or community repositories.

Select the Target Architecture: Choose the appropriate architecture for the binary. If the binary is intended for an ARM-based device, for example, make sure that the ARM emulator is enabled. You can configure this from the Ghidra project's settings.

Launch the Emulator: Once the setup is complete, you can begin emulating the binary by selecting the Emulate option from the Ghidra toolbar. This will launch the emulator and begin simulating the program's execution.

Monitor the Emulated Execution: As the program runs in the emulator, you can observe the flow of execution in real-time. This allows you to track how the program manipulates memory, handles input/output, and interacts with other system resources.

Common Use Cases for Emulation in Reverse Engineering

Malware Analysis: Emulation is especially valuable in malware analysis, as it allows you to simulate the behavior of potentially harmful code without executing it on a real system. This makes it easier to identify malicious activities, such as network connections, file modifications, or attempts to exploit vulnerabilities.

Firmware Analysis: Many embedded systems rely on firmware that is difficult to analyze without the original hardware. Emulation provides a way to simulate the behavior of firmware and analyze its interactions with the system. This is particularly useful when working with proprietary firmware or embedded software for which the hardware is unavailable.

Exploit Research: Emulation can be used to simulate various exploit scenarios, including buffer overflows and stack smashing attacks. By observing the effects of different input values on the program's execution, you can better understand how exploits work and how to mitigate them.

Software Debugging: While debugging tools allow you to interact with live executions, emulation can be used when the program cannot be executed in a real debugger environment. Emulation allows you to simulate an execution flow, analyze it, and detect bugs, all within a safe environment.

Reverse Engineering Complex Code: Some software may be designed to detect or prevent analysis. In these cases, running the program in an emulator provides a way to bypass certain protections (such as anti-debugging or anti-VM techniques) and gain insight into its functionality.

Challenges and Limitations of Emulation

While emulation is a powerful tool, it does come with certain limitations:

Performance Overhead: Emulating a program can be slower than running it natively on a physical machine, particularly for complex or large programs. This may result in delays during the analysis process.

Limited Hardware Support: Not all hardware configurations can be emulated perfectly. Some specific hardware features may be difficult to replicate, which may limit the effectiveness of emulation in certain cases.

Incomplete Emulation: While emulation can simulate the execution of code, it may not perfectly reproduce the full behavior of the program. Certain low-level system interactions, such as direct hardware access or specific operating system behavior, may not be fully emulated, leading to discrepancies in the analysis.

Complex Configuration: Setting up emulation in Ghidra requires some familiarity with the tool and the binary being analyzed. Configuring emulation for specific architectures or platform types may be challenging for beginners.

Emulation in Ghidra offers a safe and controlled way to simulate the execution of machine code, providing valuable insights into how a program operates at runtime. By using emulation in conjunction with static analysis and debugging tools, you can create a comprehensive analysis environment for reverse engineering binaries, malware, and embedded systems. Although there are some limitations to the emulation process, it remains an invaluable technique in the reverse engineer's toolkit, particularly for scenarios where real-world execution is impractical or dangerous. Through careful setup and execution, emulation can help you understand complex code, identify vulnerabilities, and enhance your reverse engineering capabilities.

8.4 Debugging Obfuscated or Encrypted Code

Obfuscation and encryption are common techniques used by software developers, malware authors, and cyber attackers to hide the true intentions of a program. In reverse engineering, the goal is to understand how a program works and identify potential vulnerabilities or malicious behavior. However, when faced with obfuscated or encrypted code, reverse engineers encounter significant challenges because the code is intentionally made difficult to understand or analyze.

This section explores strategies for debugging obfuscated or encrypted code within Ghidra, providing techniques and tools that can help reverse engineers tackle these advanced challenges. We will cover both obfuscation techniques and encryption methods, discussing how they impact debugging, and then focus on specific approaches and tools in Ghidra to mitigate these difficulties.

What is Code Obfuscation and Encryption?

Code Obfuscation refers to techniques used to deliberately make the code difficult to understand. This can be done by renaming variables and functions to meaningless names, changing the control flow of the program, or using complicated algorithms to achieve simple tasks. The objective is to make reverse engineering more difficult, often to hide malicious behavior or to prevent cracking or unauthorized analysis.

Code Encryption involves encrypting parts of the code or entire binaries to make the actual content unreadable. Malware often encrypts its payloads to avoid detection by antivirus or security tools. In such cases, the binary may only decrypt and execute its malicious code during runtime, making static analysis impossible without proper decryption keys or techniques.

Both of these methods aim to hinder or obscure the reverse engineering process, but they also leave clues and patterns that can be exploited with the right debugging strategies.

Challenges of Debugging Obfuscated and Encrypted Code

Obfuscated and encrypted code present several difficulties for reverse engineers:

Loss of Readability: Obfuscated code is hard to follow because it lacks meaningful identifiers and often uses convoluted control flow. This can make identifying functions, understanding program logic, and tracking data flow especially difficult.

Analysis of Encrypted Payloads: In the case of encrypted code, the actual program functionality is hidden until the code is decrypted during execution. Without the decryption key or understanding the encryption method, it becomes nearly impossible to analyze the encrypted sections of the binary.

Anti-Debugging Techniques: Obfuscated code may also contain anti-debugging mechanisms that attempt to detect the presence of debuggers or virtual environments. These mechanisms can break debugging sessions or mislead the reverse engineer.

Complex Control Flow: Obfuscated code often involves complex or non-linear control flow, such as jumps, indirect calls, or self-modifying code, that make stepping through the binary difficult and slow.

Approaches to Debugging Obfuscated or Encrypted Code

To effectively debug and reverse engineer obfuscated or encrypted code, reverse engineers need to employ specific strategies and techniques to bypass or handle these obstacles. Here are several methods to overcome these challenges:

1. Identify and Bypass Obfuscation Techniques

Obfuscation can take many forms, from simple renaming to complex control flow manipulation. Here's how to address different types of obfuscation:

Control Flow Obfuscation: Programs may use indirect function calls or jump tables to confuse the control flow. Ghidra provides powerful analysis tools such as Control Flow Graphs (CFGs) to help visualize and trace the flow of execution. By manually or automatically analyzing the CFG, you can reconstruct the original control flow and begin understanding the program's logic.

String Obfuscation: Obfuscators often hide strings by encoding them in different formats (e.g., base64 encoding, XOR encoding). To identify obfuscated strings, you can use Ghidra's search functionality to look for suspicious patterns like common encoding schemes or known encryption functions. Once detected, these strings can be decoded manually or with a script.

Renaming and Refactoring: Ghidra provides tools for renaming functions, variables, and other symbols to make the code more understandable. By using its Symbol Renaming feature, you can replace meaningless names with more informative labels as you analyze the code. This is especially useful when dealing with heavily obfuscated code.

2. Dealing with Encrypted Payloads

Encryption, especially in the context of malware, presents another significant challenge. The key issue is that the actual malicious code or logic is hidden behind an encryption layer, which is only decrypted at runtime. Here's how to approach debugging encrypted binaries:

Track the Decryption Routine: Often, malware or obfuscated code will include a decryption routine that decrypts its payload when executed. Your goal is to find this decryption code and determine how it works. In Ghidra, you can locate decryption routines by identifying suspicious functions that manipulate data in an unusual way (e.g., XOR operations, byte manipulations, or the use of cryptographic libraries). Once located, you can analyze the function to understand how the decryption is performed and reconstruct the plaintext payload.

Emulate or Debug the Decryption: Emulation and debugging can be particularly useful in cases where encrypted data is being decrypted dynamically. By using Ghidra's Debugger and Emulator tools, you can step through the code, monitoring memory and registers as the program decrypts its payload. By observing the decryption process in real-time, you can extract the key or fully decrypt the content without having to rely on static analysis alone.

Look for Known Encryption Patterns: Many encryption techniques are based on well-known algorithms, such as AES, RC4, or XOR. If you identify a pattern (e.g., repetitive byte sequences or standard block sizes), you may be able to recognize the encryption method and decrypt the payload manually or with a script.

3. Dealing with Anti-Debugging and Anti-VM Techniques

Many obfuscated programs, especially malware, incorporate anti-debugging or anti-virtual machine (VM) techniques designed to detect when they are being analyzed in a debugger or sandbox environment. These techniques can interfere with the debugging process by detecting the presence of breakpoints, virtual environments, or known debugger behaviors.

Bypass Anti-Debugging Measures: Ghidra's debugger can be combined with techniques like patching to bypass anti-debugging measures. For example, if the program checks for the presence of a debugger by inspecting specific system registers or API calls (e.g., IsDebuggerPresent on Windows), you can modify the binary to remove or bypass these checks. You can also use Ghidra's scripting capabilities to automatically patch the binary during debugging to prevent anti-debugging techniques from triggering.

Use Multiple Debugging Strategies: Anti-debugging techniques can sometimes be bypassed by using a mix of static analysis, dynamic analysis, and emulation. For instance, if a debugger is being detected, you can switch to emulation mode or use a different debugger. Emulators, like Ghidra's emulator, allow you to simulate execution and observe code behavior without triggering anti-debugging techniques that would normally break traditional debugging.

4. Leveraging Ghidra's Scripting and Automation

Obfuscated or encrypted code often requires repetitive tasks, such as searching for encryption patterns, renaming symbols, or tracking specific instructions. Ghidra's scripting environment allows you to automate these tasks, reducing the time spent on manual analysis.

Custom Scripts: Using Ghidra's built-in scripting capabilities (which support languages like Python and Java), you can write custom scripts to identify and handle obfuscation techniques. For example, a script could be written to automatically detect and decode obfuscated strings, or to analyze suspicious byte patterns associated with decryption routines.

Automated Analysis: Ghidra's Automated Analysis tool can be configured to run analysis processes like disassembly, function identification, and control flow reconstruction automatically. By fine-tuning the settings, you can speed up the process of analyzing complex binaries, especially when dealing with obfuscation.

Debugging obfuscated or encrypted code is one of the most challenging tasks in reverse engineering, but it is also one of the most rewarding. Ghidra provides a wide range of tools and techniques that can help reverse engineers tackle these challenges, from analyzing obfuscated control flows to tracking down decryption routines and bypassing anti-debugging measures. By combining static analysis with dynamic debugging and emulation, reverse engineers can effectively peel back the layers of obfuscation and encryption, ultimately gaining a deep understanding of a program's behavior. Whether you are dealing with malware, cracking challenges, or protecting software from reverse engineers, mastering these techniques will significantly enhance your reverse engineering expertise.

8.5 Capturing and Interpreting Runtime Behavior

Capturing and interpreting runtime behavior is a critical aspect of reverse engineering, especially when dealing with complex or dynamically changing code such as malware, software exploits, or applications that utilize self-modifying techniques. Understanding how a binary behaves during execution gives you insights into its functionality, potential vulnerabilities, and any malicious activities that may be present. In this section, we will explore the methods and tools available in Ghidra for capturing and analyzing runtime behavior, equipping you with techniques to effectively monitor and interpret how code operates during execution.

Why Capturing Runtime Behavior Is Crucial

Static analysis, which involves studying the binary without executing it, is often insufficient to fully understand the behavior of a program, especially when dealing with dynamic elements such as encrypted code, self-modifying code, or malware that performs runtime unpacking. By capturing runtime behavior, reverse engineers can observe the code as it interacts with the operating system, hardware, and other software components in real time.

Key aspects of runtime behavior that may need to be analyzed include:

Memory Access Patterns: Analyzing how the program accesses, modifies, and allocates memory during execution is crucial for understanding data handling, function calls, and identifying buffer overflow vulnerabilities.

System Call Monitoring: Observing system calls (such as file I/O operations, network requests, or process creation) provides insights into how the program interacts with the operating system and external resources, which is particularly useful for detecting malicious activity.

Data Manipulation: Some programs (especially malware) manipulate data in ways that aren't apparent in the static code, such as decrypting or encoding data during runtime. Capturing this manipulation reveals crucial information about the program's logic and payload.

API and Function Call Monitoring: Monitoring which functions are called and which libraries or APIs are being used during execution allows reverse engineers to track critical functionality and identify suspicious or unauthorized operations.

By analyzing the runtime behavior of a binary, reverse engineers can identify code paths that are not visible in the static analysis, debug complex functions, bypass anti-debugging techniques, and more accurately reconstruct the functionality of the program.

Methods for Capturing and Interpreting Runtime Behavior in Ghidra

Ghidra provides several tools and techniques to capture and interpret the runtime behavior of a binary. These tools allow reverse engineers to track the execution flow, inspect memory states, and monitor the program's interactions with the operating system. Let's explore some of the key methods you can use.

1. Using the Debugger in Ghidra

The built-in Debugger in Ghidra enables real-time monitoring of a program's execution. By running the binary in a controlled environment, reverse engineers can observe how the program behaves while it is executing. Here are the steps to capture runtime behavior with Ghidra's debugger:

Breakpoints: Setting breakpoints at key points in the program (e.g., at the beginning of critical functions, loops, or system calls) allows you to pause execution and inspect the state of registers, memory, and stack variables. This gives you visibility into how specific code sections behave during execution.

Step Through Execution: By stepping through the program one instruction at a time, you can observe how data flows through the program, how memory is modified, and how different functions interact. This is useful when dealing with complex code or when reverse engineering malware that hides its behavior.

Watch Variables and Memory: Ghidra's debugger allows you to watch variables and track how their values change during execution. You can also watch memory regions to detect memory writes, access patterns, and any unusual changes, such as modifications to code or data regions, which may indicate malicious behavior.

Call Stack and Register Inspection: By inspecting the call stack and registers, you can determine which functions are being executed and track how the program is utilizing the CPU's registers and memory. This is particularly useful for tracking dynamic function calls or identifying function return addresses that may be part of an attack (e.g., a buffer overflow exploit).

2. Emulating Code with Ghidra

Ghidra's Emulator allows for simulating the execution of a binary without the need to run it on actual hardware. This is useful for analyzing software in a safe, isolated environment, especially when dealing with unknown or potentially dangerous code. Emulation allows reverse engineers to monitor runtime behavior in a controlled environment.

Simulated Execution: By using Ghidra's emulator, you can simulate the execution of a binary on different processor architectures (e.g., x86, ARM). This allows you to capture and analyze the program's behavior in terms of instructions executed, memory access, and data manipulation.

Interpreting Memory Modifications: When emulating the program, Ghidra tracks all memory modifications made during the execution. You can monitor how the memory is accessed and altered in real time, which can be helpful for identifying malicious payloads, memory corruption, or vulnerabilities like buffer overflows.

Handling System Calls: Emulation allows you to simulate system calls made by the program to interact with the operating system or external resources. By capturing these calls, you can track the program's interactions with the file system, network, or other resources, which is particularly important for malware analysis.

3. Logging System Calls and API Calls

Another method for capturing runtime behavior is logging system and API calls. These logs provide valuable insights into how the program interacts with the operating system and external resources.

System Call Logging: By monitoring system calls such as file reads/writes, memory allocations, network activity, and process creation, you can gain insight into the high-level behavior of the program. In the context of malware, for instance, these logs may reveal when the malware tries to access sensitive files or contact a remote server.

API Call Tracing: Some reverse engineers use external tools like API monitors to trace function calls to specific APIs, such as cryptographic functions, file system operations, or network requests. This allows for deeper understanding of how the program performs its tasks and helps reveal obfuscated or encrypted operations.

4. Dynamic Analysis Tools and Sandbox Environments

While Ghidra provides strong debugging and emulation capabilities, dynamic analysis tools and sandbox environments can further aid in capturing and interpreting runtime behavior.

Sandboxes: Running the binary inside a sandbox environment (such as Cuckoo Sandbox or a custom VM) allows for safe, isolated analysis of the program's runtime behavior. These environments track system calls, network activity, file system changes, and other runtime events that may occur as the program executes.

Dynamic Analysis Frameworks: Using frameworks like Frida or Pin in conjunction with Ghidra's debugger or emulator can enhance runtime analysis. These tools allow you to inject custom scripts into running processes to intercept and monitor function calls, memory modifications, and other aspects of program behavior.

Network Traffic Analysis: For programs that communicate over a network, capturing and analyzing network traffic is essential. Tools like Wireshark can capture and log network activity, which can be analyzed to understand the program's interactions with remote servers or other systems.

5. Post-Execution Analysis with Ghidra's Analysis Tools

After capturing runtime behavior, Ghidra provides powerful tools to help interpret and analyze the captured data. Once execution is complete, you can use the following techniques:

Memory Dumps: A memory dump captures the entire contents of memory at a particular point in time, allowing you to examine memory states, track changes, and inspect data structures. By analyzing memory dumps, you can uncover sensitive information, decrypt encrypted sections, or identify hidden code.

Log Analysis: Logs captured during execution (such as system call logs or debugger output) can be loaded into Ghidra for post-analysis. By cross-referencing logs with the binary's structure, you can correlate the actions performed by the program with specific sections of code.

Function Tracking: By analyzing the call stack and tracking functions executed during runtime, you can identify the functions responsible for key actions (e.g., encryption, network communication) and further investigate their purpose.

Capturing and interpreting runtime behavior is essential for gaining a deeper understanding of how a program operates. Ghidra, combined with debugging, emulation, and dynamic analysis tools, provides reverse engineers with the capabilities needed to observe and analyze the execution of a binary. Whether you are analyzing malware, debugging complex software, or reverse engineering unknown binaries, these techniques will help you capture and interpret runtime behavior effectively, leading to valuable insights that enhance your reverse engineering work.

Chapter 9: Patching and Modifying Binaries

In this chapter, we dive into the practice of patching and modifying binaries, an essential skill for reverse engineers looking to change the behavior of a program. You'll start by learning how to identify specific areas of code or data that can be modified within a binary, such as altering instructions, modifying constants, or bypassing security checks. We'll guide you through the process of applying patches using Ghidra's built-in tools, showing you how to safely edit and test your changes within the binary. You'll also explore the concepts of binary injection and code hooking, techniques often used in malware analysis or exploit development. Additionally, we'll cover practical use cases, such as cracking software or bypassing licensing mechanisms, and how to reverse engineer these protections. We'll also discuss the importance of preserving the integrity of a binary when making modifications and best practices to ensure your patches don't inadvertently corrupt or destabilize the program. By the end of this chapter, you'll be proficient in patching and modifying binaries, a powerful skillset for any reverse engineer.

9.1 Editing Assembly Code Directly

Editing assembly code directly is a powerful technique in reverse engineering that allows you to modify and manipulate the instructions of a binary to achieve specific objectives. Whether you're patching a binary to remove a restriction, bypassing a security check, or adjusting the logic of the code to understand its behavior, editing assembly code is a fundamental skill. Ghidra, as a comprehensive reverse engineering tool, allows users to edit assembly code directly, providing an environment for dynamic analysis, debugging, and code modification. In this section, we will explore the basics of editing assembly code within Ghidra, and how it can be used to patch or modify binaries effectively.

Why Edit Assembly Code?

Assembly code provides a low-level view of how a program operates on the CPU. Directly editing assembly allows you to:

Patch Binaries: You can modify assembly instructions to change a program's behavior without needing access to the source code. This is commonly used to patch software for debugging, cracking, or removing protections like licensing checks or registration requirements.

Fix Bugs or Alter Logic: In reverse engineering, modifying assembly instructions can be useful for testing different program behaviors, fixing bugs, or modifying program flow to study its effects.

Bypass Anti-Analysis or Anti-Debugging: Some software includes anti-debugging or anti-reverse engineering techniques. Directly editing the assembly code can help you bypass these protections by changing or removing problematic instructions.

Malware Analysis: In the context of malware analysis, editing the assembly code can help in disabling malicious routines, tracking down hidden payloads, or controlling the flow of execution to better understand a malware sample.

Preparing to Edit Assembly Code in Ghidra

Before jumping into editing assembly code, it's essential to properly set up the environment in Ghidra to ensure that changes are made effectively and safely. Below are the steps to prepare your workspace:

Import the Binary: Start by importing the binary you want to edit into Ghidra. Once the binary is imported, Ghidra will automatically perform an initial analysis, disassembling the code and creating a program structure that includes functions, data, and references.

Navigate to the Assembly Code: Ghidra's CodeBrowser tool allows you to navigate through the disassembled code. From the function list or the program flow, you can select and view the assembly code of interest. You can use the Listing window to see the raw assembly instructions and their corresponding addresses.

Set Up a Safe Workspace: Before editing the code, it's essential to back up the original binary. While Ghidra provides a "undo" feature in the disassembly, making changes to a binary at the assembly level can introduce unintended consequences. Saving multiple versions of the binary ensures you can always return to the original state.

Editing the Assembly Code

Once you're set up and ready to make changes, follow these steps to edit assembly code directly in Ghidra:

1. Using the Listing Window

The Listing window is the main interface where assembly instructions are displayed. You can interact with the instructions in this window by modifying individual opcodes or even entire instruction sequences.

Select the Instruction: To edit an assembly instruction, right-click on the instruction you want to modify. This can be a single instruction or an entire block of code.

Choose "Patch Instruction": Right-clicking on the instruction and selecting "Patch Instruction" opens a dialog where you can replace the current instruction with a new one. You can type the new opcode manually or use a hexadecimal value that corresponds to the desired instruction.

Editing Opcodes: When you select an instruction to edit, you can directly modify the assembly code. For example, replacing a jump instruction (jmp) with a nop (no operation) to bypass a code section or changing a conditional jump (jne) to an unconditional jump (jmp).

2. Adding or Removing Instructions

You may need to add new instructions or remove unnecessary ones to alter the program flow:

Inserting Instructions: You can insert new assembly instructions at a specific address using the Patch Instruction option. If you're adding a jump or other control flow instructions, ensure that the new instructions do not corrupt the memory or data.

Removing Instructions: Removing instructions is equally simple. Right-click on the instruction you wish to remove and select Delete Instruction. This can be useful when you want to disable a specific function or security check.

3. Modifying Registers and Memory Access

Assembly code operates heavily on registers and memory locations. Sometimes, editing assembly code requires altering how registers are used or how memory is accessed:

Changing Register Values: In assembly, registers are used to store temporary data. Modifying register values can change the behavior of certain operations. For example, if you see a function that checks if a register holds a certain value, you could modify the value to manipulate the flow.

Memory Access: If the program interacts with memory (e.g., reading or writing to specific locations), you can edit the instructions that access these addresses to alter how data is fetched or written. This can be helpful in bypassing checks or patching incorrect data.

4. Redirecting Control Flow

A common use case for editing assembly code is redirecting the program's control flow:

Jumping to Specific Functions: If you want the program to skip certain functions or go to a different location in the binary, you can modify jump instructions. This is particularly useful for bypassing checks or forcing specific behavior. For example, changing a conditional jump (je) to an unconditional jump (jmp) causes the program to skip the conditional check and proceed to the next block.

NOP Sleds: In some cases, you might want to "neutralize" a section of code without changing much. This can be done by replacing a sequence of instructions with NOP (no operation) instructions, effectively "skipping" over the targeted code. This technique is often used for patching checks or nullifying specific features like authentication prompts.

Testing the Modifications

After editing the assembly code, it is essential to test the modified binary to ensure that the changes produce the desired outcome and do not introduce new issues. Ghidra's Debugger and Emulator can be used to step through the modified code to confirm that the changes work as intended:

Debugging: You can run the modified binary in Ghidra's debugger to step through the code and observe the behavior after the patch. This allows you to verify that the changes did not break the program or introduce new errors.

Running in Safe Environment: Always test the modified binary in a safe, isolated environment such as a virtual machine or sandbox. This is especially important when dealing with unknown or potentially dangerous binaries, such as malware.

Editing assembly code directly is one of the most effective techniques for reverse engineering and modifying binaries. Ghidra's powerful set of tools enables users to navigate, modify, and patch assembly code to better understand, manipulate, and debug software. Whether you're bypassing restrictions, fixing bugs, or exploring malware, knowing how to edit assembly code directly is an invaluable skill in the reverse engineer's toolkit. While powerful, it requires a good understanding of assembly language, CPU architectures, and how programs execute at a low level to ensure that modifications are made safely and effectively.

9.2 Reassembling and Rebuilding Patched Binaries

Once you've edited assembly code directly in Ghidra, the next step is to ensure that your changes are properly integrated into the binary. This involves reassembling and rebuilding the patched binary so that it can be executed with the desired modifications. This process requires careful attention to how the assembly code is translated back into machine code and how any changes impact the overall structure of the binary. In this section, we will explore the reassembly process in Ghidra, including how to handle changes in the binary, preserve the integrity of the patched file, and create a working executable after modifications.

Why Reassemble and Rebuild Patched Binaries?

When you modify a binary at the assembly level, you alter the instructions that the CPU will execute. However, these changes are not reflected in the machine code of the binary unless you reassemble and rebuild the patched binary. Reassembling ensures that:

- **Machine Code Matches Modified Assembly**: After editing assembly instructions, the machine code needs to be re-generated so that the executable can run with the new, patched behavior.
- **File Integrity**: The binary's structure (such as headers, sections, and segments) must remain intact so that the file remains executable. If the patched binary has incorrect file headers or section sizes, it may fail to load or crash when executed.
- **Avoid Corruption**: The process of rebuilding ensures that memory regions (such as code, data, and stack) are correctly aligned, avoiding potential crashes or undefined behavior after modification.

Key Concepts in Reassembling Binaries

Before diving into the specifics of reassembling binaries in Ghidra, it's important to understand a few fundamental concepts:

Disassembly and Assembly Code: Disassembly is the process of converting machine code into assembly code, which is human-readable. Conversely, assembly code is converted back into machine code during reassembly. When you edit the assembly code in Ghidra, you are changing the human-readable instructions that the CPU will execute when converted back into machine code.

Relocation and Addressing: When editing the assembly code, especially if you add or remove instructions, the addresses of functions, variables, and other elements within the binary might shift. Rebuilding the binary involves ensuring that all addresses and references are correctly updated and that no invalid memory references exist.

Binary Sections: A binary is typically divided into different sections, such as the .text section (for code), .data section (for initialized data), and .bss section (for uninitialized data). Editing the assembly may alter the size or content of these sections, requiring adjustments during reassembly.

Steps for Reassembling and Rebuilding Patched Binaries in Ghidra

1. Make Necessary Edits to the Assembly Code

Before you can rebuild the binary, ensure that you have made all the necessary modifications to the assembly code. This could involve altering control flow, modifying instructions, inserting or deleting code, and bypassing specific checks or protections.

Patch Instructions: After editing the instructions, ensure the program logic flows as intended. You might have patched jump instructions, changed values in registers, or even replaced sections of the code with NOPs (No-Op instructions).

Ensure Consistency: After modifications, check if the program's structure is consistent with the original. Ensure that sections like code, data, and stack are correctly defined, and addresses of functions are accurately aligned.

2. Review Changes to the Binary Structure

After editing the assembly code, examine how the changes impact the structure of the binary. Some key areas to review include:

Address Modifications: When you change the code (e.g., by adding new instructions or modifying existing ones), the addresses of subsequent instructions may change. Ensure that references to functions, variables, or memory addresses are correctly updated, especially if you added or removed code sections.

Section Size and Alignment: Adding or removing code could change the size of the .text section (the section containing the machine code). Ghidra will need to recompute the sizes and offsets of sections to ensure proper alignment. This is crucial for the binary to be correctly loaded into memory at runtime.

Relocations: If your modifications impact the binary's address space, such as by inserting new code or altering memory references, the binary will need to handle relocations. Ghidra may help by updating the relocation table to reflect these changes.

3. Reassemble the Code

Once you've confirmed that the assembly code modifications are complete, Ghidra allows you to reassemble the code and integrate it back into the binary.

Rebuild the Binary: In Ghidra, once you modify the assembly code, the tool will automatically update the underlying machine code in memory. To finalize your changes, you need to write the modified code back into the binary.

Save Patched Binary: After reassembling, you can save the modified binary with the changes applied. You can export the patched file by selecting "File" > "Export" from Ghidra's CodeBrowser tool, choosing a suitable file format (e.g., ELF, PE), and specifying the output location.

4. Adjust for Header Changes

When reassembling and rebuilding the binary, it's important to ensure that the headers (e.g., the program header table, section headers, and entry points) are correctly adjusted to reflect any changes you made to the code.

Entry Point: If your modifications change the program flow significantly, you may need to update the entry point to reflect the new starting address of the code.

Section Headers: Ensure the section headers are updated to account for the new sizes of the code, data, and other sections. If you added new sections, make sure they are included in the binary's section table.

Relocation Entries: If you've modified code that references other parts of the binary (e.g., external libraries or internal functions), you may need to update relocation entries. This ensures that references to memory addresses are accurate after reassembly.

5. Test the Patched Binary

After reassembling and rebuilding the patched binary, the next step is to test it to ensure that it functions correctly and that your changes have been successfully implemented.

Run in a Safe Environment: Test the modified binary in a controlled, isolated environment, such as a virtual machine or sandbox. This ensures that the patched binary runs as expected without causing any unintended side effects.

Debugging: Use Ghidra's debugger or external debugging tools to step through the patched binary and monitor its behavior. Make sure that the logic changes are effective and that the binary no longer crashes or behaves unexpectedly.

Verify Integrity: Check the integrity of the binary to ensure that the modifications haven't corrupted the executable. You may want to compare the modified binary with the original (pre-patched version) to verify that only the intended changes were applied.

6. Distribute or Deploy the Patched Binary

Once you have verified that the patched binary works as intended, you can proceed to distribute or deploy it as needed. This could involve packaging the binary for further analysis, deploying it as part of a software update, or using it for penetration testing or malware analysis.

Tips for Successful Reassembly and Rebuilding

Backup the Original: Always keep a backup of the original binary before making any changes. This ensures that you can revert to the unmodified version if needed.

Careful with Memory Modifications: When altering memory access, be mindful of alignment and access patterns. Incorrect memory changes can lead to crashes or unexpected behavior in the binary.

Use Debugging Tools: After rebuilding the binary, use debugging tools to verify that your changes do not introduce new bugs or break the program. Debugging allows you to step through your changes in real time and identify any issues early.

Reassembling and rebuilding patched binaries is a critical part of the reverse engineering process, especially when modifying a binary at the assembly level. Ghidra provides the necessary tools to make direct modifications to the assembly code, reassemble the binary, and ensure that your changes are successfully integrated into the executable. By carefully reviewing changes to the binary structure, adjusting headers, and testing the patched binary, you can achieve the desired behavior while preserving the integrity and functionality of the binary. Whether you're patching software, bypassing protections, or analyzing malware, mastering the reassembly process in Ghidra is an essential skill for effective reverse engineering.

9.3 Injecting Custom Code into an Existing Binary

Injecting custom code into an existing binary is one of the most powerful techniques in reverse engineering and binary modification. This process allows you to alter the behavior of a program, extend its functionality, or even introduce entirely new features, all without access to the source code. Whether you're patching a program to add a backdoor, modifying a function to alter its behavior, or implementing new functionality for analysis, code injection is a crucial skill in the reverse engineer's toolkit.

In this section, we will explore the process of injecting custom code into a binary using Ghidra, discussing the key concepts, techniques, and best practices for successful code injection. We will break down the process into clear steps, from identifying where to inject code to testing the modified binary.

Why Inject Custom Code into a Binary?

Injecting custom code into a binary is useful for several reasons:

Enhancing Functionality: You might want to add new features or modify the way the binary behaves. For example, adding logging capabilities, changing output formats, or adding a new user interface.

Bypassing Protections: Many binaries implement protections such as anti-debugging, anti-reverse engineering, or licensing checks. Injecting code can help you bypass or disable these protections by altering the program's flow.

Malware Analysis: When analyzing malware, you may need to inject custom code to observe how the malware interacts with its environment or to test different exploitation scenarios. For instance, injecting code to log memory writes or network activity.

Patching Bugs: If you come across a bug in the binary, you can inject code that fixes the issue. This could involve fixing memory leaks, correcting logic errors, or improving the performance of certain functions.

Creating a Backdoor: In some cases, injecting code can be used to add a backdoor to the program, allowing you to control or monitor the program remotely or even from within a local context.

Preparing for Code Injection

Before you begin injecting custom code into a binary, it's essential to prepare by setting up a proper environment, making backups, and understanding the program's structure. Here are the key steps to take before starting the injection process:

1. Backup the Original Binary

Always make a backup of the original binary before making any changes. This ensures that you can revert to the unmodified version if anything goes wrong.

2. Understand the Binary Format

Familiarize yourself with the binary format, including the type of binary (e.g., PE, ELF, Mach-O), its sections (e.g., .text, .data, .bss), and its structure. Ghidra will help by performing an initial analysis on the binary, but understanding its layout and memory management is crucial for successful code injection.

3. Choose a Target Location for Injection

Decide where in the binary you want to inject your custom code. The choice depends on your objectives and the binary's structure:

- **Code Injection**: You can inject your code into the .text section, which holds the executable code. You may need to find an unused space within the .text section or overwrite existing instructions that are no longer necessary.
- **Data Injection**: Sometimes, injecting data into the .data or .bss section is necessary, especially if you're dealing with new variables or strings that your custom code will need.
- **Function Replacement**: If your goal is to replace an existing function, you'll need to identify the function's address and modify the program's control flow to redirect it to your custom code.

4. Determine the Custom Code to Inject

Once you've decided where to inject the code, you need to determine what code to inject. This could be a simple operation, such as adding a jump instruction to a specific function, or something more complex, like inserting a new function or modifying existing functionality.

- **Custom Code**: Write the code you want to inject in assembly or machine code. You may also need to account for calling conventions and how the new code will interact with the rest of the program.
- **Code Size**: Ensure that the size of the injected code fits in the available space within the binary. If you don't have enough space, you might need to relocate other sections of the binary or adjust the program's structure.

Injecting Custom Code into the Binary Using Ghidra

Once you've completed the preparations, you can begin the process of injecting custom code. Ghidra provides several tools for this process, but the general steps are as follows:

1. Identify Injection Points

Start by identifying an appropriate location within the binary to insert the custom code. Ghidra's CodeBrowser tool is the most useful for this:

Search for Free Space: Look for unused space or padding within sections like .text or .data where your code can be inserted without interfering with other program components. You can use Ghidra's Listing window to inspect the disassembled code and check for gaps or padding.

Function Boundaries: If you are replacing or modifying a function, identify the start and end points of the function. You can use Ghidra's Function view to locate functions and navigate through their code.

2. Inject Code Using the "Patch Instruction" Feature

Once you've located an appropriate injection point, you can begin editing the assembly code to insert your custom code:

Access the Code Browser: Open the CodeBrowser tool in Ghidra and navigate to the location where you want to insert the custom code.

Patch Instructions: Right-click on the target instruction or address and select the Patch Instruction option. This allows you to modify or replace existing code with your custom instructions.

Insert Custom Code: Using the Patch Instruction feature, you can write your custom assembly code at the desired location. If you're injecting new functionality, you may need to write multiple instructions, such as pushing registers, jumping to your custom function, or manipulating memory.

3. Redirect Control Flow (If Necessary)

If your injected code needs to take control of the program flow, you will need to modify the existing control flow to point to your custom code. This is typically done using jump instructions, which can redirect execution to the injected code.

Use Jumps and Calls: For example, you can replace a function call with a jump to your custom function. If you're injecting code into an unused section, you may need to add a jump to the beginning of your new code so that it can execute when the program reaches that point.

Modify Return Addresses: If your custom code is a function or subroutine, make sure that the return address is correctly adjusted, so the program continues to execute as intended after the custom code is executed.

4. Handle Dependencies

If your custom code relies on external functions, variables, or libraries, make sure those dependencies are correctly handled:

Injecting Data: If your custom code requires new data (such as variables, strings, or buffers), you can inject this data into the binary's .data or .bss sections.

Linking to External Libraries: If your injected code depends on external functions, ensure that these functions are correctly linked or available at runtime.

5. Rebuild the Binary

After injecting your custom code and ensuring all references are correctly updated, the next step is to rebuild the binary.

Rebuild Sections: Ghidra will update the relevant sections (like .text, .data, and .bss) to accommodate the injected code. Make sure that the section headers and memory addresses are updated accordingly.

Save Patched Binary: Save the modified binary to a new file. You can do this through File > Export, ensuring that you specify the appropriate file format (PE, ELF, etc.).

Testing and Debugging the Patched Binary

After injecting custom code, it's crucial to test the modified binary to ensure that the injected code behaves as expected and that the binary's integrity is maintained.

1. Debugging the Binary

Use Ghidra's built-in Debugger or external debuggers to step through the modified binary. This will allow you to verify that the injected code runs correctly and that the program's overall functionality is intact.

Step Through Code: Use breakpoints and step-through features to observe the program's flow and monitor how your injected code interacts with the rest of the binary.

Check for Crashes: Look for any crashes, unexpected behaviors, or incorrect outputs during testing. Debugging tools can help pinpoint where the code injection might have gone wrong.

2. Verify Functionality

Make sure that the injected code performs its intended task and doesn't break any other functionality in the binary. For example, if you added a logging feature, verify that it works as expected. If you bypassed a protection mechanism, confirm that the bypass works and the program behaves normally afterward.

3. Run in a Safe Environment

Always test the modified binary in a controlled environment, such as a virtual machine or a sandbox, especially if you're working with sensitive or potentially harmful binaries (e.g., malware samples).

Injecting custom code into an existing binary is a powerful technique for modifying software, performing advanced reverse engineering tasks, and experimenting with different program behaviors. By using Ghidra's tools, you can effectively identify injection points, modify assembly code, and ensure the injected code integrates seamlessly into the binary. With the right precautions and testing, you can successfully inject custom code to add functionality, bypass protections, or analyze software in ways that would otherwise be impossible. As with any reverse engineering task, remember to work carefully and ethically, and always back up your original binaries before making any changes.

9.4 Validating Changes with Ghidra Tools

Once you have successfully injected custom code into a binary, the next crucial step is validating those changes to ensure that the binary behaves as expected. Without proper validation, there's a risk that your modifications could break the program, introduce bugs, or create security vulnerabilities. Ghidra provides a set of tools that are essential for validating and testing changes, ensuring that your injected code integrates smoothly into the binary.

In this section, we will explore how to use Ghidra's built-in tools to verify that the changes you have made are functional, stable, and do not negatively affect the rest of the program. Validation involves checking various aspects, such as memory, control flow, and functionality, as well as ensuring that the overall integrity of the binary is maintained.

Key Areas of Validation

Memory Integrity and Correctness One of the first things you need to verify after injecting code is that the memory structure of the binary remains intact. Injected code, especially if it manipulates the program's flow or data sections, can lead to unexpected memory corruption or errors if not correctly validated. Ghidra provides tools to inspect memory and identify any issues.

- **Memory Viewer**: The Memory window in Ghidra allows you to view the contents of the binary's memory. After modifying the binary, you can use this tool to check that the memory structure is consistent and has not been corrupted during the injection process.
- **Data Integrity**: If you injected data into sections like .data or .bss, ensure that it has been correctly written and that other parts of the binary do not inadvertently overwrite or corrupt it.

- **Pointer Analysis**: If your injected code involves modifying pointers or memory addresses, it's crucial to validate that all pointers now reference valid memory locations. Ghidra can automatically track and display memory references and pointer relationships, making it easier to spot any issues.

Control Flow and Functionality Since you likely modified or redirected control flow to integrate custom code, it's essential to validate that these changes don't cause unexpected jumps or crashes.

- **Control Flow Graph (CFG)**: The Control Flow Graph in Ghidra helps you visualize how different sections of the program flow from one to another. After your code injection, Ghidra can regenerate the control flow graph and highlight the newly added control flow changes. Verify that the graph correctly reflects the new functionality you've introduced.
- **Function Integrity**: If you replaced or modified existing functions, make sure that the function's entry and exit points have been correctly adjusted. Ghidra's Function window lets you verify the start and end of each function and ensures that your modifications don't disrupt the overall control flow.
- **Cross-References**: Use Cross-References in Ghidra to validate that all functions and variables related to your injected code are correctly referenced throughout the binary. Ensure there are no orphaned references or misdirected function calls that could lead to issues during execution.

Static Analysis with Ghidra's Analysis Tools Ghidra includes a set of analysis tools that automatically check for common problems in the binary. These tools are helpful in detecting issues that might arise from your code injection, such as incorrect function signatures, misaligned instructions, or broken data structures.

- **Auto-Analysis**: After modifying the binary, rerun Ghidra's auto-analysis to ensure that all functions, variables, and memory sections are correctly recognized and analyzed. The tool will check for any discrepancies and ensure that your changes align with the overall structure of the binary.
- **Data Type Analysis**: If your custom code involves new data structures or data types, Ghidra's Data Type Manager will help you inspect them for accuracy. This feature ensures that injected data types are properly aligned with existing data structures, preventing misalignment or memory access errors.
- **Symbol and String Analysis**: If you injected new symbols or strings into the binary, use Ghidra's Symbol Table and String Table features to ensure they have been correctly integrated. These tools will allow you to check if the new symbols are correctly defined and if there are any conflicts with existing symbols.

Dynamic Validation Using Ghidra's Debugger Static analysis is helpful, but dynamic testing is often necessary to confirm that the changes you made are functioning as expected in real-world execution conditions. Ghidra includes a powerful debugger that can be used to test your modified binary in a controlled environment.

- **Debugging the Modified Binary**: Once you've injected code into the binary, the next step is to load the modified binary into Ghidra's debugger and step through it. Set breakpoints at key locations where your injected code is located and carefully observe the program's behavior as it runs.
- **Checking for Crashes or Unexpected Behavior**: While debugging, pay close attention to whether the binary crashes, enters an infinite loop, or behaves unexpectedly. Use the Stack Trace and Registers windows to monitor the program's execution state and check for any anomalies.
- **Monitor Register and Memory States**: Use the debugger to inspect the contents of registers and memory as the program executes. This helps you ensure that the injected code modifies the program's state as intended without causing errors or memory corruption.

Testing for Compatibility and Security If you modified the binary for practical purposes like malware analysis or functionality enhancement, it's essential to test for compatibility with various environments and security vulnerabilities.

- **Platform-Specific Compatibility**: Test your modified binary across different operating systems or environments, especially if you're working with binaries designed for multiple platforms (e.g., cross-platform ELF, PE, or Mach-O binaries). This ensures that your changes don't introduce compatibility issues.
- **Security Validation**: For security-focused reverse engineering tasks, use Ghidra to validate that the injected code does not introduce new vulnerabilities. Look for common issues such as buffer overflows, improper memory access, or unhandled exceptions that could lead to security risks.
- **Reversibility of Changes**: It's also good practice to verify that your changes can be undone if necessary. Using Ghidra's history tracking, you can check previous versions of the binary and compare them with the modified version to ensure that your changes don't unintentionally lock you out of future analysis.

Regression Testing After validating your changes with Ghidra's tools, it's important to perform regression testing to ensure that your modifications haven't broken any other functionality of the binary.

- **Test Cases**: If possible, run a set of pre-defined test cases that cover the major functionalities of the binary. This will help you confirm that the core functionality of the program is still intact.
- **Compare with Original Behavior**: Where feasible, compare the modified binary's behavior with that of the original, unmodified binary. This comparison can be performed through automated testing tools, or manually by observing specific program behaviors and outputs.

Validating changes to a binary after code injection is an essential part of the reverse engineering process. With Ghidra's extensive toolset, you can ensure that your modifications are correct and that the integrity of the binary is maintained. From memory integrity checks and static analysis to dynamic debugging and compatibility testing, Ghidra provides a comprehensive environment for verifying that your changes function as intended and don't introduce new issues. Always remember to test thoroughly and validate each modification to avoid unintended consequences in your analysis or projects.

9.5 Practical Applications: Fixing Bugs and Removing Protections

One of the most powerful and practical uses of reverse engineering tools like Ghidra is the ability to fix bugs or remove protections from a binary. Whether you're working with a legacy software project, conducting malware analysis, or simply reverse engineering a piece of software for educational purposes, Ghidra provides the necessary features to help you identify and resolve issues in compiled code. This section will cover the practical applications of Ghidra for fixing bugs and removing protections, providing detailed strategies for applying your reverse engineering skills effectively.

Fixing Bugs in Compiled Code

In software development, it's common to encounter situations where bugs manifest after compilation, but the source code is unavailable or too complex to debug in its original form. In such cases, reverse engineering can be the only practical solution for identifying and fixing bugs.

Identifying the Root Cause

The first step in fixing a bug using Ghidra is identifying the root cause. Typically, bugs arise from issues with memory access, control flow, or improper handling of functions. By disassembling the binary and using Ghidra's analysis features, you can trace the program's execution and identify the exact location where the bug occurs. Look for uninitialized variables, incorrect function calls, or memory corruption that might be causing unexpected behavior. Ghidra's Decompiler and Disassembler views will be especially useful for this task, as they allow you to observe the code at different levels of abstraction.

Modifying the Code

Once you've identified the bug, the next step is to modify the binary to fix the issue. You might need to adjust function calls, change memory addresses, or fix logical errors in the assembly code. Ghidra allows you to directly edit the assembly code in its CodeBrowser tool. You can apply fixes like changing jump addresses, modifying conditional branches, or altering data values. After making the necessary adjustments, Ghidra provides real-time feedback on the changes, allowing you to verify that your fix is effective.

Testing the Fix

Once you've patched the bug, it's essential to test the binary thoroughly to ensure that the fix works and hasn't introduced any new issues. Use Ghidra's Debugger to run the binary in a controlled environment and step through the modified code. Check whether the bug still manifests and whether the overall behavior of the program remains correct. Dynamic analysis tools, such as Emulation or Runtime Debugging, will help you validate that your changes have resolved the problem without causing other errors.

Regression Testing

After fixing a bug, it's always important to perform regression testing. Even though you fixed the specific issue, changes to one part of the binary can inadvertently affect other parts of the program. By running a suite of test cases or checking the program's overall behavior, you ensure that the fix hasn't compromised other features or functionalities. Ghidra can help automate some aspects of this process, but manual inspection and testing may still be required to confirm that no new bugs have been introduced.

Removing Protections from Binaries

Removing software protections is one of the most common reverse engineering tasks, especially when working with obfuscated, cracked, or protected applications. These protections may include mechanisms such as anti-debugging, anti-tampering, or licensing checks that prevent unauthorized use of software. By understanding and bypassing these protections, you can gain full access to a program's features or remove restrictions that are no longer needed.

Identifying Protection Mechanisms

The first step in removing protections is identifying the protection mechanisms in place. Common protections include:

- **Anti-Debugging**: This prevents the binary from being analyzed or debugged by tools like Ghidra or IDA Pro. The binary may contain code designed to detect if a debugger is attached and behave differently or crash if one is detected.
- **Code Obfuscation**: This makes the code difficult to understand by renaming variables, adding unnecessary complexity, or inserting redundant operations.
- **Anti-Tampering**: Many binaries include checks that ensure the binary hasn't been modified in any way. These checks can be used to verify the integrity of the program during execution.
- **License and Activation Checks**: These checks ensure that a valid license is used to run the software and prevent unauthorized usage.

Ghidra's Disassembly and Decompiler views, along with its Function Graph tool, are invaluable for identifying these protections. You can use these tools to spot specific functions or code patterns that correlate with anti-debugging or anti-tampering techniques.

Bypassing Anti-Debugging Protections

To bypass anti-debugging protections, you need to identify where and how the binary detects the presence of a debugger. In some cases, the binary may check for debugging-related system calls or specific flags that indicate the presence of a debugger. Once identified, you can modify the instructions that trigger these checks or neutralize the functions responsible for detecting the debugger. Ghidra's Disassembler lets you edit assembly code directly, which can be used to patch out these anti-debugging checks. Common methods include:

- **NOPing Out Instructions**: Inserting no-op (NOP) instructions to replace code that checks for debuggers.
- **Modifying Conditional Branches**: Changing jump conditions to bypass checks that detect a debugger.

Removing Code Obfuscation

Code obfuscation is designed to confuse reverse engineers by making the code harder to understand. To remove obfuscation, you'll need to identify the areas of the code that have been obfuscated. This often involves recognizing patterns of redundant operations, confusing variable names, or unusual control flow. Ghidra's Decompiler tool will help you to simplify these sections of the binary, making them more readable and allowing you to understand the obfuscated logic. In some cases, you may need to manually clean up the decompiled output, renaming variables and functions to more meaningful names, and simplifying complex expressions.

Bypassing Integrity and Anti-Tampering Checks

Many software protections include integrity checks that compare the current binary against a known hash or signature. If the binary is modified, these checks will typically cause the program to exit or behave incorrectly. By identifying the location of these checks in the binary (using Ghidra's Cross-References tool), you can disable or bypass them. Common techniques include:

- **Patching Integrity Check Functions**: Modify the logic that performs integrity checks to always return success or bypass the failure conditions.
- **Disabling Checksums or Hash Verifications**: Replace the integrity check algorithms with NOPs or modify their output so that it always matches the expected value.

Disabling License and Activation Checks

License and activation checks are commonly found in commercial software to ensure that users have a valid license. These checks often involve comparing serial numbers, activation keys, or online validation. If you want to remove these protections, you'll need to identify the sections of the binary that validate the key or serial number. Ghidra's Decompiler and Search tools can help pinpoint the locations where the software compares user input to the expected license information. Once found, you can patch these sections to disable the check or hard-code a valid license.

Testing After Removal

After removing the protection mechanisms, it is crucial to thoroughly test the binary to ensure that it works as expected. Debug the modified binary and step through the areas where the protection was removed. Use Ghidra's Debugger and Emulator to test the binary in a safe environment and verify that it functions properly without the protections.

If necessary, perform a clean reinstall of the software on a test system to ensure that the protections are completely bypassed and the software runs as intended.

Fixing bugs and removing protections from binaries are two of the most common and practical applications of reverse engineering. Ghidra's comprehensive suite of tools, including its disassembler, decompiler, debugger, and code analysis capabilities, makes it an invaluable resource for reverse engineers looking to address issues in compiled code. By understanding the root causes of bugs, modifying the code appropriately, and removing protection mechanisms, reverse engineers can gain full control over a binary, making it possible to fix problems, unlock features, and ensure that the binary behaves as expected. Always remember to test thoroughly after making modifications to confirm that your changes have not introduced any unintended side effects.

Chapter 10: Scripting and Automation with Ghidra

In this chapter, we explore the power of scripting and automation within Ghidra, which allows you to streamline repetitive tasks, extend Ghidra's capabilities, and enhance your reverse engineering workflow. You'll begin by learning how to write and run Ghidra scripts using the built-in Java and Python (Jython) environments. We'll cover the basics of scripting, such as interacting with Ghidra's API to manipulate program data, navigate functions, and automate tasks like renaming symbols, analyzing code, and extracting information. You'll also discover how to create custom scripts that can be reused across different projects, making your reverse engineering process faster and more efficient. Along the way, we'll dive into automation techniques for bulk analysis, batch processing of files, and integrating Ghidra with external tools for extended functionality. We'll also discuss how to debug and optimize your scripts to ensure they perform as expected. By the end of this chapter, you'll be able to harness the full power of Ghidra's scripting capabilities, unlocking greater flexibility and efficiency in your reverse engineering tasks.

10.1 Overview of Scripting Languages: Java vs. Python

When it comes to automation and scripting in Ghidra, the two most commonly used languages are Java and Python. Both languages offer unique strengths and serve distinct purposes in the reverse engineering and security analysis fields. Ghidra, being developed by the National Security Agency (NSA), leverages both Java and Python as part of its scripting infrastructure, allowing reverse engineers to enhance their workflow, automate tasks, and extend the tool's functionality.

In this section, we will provide a comparative overview of Java and Python in the context of Ghidra scripting, outlining their features, benefits, and use cases.

1. Java in Ghidra Scripting

Java is the primary language used for the development of Ghidra itself, and it offers several advantages when used for scripting within the platform. Ghidra's core functionality is built with Java, which makes it a natural fit for writing plugins and advanced scripts that require deep integration with Ghidra's API.

Advantages of Using Java in Ghidra:

- **Deep Integration with Ghidra's Core**: Since Ghidra is built in Java, scripts written in Java can directly interact with Ghidra's internal APIs, providing access to all of its functionality.
- **Rich Ecosystem**: Java benefits from a robust ecosystem of libraries and frameworks, making it ideal for tasks that require advanced data structures, concurrency, or complex operations. If a task needs to interact with Ghidra's data models and structures in a way that Python cannot handle efficiently, Java is a solid choice.
- **Performance**: Java generally outperforms Python in terms of execution speed, especially for computationally intensive tasks. While Ghidra's core runs in Java, scripts written in Java often have better performance when processing large binaries or running complex algorithms.
- **Error Handling and Robustness**: Java has strong error handling features, such as exception handling and type safety, which can be useful when dealing with larger, more complex scripts or systems where stability is crucial.

Common Use Cases for Java:

- **Advanced Plugin Development**: Java is typically used for creating plugins or custom extensions within Ghidra, as the platform itself is built on the Java programming language.
- **Complex Task Automation**: When working with large datasets, or requiring advanced concurrency (multi-threading) capabilities, Java scripts are ideal for automating tasks that involve significant computation.
- **Developing Custom Tools**: For tasks that require integration with Ghidra's GUI or advanced data analysis (e.g., large-scale binary analysis or new disassembly techniques), Java offers deeper access to Ghidra's internal libraries and tools.

How to Script in Java in Ghidra:

Java scripts are typically written within Ghidra's Script Manager, a built-in tool that allows you to write, edit, and execute Java scripts directly in the Ghidra interface. To create a Java script, users should select the "New Java" script option in the Script Manager and begin writing their code using Ghidra's extensive Java API.

2. Python in Ghidra Scripting

Python, a dynamic and high-level language, is also supported by Ghidra for scripting purposes. Python offers a more accessible, lightweight, and user-friendly experience for users who may not be familiar with Java or prefer a simpler syntax for their scripting tasks.

Advantages of Using Python in Ghidra:

- **Ease of Use**: Python is known for its simple, readable syntax, making it ideal for quick prototyping, automation of common tasks, or for beginners who are learning reverse engineering or programming.
- **Rapid Prototyping**: With Python, you can quickly write and test scripts without needing to deal with the verbosity or boilerplate code that is common in Java. This makes it perfect for iterative processes or proof-of-concept scripts.
- **Dynamic Typing**: Python's dynamic typing system allows for faster script development and flexibility. You don't need to declare variable types explicitly, which simplifies the process of writing and testing scripts on the fly.
- **Extensive Libraries**: Python comes with a rich ecosystem of libraries and modules, which can be extremely useful for tasks like file manipulation, cryptography, or interacting with web services. The availability of third-party packages makes Python an excellent choice for tasks that go beyond the core capabilities of Ghidra.
- **Integration with Other Tools**: Python has wide compatibility with other tools and systems, making it ideal for integrating Ghidra with external systems or performing additional analyses like interacting with databases, running machine learning models, or querying network resources.

Common Use Cases for Python:

- **Quick Scripting and Automation**: Python is commonly used for scripting repetitive tasks such as scanning binaries for specific patterns, extracting functions, or collecting metadata from a binary.
- **Interfacing with External Tools**: Python is often used to integrate Ghidra with external tools (e.g., Metasploit, network analyzers, or databases) to enhance the reverse engineering workflow.
- **Custom Analysis**: Python is widely used for custom analysis, such as searching for specific byte patterns, manipulating binary data, or extracting function signatures, all of which are common tasks during reverse engineering projects.
- **Education and Rapid Development**: Python's simplicity and readability make it an excellent choice for educational purposes or for rapid prototyping when you're exploring Ghidra's capabilities.

How to Script in Python in Ghidra:

Python scripts in Ghidra can be executed via the Script Manager, just like Java scripts. However, the scripting environment can be accessed by selecting the "Python" option when creating a new script. Once you have selected the Python script type, you can utilize Ghidra's Python API (based on Jython, the Java implementation of Python) to interact with the Ghidra environment and perform reverse engineering tasks.

3. Which Language Should You Use?

The choice between Java and Python for Ghidra scripting depends on the specific goals of your project:

- Choose Java if you require deep integration with Ghidra's core features, need to develop high-performance plugins, or are working on complex binary analysis tasks that require the power of Java's robust type system and advanced concurrency features.
- Choose Python if you need to quickly prototype an idea, automate repetitive tasks, integrate Ghidra with other tools, or perform custom analysis on smaller to medium-sized binaries. Python is also great if you want to focus more on the reverse engineering tasks and less on the coding side.

Both Java and Python are excellent choices for scripting in Ghidra, each offering distinct advantages depending on the task at hand. Java is perfect for larger, more complex projects that require deep integration and high performance, while Python is ideal for rapid scripting and automation with its simple syntax and extensive libraries. Understanding when to use each language is key to maximizing the efficiency and effectiveness of your reverse engineering workflow. Ghidra's support for both Java and Python provides a flexible environment, allowing you to choose the best tool for the job.

10.2 Writing Simple Scripts for Automation

One of the key strengths of Ghidra is its ability to automate repetitive tasks through scripting, which can save you significant time and effort during reverse engineering. Ghidra supports both Java and Python scripting, with Python often being the preferred choice for simple scripts due to its easy-to-read syntax and fast development cycle. In this section, we'll go over how to write simple automation scripts in Ghidra, walk you through a few examples, and provide tips to get you started.

1. Getting Started with Scripting in Ghidra

Before diving into writing scripts, let's quickly go over how to set up your scripting environment in Ghidra:

Accessing the Script Manager: To start writing scripts, open the Script Manager in Ghidra, which you can access from the Window menu. This tool will allow you to create, edit, and execute scripts directly from within Ghidra.

Selecting the Script Type: In the Script Manager, you can choose the language you want to use for your script. You can select Python for quick automation scripts, or Java for more complex and performance-intensive tasks.

Creating a New Script: Click the New button in the Script Manager and select Python as your scripting language. This will open an editor window where you can start writing your script.

Running the Script: Once you've written your script, you can run it directly from the Script Manager by selecting the script and clicking the Run button.

2. Example 1: Automating Function Renaming

A common task during reverse engineering is renaming functions to something more meaningful based on your understanding of the binary. This can help improve the readability of the disassembly and simplify the analysis process.

Let's write a simple Python script that automatically renames functions based on a specific pattern or criteria.

Python Script to Rename Functions:

```
# Importing necessary Ghidra API classes
from ghidra.program.model.listing import Function
from ghidra.program.model.symbol import SourceType

# Define the criteria for renaming functions (e.g., rename functions with a specific name)
pattern_to_rename = "sub_"

# Get the current program (the loaded binary)
current_program = currentProgram
```

```
# Get the function manager from the program
function_manager = current_program.getFunctionManager()

# Loop through all functions in the program
for function in function_manager.getFunctions(True):
    # Check if the function name starts with the specified pattern
    if function.getName().startswith(pattern_to_rename):
        new_name = "Renamed_" + function.getName()

        # Rename the function
        function.setName(new_name, SourceType.USER_DEFINED)

        # Print out the renaming action
        print(f"Renamed function {function.getName()} to {new_name}")
```

How This Script Works:

- The script accesses the current program (the loaded binary) and gets the Function Manager which allows us to interact with the functions in the program.
- It loops through each function and checks if its name starts with the specified pattern (e.g., "sub_").
- If a match is found, the function is renamed with a new name (in this case, the prefix "Renamed_").

Finally, the script outputs the renamed functions to the Ghidra console for feedback.
Benefits of This Script:

- **Automation**: This simple script automates the process of renaming multiple functions based on a naming pattern, which can save time when analyzing complex binaries.
- **Clarity**: Renaming functions allows you to better understand the logic of a binary and make reverse engineering more efficient.

3. Example 2: Searching for Specific Byte Patterns

Another common task in reverse engineering is searching for specific byte patterns (e.g., signatures of known functions, magic numbers, or key indicators). This type of search can help you quickly identify areas of interest in a binary.

Let's write a Python script to search for a specific byte pattern in the binary and highlight those areas.

Python Script to Search for Byte Pattern:

```python
# Importing necessary Ghidra API classes
from ghidra.program.model.address import Address

# Define the byte pattern we are looking for (e.g., '90 90 90' for NOP sleds)
byte_pattern = bytearray([0x90, 0x90, 0x90])

# Get the current program's memory
memory = currentProgram.getMemory()

# Start searching from the beginning of the program
start_address = currentProgram.getMinAddress()
end_address = currentProgram.getMaxAddress()

# Loop through the program's memory
address = start_address
while address < end_address:
    # Search for the byte pattern at the current address
    if memory.getByte(address) == byte_pattern[0]:
        if memory.getBytes(address, len(byte_pattern)) == byte_pattern:
            print(f"Pattern found at {address}")
            # Optionally, highlight the found pattern (e.g., mark it in the disassembly)
            # (Additional steps can be added here to mark or annotate the found pattern in Ghidra)

    address = address.add(1)  # Move to the next byte
```

How This Script Works:

- The script defines the byte pattern to search for (in this case, a sequence of NOP instructions, represented by 0x90).
- It then gets the program's memory and iterates through each byte to look for the pattern.
- Once it finds the pattern, it outputs the address where the pattern is located.
- The script can also be modified to highlight the found pattern in the disassembly, making it easier to spot during analysis.

Benefits of This Script:

- **Pattern Search**: This script automates the process of searching for specific byte patterns, making it faster to locate known function signatures or vulnerabilities.
- **Efficiency**: By quickly pinpointing areas of interest, you can save time during the reverse engineering process.

4. Example 3: Extracting Function Signatures

Often, reverse engineers need to extract function signatures to identify particular functions across different binaries. This task can be automated with a simple Python script that pulls function names, start addresses, and sizes for analysis.

Python Script to Extract Function Signatures:

```
# Importing necessary Ghidra API classes
from ghidra.program.model.listing import Function

# Get the current program's function manager
function_manager = currentProgram.getFunctionManager()

# Loop through all functions in the program and extract their names, addresses, and
sizes
for function in function_manager.getFunctions(True):
    name = function.getName()
    start_address = function.getEntryPoint()
    size = function.getBody().getSize()

    # Output function signature information
    print(f"Function Name: {name}")
    print(f"Start Address: {start_address}")
    print(f"Size: {size} bytes")
    print("-" * 40)
```

How This Script Works:

- The script accesses the Function Manager and loops through all the functions in the current program.
- For each function, it extracts the function name, start address, and size (in bytes).

- It then prints this information to the Ghidra console, which can be useful for creating a list of function signatures or exporting the data for further analysis.

Benefits of This Script:

- **Signature Extraction**: Automates the extraction of function signatures, which can be useful for building a database of known functions across different binaries.
- **Data Organization**: Helps organize and present the extracted data in a clear format for further analysis.

5. Best Practices for Writing Scripts in Ghidra

While writing simple automation scripts, keep the following best practices in mind:

- **Use Meaningful Variable Names**: Clear, descriptive names for variables and functions will make your scripts easier to understand and maintain.
- **Comment Your Code**: Even simple scripts should be well-commented to explain what each section does. This will help you, and others, understand the script's purpose.
- **Test in Small Batches**: When writing scripts for Ghidra, especially if you're automating actions like renaming functions or searching for byte patterns, always test the script on a small binary or a limited section of a binary first.
- **Error Handling**: Add error handling to your scripts to ensure they can handle edge cases (e.g., invalid memory addresses, missing data, etc.) gracefully.

Writing simple automation scripts in Ghidra can significantly improve your efficiency and make your reverse engineering tasks more manageable. By leveraging Python or Java, you can automate repetitive tasks like renaming functions, searching for byte patterns, or extracting function signatures. These scripts can save you time and help focus on the more complex aspects of reverse engineering. With practice and experience, you'll be able to write more advanced scripts tailored to your specific needs.

10.3 Exploring the Ghidra API for Custom Solutions

The Ghidra API provides powerful functionality to extend and customize Ghidra's capabilities beyond its built-in features. Whether you're automating specific tasks, creating custom analysis tools, or integrating Ghidra with external systems, understanding the Ghidra API is essential for building tailored solutions. In this section, we'll introduce you to the core components of the Ghidra API, explain how it can be used to develop custom functionality, and provide practical examples to get you started.

1. Overview of the Ghidra API

The Ghidra API is a set of Java-based classes and interfaces that provide access to Ghidra's internal data structures and tools. The API allows you to interact programmatically with Ghidra, enabling you to automate analysis, manipulate data, and create custom features. It is organized into several packages, each focusing on different aspects of the program:

- **Program Model**: This package provides access to the internal representation of the loaded program, including functions, data, and memory.
- **Listing**: Contains classes for managing code and data in Ghidra's disassembly view (e.g., functions, instructions).
- **Symbol Table**: Allows you to manipulate the program's symbols (i.e., function names, variable names, etc.).
- **Memory**: Interacts with the memory of the loaded binary to perform operations like reading, writing, or searching.
- **Decompiler**: Provides access to Ghidra's decompiler, enabling custom decompilation and analysis of binary code.
- **Utilities**: Includes various utility classes that help with tasks like file handling, logging, and string manipulation.

Understanding these core components will help you leverage the Ghidra API to create custom solutions.

2. Setting Up Your Development Environment for API Access

Before you start writing custom scripts or tools using the Ghidra API, you need to set up your development environment:

Install Ghidra: Ensure that you have a working installation of Ghidra. You can download it from the official website.

Create a Script in Ghidra: Open the Script Manager from within Ghidra to create a new script. In the Script Manager, select Java as the scripting language if you're working directly with the Ghidra API (Java is the primary language for interacting with the Ghidra API).

Accessing the API: Once your script is set up, you can start writing Java code that accesses the Ghidra API. Scripts in Ghidra run within the context of the current project, meaning they have access to all data and analysis that have been loaded in Ghidra.

3. Accessing the Program Data Using the API

One of the most common tasks in reverse engineering is manipulating the program's data. The Ghidra API makes it easy to access and manipulate functions, instructions, and memory.

Accessing Functions

To get a list of functions within a program, you can use the FunctionManager class, which provides methods for fetching all functions or finding a specific function by its address.

```
import ghidra.program.model.listing.Function;
import ghidra.program.model.listing.FunctionManager;

FunctionManager functionManager = currentProgram.getFunctionManager();
FunctionIterator functions = functionManager.getFunctions(true); // Iterate through all functions

while (functions.hasNext()) {
    Function function = functions.next();
    System.out.println("Function: " + function.getName() + " at " +
function.getEntryPoint());
}
```

This script will print out the names and entry points of all functions in the current program.

Accessing Memory

The Memory API allows you to read and write memory in the loaded program. You can access raw data in the program's memory for analysis or modification.

```
import ghidra.program.model.memory.Memory;

Memory memory = currentProgram.getMemory();
byte[] data = new byte[4];
```

Address address = currentProgram.getAddressFactory().getAddress("0x00400000"); // Example address

memory.getBytes(address, data);
System.out.println("Data at 0x00400000: " + Arrays.toString(data));

This script reads 4 bytes of data from the address 0x00400000 and prints them out.

4. Using the Decompiler API

The Decompiler API allows you to interact with Ghidra's decompiler, which converts assembly code into a higher-level representation like C code. This can be useful for creating custom analysis tools that need to operate at a higher abstraction level.

Decompiling a Function

You can decompile a specific function to obtain a high-level representation of its behavior.

import ghidra.app.decompiler.;*
import ghidra.program.model.listing.;*

DecompInterface decompiler = new DecompInterface();
decompiler.openProgram(currentProgram);

Function function =
currentProgram.getFunctionManager().getFunctionAt(currentAddress); // Example address
DecompileResults results = decompiler.decompileFunction(function, 30,
TaskMonitor.DUMMY); // 30 second timeout

if (results != null) {
*   String decompiledCode = results.getDecompiledFunction().getC();*
*   System.out.println("Decompiled Code:\n" + decompiledCode);*
}

This script decompiles a function and prints out the C code generated by Ghidra's decompiler. You can adjust the timeout to allow for more time-intensive decompilation tasks.

5. Custom Tools and Automation

The Ghidra API allows you to build custom tools and automations that can significantly speed up your reverse engineering workflow. These tools can be built as standalone scripts or integrated into Ghidra's user interface.

Creating a Custom Search Tool

Suppose you want to automate the search for certain types of instructions (e.g., finding all instances of a specific instruction). You can use the Listing API to access the disassembled code and look for specific instructions.

```
import ghidra.program.model.listing.*;
import ghidra.program.model.mem.*;

Listing listing = currentProgram.getListing();
CodeUnitIterator iter = listing.getCodeUnits(currentProgram.getMinAddress(), true);

while (iter.hasNext()) {
    Instruction instruction = (Instruction) iter.next();
    if (instruction.getMnemonicString().equals("mov")) {
        System.out.println("Found 'mov' instruction at " + instruction.getAddress());
    }
}
```

This script iterates through all instructions in the disassembled code and prints the address of any mov instruction found.

Automating Data Collection

Another use of the Ghidra API is automating the collection of data. For example, you could write a script that automatically extracts all function names, sizes, and arguments, then exports them to a CSV file.

```
import java.io.*;
import ghidra.program.model.listing.*;

FileWriter writer = new FileWriter("functions.csv");
BufferedWriter bufferedWriter = new BufferedWriter(writer);
FunctionManager functionManager = currentProgram.getFunctionManager();
FunctionIterator functions = functionManager.getFunctions(true);
```

```
while (functions.hasNext()) {
    Function function = functions.next();
    String functionName = function.getName();
    String functionSize = String.valueOf(function.getBody().getSize());
    String arguments = function.getSignature().toString();

    bufferedWriter.write(functionName + "," + functionSize + "," + arguments + "\n");
}

bufferedWriter.close();
System.out.println("Data exported to functions.csv");
```

This script exports a list of functions with their names, sizes, and argument signatures into a CSV file, which can be further analyzed using spreadsheet software.

6. Integrating with External Tools

One of the most powerful aspects of the Ghidra API is its ability to integrate with external tools and systems. You can create custom integrations, such as:

- Calling external services to analyze data or interact with other security tools.
- Exporting data to external formats such as XML, JSON, or databases.
- Automating interactions with external debuggers or fuzzers.

For example, you could write a script that communicates with an external static analysis tool to analyze functions or malware, and then imports the results into Ghidra for further investigation.

7. Best Practices for Working with the Ghidra API

When working with the Ghidra API, consider the following best practices:

- **Modularize Your Code**: Break your code into smaller functions to make it easier to debug and maintain.
- **Use Logging**: The Ghidra API provides support for logging. Use it to track script execution and debug issues.
- **Handle Errors Gracefully**: Always include error handling in your scripts to prevent crashes or unexpected behavior.

- **Test on Sample Binaries**: Before running custom tools or scripts on important binaries, test them on smaller or sample binaries to ensure they work as expected.
- **Consult the Ghidra API Documentation**: The Ghidra API documentation is a valuable resource for understanding the classes and methods available. The API documentation is accessible directly within the Ghidra script manager and also online.

The Ghidra API provides vast opportunities to enhance and customize the reverse engineering workflow. By leveraging the API, you can automate tasks, create custom tools, and integrate with other systems, enabling a more efficient and tailored reverse engineering process. Whether you're working with disassembled code, memory, or decompiled functions, the Ghidra API is a versatile tool that can help you build the solutions you need.

10.4 Debugging and Testing Your Scripts

Debugging and testing scripts is a critical part of developing custom automation and analysis tools using the Ghidra API. Since reverse engineering tasks are often complex and involve analyzing large and intricate binaries, it's essential that your scripts work reliably and produce accurate results. In this section, we will explore techniques for debugging and testing your Ghidra scripts, helping you ensure that your custom solutions are robust and efficient.

1. Debugging Strategies for Ghidra Scripts

Debugging Ghidra scripts requires a combination of traditional debugging techniques and tools within the Ghidra environment. Since scripts run inside the Ghidra framework, it's important to leverage both Ghidra's native debugging features and standard Java debugging practices.

Using Ghidra's Script Console for Immediate Feedback

When you run a script within Ghidra, the Script Console provides a real-time output of your script's execution. This can be used for immediate feedback, such as printing debug information, displaying variable values, or tracking the flow of your script.

Print Debugging: A simple but effective technique is to insert println() statements throughout your code to track the script's execution. This can help you understand what parts of your code are being executed and what the values of key variables are at different stages.

System.out.println("Function Name: " + function.getName());

Tracking Flow: Insert println() statements at key points in your script to see how the flow progresses, which functions are called, and what data is being processed.

System.out.println("Processing function at address: " + currentAddress);

Error Messages: If something goes wrong, consider adding custom error messages to help identify the specific part of the code causing the issue.

if (function == null) {
*   System.out.println("Error: Function not found at address " + currentAddress);*
}

Using TaskMonitor for Real-Time Updates

For longer-running scripts, Ghidra provides a TaskMonitor class that allows you to manage and monitor script execution. It can also be used for debugging purposes by updating the task's progress and reporting status.

import ghidra.util.task.TaskMonitor;

TaskMonitor monitor = TaskMonitor.DUMMY; // Replace with your TaskMonitor if necessary
monitor.setMessage("Starting analysis...");
// Example: Update progress periodically
monitor.setProgress(50); // Progress value between 0 and 100

This can be useful when your script is processing large amounts of data, allowing you to see its progress and prevent it from becoming unresponsive.

Using Java Debugger (JDB) for In-Depth Debugging

While the println() and TaskMonitor techniques can be helpful, for more in-depth debugging, you can use the Java Debugger (JDB) or an Integrated Development Environment (IDE) such as Eclipse or IntelliJ IDEA. To debug your Ghidra scripts using a Java IDE, follow these steps:

- **Configure the Ghidra Script Project**: Set up your Ghidra scripts as a project in your IDE.
- **Attach to Ghidra**: Launch Ghidra with your script in debug mode, and attach your IDE's debugger to the running Ghidra process.
- **Set Breakpoints**: Place breakpoints in your script to pause execution at key points.
- **Step Through Code**: Use the IDE's debugging tools to step through your code line by line, inspect variable values, and trace the execution flow.

2. Testing Your Scripts

Testing scripts is equally important as debugging, especially when your script is part of a larger reverse engineering workflow. A well-tested script will handle edge cases, ensure the accuracy of results, and behave as expected under different conditions.

Unit Testing for Ghidra Scripts

Unit testing is a software testing technique where individual parts of the program (functions or methods) are tested in isolation. Although Ghidra scripts typically run inside the Ghidra environment, you can still employ unit testing frameworks like JUnit to test smaller units of functionality in isolation.

Set Up JUnit in Ghidra: Ghidra supports using JUnit for testing scripts. To get started:

- Download and configure JUnit in your development environment.
- Create a separate project or module specifically for unit tests.

Write Test Cases: Design unit tests that focus on the core functionality of your script. For example, if your script manipulates functions or analyzes specific data, write tests to check the expected results for different inputs.

```
import org.junit.Test;
import static org.junit.Assert.*;

public class FunctionAnalyzerTest {
    @Test
    public void testFunctionExtraction() {
        Function function = getFunctionAtAddress("0x00400000");
        assertNotNull(function);
```

```
    assertEquals("expectedFunction", function.getName());
  }
}
```

In this simple unit test, we check if a function at a given address exists and if its name matches the expected result.

Run Tests: Execute the tests from within your IDE to confirm the accuracy of your functions. If any test fails, examine the error messages to identify where things went wrong.

Integration Testing with Full Programs

While unit testing is effective for isolated components, integration testing involves testing the complete functionality of your script within Ghidra. This includes running the script on a variety of binary samples to verify its real-world performance.

Use a Test Set of Binaries: Collect a set of test binaries (preferably with known behavior) that your script can process. These binaries should cover various edge cases, such as obfuscated code, packed binaries, or unusual instruction patterns.

Test Script on Binaries: Run your script on these binaries and check whether it behaves as expected. This might involve verifying that the output matches the expected results or ensuring that no errors or crashes occur.

Handle Edge Cases: Test your script with edge cases such as:

- Large binaries with many functions
- Corrupted binaries
- Binaries with unusual instruction sets or encryption

You may want to automate this testing process by writing a script that runs your tool on several binaries and logs the results.

3. Best Practices for Debugging and Testing

While debugging and testing, consider the following best practices to ensure your scripts work effectively and efficiently:

Isolate Problems with Minimal Test Cases

If you're encountering issues, simplify your script and test it with minimal input to isolate the problem. Start by testing a basic function, then add complexity incrementally. This will help you identify the root cause of issues without unnecessary noise.

Keep Your Code Modular

Write your code in a modular way, breaking it down into smaller, manageable functions. This approach not only makes your code easier to maintain but also makes it easier to isolate and test individual components.

Test in a Controlled Environment

Test your scripts in a controlled environment to avoid accidental damage or incorrect analysis. Ensure that you have a backup of your project or work on a copy when experimenting with new scripts or testing them in real-world scenarios.

Use Logs to Track Errors and Results

When testing complex scripts, consider adding logging at various levels (info, debug, error) to capture the execution flow. Logging can help you trace exactly where things went wrong if the script does not produce the expected results.

import java.util.logging.Logger;

Logger logger = Logger.getLogger("MyGhidraScriptLogger");
logger.info("Starting function extraction.");
Validate Results and Analyze Output

After running your script, verify that the output is accurate. Compare the results with known values, use manual inspection when necessary, and validate that your script hasn't caused unintended modifications to the binary or project.

4. Debugging Obfuscated or Packed Binaries

Dealing with obfuscated or packed binaries adds an extra layer of complexity to debugging and testing. These types of binaries often involve code that is intentionally difficult to understand or analyze, making it challenging to debug your scripts.

Dealing with Obfuscation: If you encounter obfuscated code, consider using Ghidra's Decompiler to simplify the code or focus on specific parts of the binary. Deobfuscating the binary can help make the output of your script more understandable.

Packed Binaries: Packed binaries often require special treatment, such as dynamic unpacking during runtime. In these cases, you may need to use external debuggers or Ghidra's Emulation features to simulate runtime behavior.

Debugging and testing are essential steps in ensuring the reliability and accuracy of your Ghidra scripts. By utilizing Ghidra's script console, Java debugger, and unit testing frameworks, you can identify and resolve issues in your scripts more effectively. Additionally, integration testing with real-world binaries will ensure that your scripts perform well in complex reverse engineering tasks. By following best practices and understanding common pitfalls, you can build robust, efficient, and reliable scripts that will enhance your reverse engineering workflows.

10.5 Use Cases: Bulk Analysis, Custom Reports, and Plugins

Ghidra's scripting capabilities open up a wide range of possibilities for automating and customizing reverse engineering workflows. By writing custom scripts, analysts can streamline repetitive tasks, automate complex analyses, and extend the tool's functionality with custom reports and plugins. In this section, we explore some of the most useful use cases for Ghidra scripting, including bulk analysis, generating custom reports, and developing plugins to enhance Ghidra's capabilities.

1. Bulk Analysis: Automating Repetitive Tasks

Reverse engineering often involves working with large sets of files or performing the same operations across multiple targets. For instance, analyzing hundreds or thousands of executables manually can be tedious and time-consuming. Ghidra's scripting features allow you to automate these tasks, performing bulk analysis on a large number of binaries or datasets.

Batch Processing of Multiple Files

Using Ghidra scripts, you can create workflows to automatically load multiple binaries into Ghidra, perform an analysis on each, and extract the results in a consistent format. For example, you can write a script that imports a directory of binaries, runs basic analysis (disassembly, function identification), and saves the results.

```
import ghidra.framework.model.Project;
import ghidra.app.util.importer.FileImporter;

File[] files = new File("path/to/binaries").listFiles();
for (File file : files) {
    if (file.isFile() && file.getName().endsWith(".exe")) {
        // Import binary file
        FileImporter.importFile(file, project);
        // Perform additional analysis...
    }
}
```

With such a script, analysts can avoid manually importing and analyzing each binary, allowing them to focus on interpreting results rather than performing repetitive tasks.

Automating Common Tasks

Certain tasks, such as identifying functions, renaming variables, or analyzing common sections of code (like encryption routines), can be automated across many binaries. Scripts can help you perform these tasks in bulk, ensuring consistency and reducing human error. For example, a script might automatically identify functions across all imported files, extract metadata, and categorize the results based on function types.

Scanning for Known Malware Indicators

A common use case for bulk analysis is malware analysis, where you might want to scan a large number of binaries for specific signatures or known indicators of compromise (IOCs). A custom script can scan each binary for known patterns or anomalies, such as suspicious function names, strings, or system calls, and generate a report of suspicious findings.

2. Custom Reports: Tailored Output for Analysis

Another powerful use case for scripting in Ghidra is the generation of custom reports. Sometimes, the data you extract from binaries using Ghidra's analysis tools needs to be presented in a specific format or with certain annotations. Custom reports allow you to automatically collect relevant information from your analysis and structure it in a way that is useful for further investigation, documentation, or collaboration.

Generating Function or Instruction-Level Reports

A simple yet valuable report might include a list of functions found in a binary, along with details about each function's address, size, and call dependencies. A script could extract this data and format it into a CSV, XML, or HTML report for further analysis.

```
import java.io.BufferedWriter;
import java.io.FileWriter;
import ghidra.program.model.listing.Function;
import ghidra.app.util.headless.HeadlessAnalyzer;

BufferedWriter writer = new BufferedWriter(new FileWriter("functions_report.csv"));
writer.write("Function Name,Address,Size\n");

for (Function function : currentProgram.getFunctionManager().getFunctions(true)) {
    writer.write(function.getName() + "," + function.getEntryPoint() + "," +
function.getLength() + "\n");
}

writer.close();
```

This report can be used by analysts to quickly identify and categorize functions within a binary, which is especially useful in malware analysis or vulnerability research.

Cross-Referencing and Dependency Reports

In addition to basic function reports, custom scripts can generate cross-reference reports, showing how functions or data structures interact. For example, a script can analyze how a particular function is called throughout a binary and output a detailed report of the calling functions, addresses, and arguments.

This is invaluable in understanding the relationships between different parts of the program, and it can be useful for security assessments, code audits, or understanding how malware components interact.

Creating Documentation for Reverse Engineering Projects

When reverse engineering a piece of software or malware, it is important to document the findings. Writing detailed reports is time-consuming, but custom reports generated through scripting can reduce this burden. Scripts can generate documentation that includes function names, variable names, memory allocations, and code structures—automatically creating a reference for the reverse engineer. These reports can be formatted in a way that's easy to share with colleagues or clients, helping to improve collaboration and communication.

3. Developing Plugins: Extending Ghidra's Functionality

One of the most powerful features of Ghidra's scripting environment is the ability to extend the tool's functionality through custom plugins. Plugins allow you to add new features, user interfaces, or tools directly to Ghidra, tailoring the software to your specific needs and workflows.

Creating Custom Analysis Tools

For analysts who have specialized needs, creating custom analysis tools through plugins can significantly enhance the efficiency of their reverse engineering work. For example, a plugin could integrate a third-party tool like a static analysis engine or an automatic disassembler, allowing it to run seamlessly within Ghidra's user interface.

```
// Example plugin to integrate a custom analysis tool
public class MyCustomAnalysisPlugin extends Plugin {
    public MyCustomAnalysisPlugin() {
        // Setup plugin
    }

    public void analyzeBinary(Program program) {
        // Perform custom analysis on the loaded program
    }
}
```

Such plugins can automate specific reverse engineering tasks, allowing analysts to quickly run specialized tools without having to leave Ghidra or manually configure external programs.

Custom User Interfaces for Specific Workflows

Sometimes, a custom user interface (UI) is needed to simplify interactions with your reverse engineering scripts. Ghidra's plugin architecture supports the creation of custom UIs that can help users navigate through analysis results, visualize data, or even control script execution. A plugin might include a GUI window for visualizing function calls, memory regions, or analysis results that can be interactively manipulated.

For example, a malware analysis plugin could allow users to quickly visualize which sections of code are related to file operations, network activity, or encryption, making the analysis process more efficient.

```
import docking.widgets.Pane;
import ghidra.framework.Application;

public class CustomUIPlugin extends Plugin {
    public void createUI() {
        Pane pane = new Pane();
        pane.addLabel("Custom Analysis Results");
        // Add custom UI elements
    }
}
```

Integrating External Tools and Databases

Plugins can also enable Ghidra to interface with external systems, such as threat intelligence databases or malware repositories. For instance, you could create a plugin that queries a malware database for known indicators or hashes while performing analysis on a binary, allowing you to automatically check for known threats and add context to your findings.

Creating Custom Exporters

Plugins can also be used to develop custom exporters that allow you to export Ghidra analysis results in proprietary formats or integrate Ghidra with other tools in your workflow. For example, you might create a plugin that exports the disassembly or decompiled code in a specific format needed by another tool or team.

Ghidra's scripting capabilities provide a robust framework for automating reverse engineering tasks, generating custom reports, and extending the tool's functionality through plugins. The ability to perform bulk analysis and generate detailed, automated reports saves time and ensures consistency, while the plugin system enables you to tailor Ghidra to your specific needs and integrate it with external tools and systems. Whether you are automating repetitive tasks, creating detailed documentation, or extending the functionality of Ghidra, scripting offers immense potential to enhance the reverse engineering process.

Part IV: Practical Applications

Part IV shifts the focus from theory and tools to practical, real-world applications of reverse engineering using Ghidra. In this section, you'll explore how the skills and techniques you've learned can be applied to solve common challenges in cybersecurity, software analysis, and malware research. Whether it's analyzing malicious software, dissecting firmware, or solving CTF (Capture The Flag) challenges, you'll gain hands-on experience with real-world scenarios that demonstrate Ghidra's versatility and power. Each chapter is designed to build on your core reverse engineering skills, providing you with the practical knowledge needed to use Ghidra to tackle complex, real-world problems with confidence and precision.

Chapter 11: Malware Analysis

In this chapter, we explore the essential process of malware analysis using Ghidra, a critical skill for identifying and understanding malicious software. You'll learn how to import and analyze suspicious binaries, uncovering how malware operates and identifying key indicators of compromise (IOCs) such as malware behavior, infection vectors, and payload delivery mechanisms. We'll walk through techniques for disassembling and decompiling malware samples to reverse engineer obfuscated code, helping you understand how the malware functions at both the code and system levels. You'll also gain insights into dynamic analysis strategies, using Ghidra in combination with external tools to track runtime behavior, such as memory manipulation, network communication, and system calls. Additionally, we'll cover how to identify common anti-analysis techniques used by malware, such as code obfuscation, packing, and anti-debugging measures, and how to bypass these protections. By the end of this chapter, you'll be equipped to analyze and understand complex malware samples, gaining valuable skills in detecting, reversing, and mitigating cyber threats.

11.1 Setting Up a Secure Environment for Malware Analysis

Malware analysis is a critical aspect of cybersecurity that involves examining malicious software to understand its behavior, identify its capabilities, and determine how to mitigate or neutralize it. However, analyzing malware can be risky because executing malicious code can compromise your system, data, or network. Therefore, creating a secure environment is essential to ensure that the malware does not cause harm while you investigate it. In this section, we will discuss how to set up a secure and isolated environment for effective and safe malware analysis.

1. Using Virtual Machines (VMs) for Isolation

Virtual machines (VMs) provide a controlled environment for malware analysis by isolating the malware from your host system. Running malware inside a VM ensures that any malicious activity is contained within the virtualized environment, minimizing the risk of affecting the host system or the broader network. VMs also allow you to create snapshots, which enable you to revert the system to a clean state after each analysis session.

Choosing the Right Virtualization Platform

Popular virtualization platforms for malware analysis include VMware, VirtualBox, and Hyper-V. Each of these platforms allows you to create isolated environments where malware can be executed safely. VMware, in particular, offers advanced features like snapshots, advanced networking options, and resource isolation, which are useful in the context of malware analysis.

Configuring the VM for Malware Analysis

When setting up a VM for malware analysis, consider the following:

- **Snapshot Strategy**: Take regular snapshots of the VM to revert to a clean state if the malware does damage or leaves traces.
- **Networking Configuration**: Disable internet access on the analysis VM to prevent the malware from communicating with external servers unless monitoring network traffic is part of the analysis.
- **Resource Limitation**: Limit the VM's resources (e.g., CPU, memory) to prevent malware from overwhelming the system and to mitigate the impact of resource-hungry malware.
- **Shared Folders**: Disable shared folders between the host and VM to avoid the possibility of malware spreading from the VM to the host.

By configuring these parameters, you ensure that the analysis environment is isolated, and the risk of infecting other systems is minimized.

2. Network Isolation and Monitoring

Malware often attempts to communicate with external servers or control systems as part of its functionality. To prevent this communication and ensure the safety of your network, the analysis environment should be isolated from the internet or external networks.

Air-Gapped Networks

One of the best practices is to air-gap the analysis machine. An air-gapped environment is a completely isolated network that does not have any physical or wireless connection to external networks, including the internet. This method prevents the malware from reaching out to its command-and-control servers or spreading over the network.

Controlled Virtual Networks

If a complete air-gap is not practical, consider using controlled virtual networks. Virtualization platforms allow you to set up virtual network interfaces that connect the VM only to specific, isolated network segments or host-only networks. These virtual networks ensure that malware cannot escape the VM and infect external devices.

Using Network Monitoring Tools

To observe the malware's behavior, including its network communications, use network monitoring tools inside the isolated environment. Tools like Wireshark, tcpdump, or even a dedicated malware analysis system (like Cuckoo Sandbox) can capture traffic and provide insights into how the malware communicates with external servers. This helps to understand the malware's objectives and capabilities.

3. Configuring Analysis Tools in the Environment

Malware analysis often requires a suite of tools for examining the behavior, code, and structure of the malware. These tools should be carefully selected and configured to avoid interactions that could lead to exposure or compromise of your system. Here's how to configure them for maximum safety:

Static Analysis Tools

Static analysis involves examining the malware's code without executing it. Tools like Ghidra, IDA Pro, and Radare2 are commonly used to analyze the disassembled or decompiled binary of malware. Since these tools do not require execution of the malware, they can be safely used in the isolated environment.

Dynamic Analysis Tools

Dynamic analysis involves running the malware in a controlled setting to observe its behavior in real time. For dynamic analysis, you can use tools like Process Monitor, RegShot, or Sandboxie. These tools allow you to monitor system changes, such as file creation, registry modifications, and network traffic, which are vital in understanding how the malware operates. These tools should also be set up in the isolated VM environment to avoid leaking information back to the host system.

Memory Dump Tools

Malware may leave traces in memory or use sophisticated techniques to evade detection. Tools like Volatility can be used to perform memory analysis, helping identify malicious activities that are not immediately visible from the file system. Ensure that these tools are configured to capture memory dumps and system states periodically during the malware's execution.

4. Handling Malware Samples Safely

To further mitigate risks, proper handling of malware samples is crucial. Here are some best practices to follow:

Storing Malware Samples in Isolated Locations

Store malware samples on removable media or network drives that are also isolated from your primary work environment. These storage devices should not be connected to your primary network and should be dedicated solely to storing and transferring malware samples.

Renaming Files

To avoid accidental execution, rename malware files to obscure names before transferring them into the analysis environment. For example, changing file extensions from .exe to .txt can prevent accidental execution if the file is mistakenly opened on a vulnerable system.

Using Hashes to Verify Integrity

When handling multiple malware samples, use cryptographic hashes (e.g., SHA-256) to verify the integrity of each sample and ensure that the sample you are analyzing has not been altered or replaced. Keeping a record of the hash values helps in confirming that you are working with the correct version of the malware.

5. Creating an Incident Response Plan

While the goal is to maintain a secure environment, there's always a possibility that malware could escape the containment or compromise the analysis system. It is essential to have an incident response plan in place to address such situations.

Network Segmentation for Detection

Use network segmentation to ensure that even if malware does manage to break containment, it has limited access to other systems. Network segmentation creates isolated zones within your organization, ensuring that if malware escapes from a VM, it cannot easily spread to critical systems or data.

Snapshot and Rollback Mechanisms

Always maintain the ability to quickly revert to a known safe state using snapshots or backups. This can be done by taking VM snapshots before and after the analysis. If anything goes wrong, you can easily restore the VM to its original, uninfected state.

Sharing Findings and Results

After analyzing the malware, document and share your findings in a structured and secure manner. If necessary, provide the information to relevant parties (e.g., your organization's cybersecurity team, CERT, or law enforcement) while ensuring the data is protected and anonymized where required.

Setting up a secure environment for malware analysis is an essential first step in performing effective and safe reverse engineering. By utilizing virtual machines, isolating the analysis environment, configuring network settings, and using appropriate analysis tools, you can significantly mitigate the risks associated with working with malware. These precautions help protect not only your system but also the broader network and data from potential threats. Proper handling of malware samples and creating a response plan ensures that your analysis can proceed with minimal risk to your infrastructure and operations. With these safety measures in place, you can confidently perform thorough and impactful malware analysis.

11.2 Identifying Obfuscation and Packing Techniques

Malware authors often employ various techniques to obscure the functionality and behavior of their malicious software in order to evade detection and analysis. These techniques, such as obfuscation and packing, are specifically designed to make reverse engineering more difficult, hindering analysts from understanding the malware's true behavior. In this section, we will explore common obfuscation and packing techniques used in malware, how to identify them, and strategies for bypassing these methods during analysis.

1. What is Obfuscation and Packing?

Obfuscation refers to the deliberate modification of code or data in a way that makes it difficult to understand while retaining its original functionality. Obfuscation can target various parts of the malware, such as function names, control flow, or even data structures. It is typically used to confuse reverse engineers and automated analysis tools, making the code harder to follow.

Packing, on the other hand, involves compressing or encrypting a binary file to make it unreadable to analysis tools like disassemblers or debuggers. The idea behind packing is to protect the payload by disguising it as benign code or making it impossible to analyze directly. When executed, a packed binary typically unpacks itself in memory, often using a custom unpacking routine to reveal the original malicious code.

Both obfuscation and packing can be used together, and identifying these techniques is crucial for malware analysts to effectively unpack and understand the true intent of a piece of malicious software.

2. Identifying Obfuscation Techniques

There are many forms of code obfuscation that malware authors can use. Here are some of the most common techniques and how to identify them:

2.1 Control Flow Obfuscation

Control flow obfuscation is a technique where the program's execution flow is altered to confuse the analysis process. The goal is to make the code more complex without changing its functionality. This can include adding unnecessary jumps, loops, or function calls that do not serve any real purpose.

How to Identify:

- **Unusual Jump Instructions**: Look for sequences of conditional and unconditional jump instructions (like JMP, JZ, JNZ, etc.) that do not appear to make logical sense.
- **Long, Unwieldy Loops**: Code that seems to involve unnecessary looping, or jumps between functions in ways that break normal program flow, can be a sign of control flow obfuscation.
- **Dynamic Control Flow**: If the control flow relies on data that changes dynamically during execution, it may be an indication of obfuscation.

2.2 String Encryption and Encoding

Malware often uses string encryption to hide critical data such as URLs, IP addresses, and file paths. Strings may be encrypted or encoded within the binary, and a decryption routine is included to decode them at runtime.

How to Identify:

- **Encrypted Strings**: Strings that appear as random characters or gibberish in the disassembled code might be encrypted. In some cases, you can search for known decryption functions (e.g., XOR, base64, RC4) within the binary.
- **Suspicious Function Calls**: Look for suspicious calls to functions that are commonly used for string manipulation or decryption, such as memcpy, strcpy, or functions that seem to handle bytes in unusual ways.

2.3 Junk Code Insertion

Junk code insertion involves adding extra, meaningless code to a program to increase its size and complexity. This code serves no real purpose other than to confuse the reverse engineer and slow down the analysis.

How to Identify:

- **Unnecessary Functions**: Identify functions or blocks of code that do not seem to serve a useful purpose in the context of the program. These can include loops that never terminate or variables that are defined but never used.
- **Obfuscated Code Sequences**: Look for large blocks of code that appear randomly inserted without clear function. These blocks may include no-operations (NOP), redundant instructions, or irrelevant calculations.

2.4 Virtual Machines (VM) and Custom Interpreters

Some advanced malware authors use virtual machines (VMs) or custom interpreters to execute their code. The malware code is translated into a VM-specific bytecode or intermediate representation, making it harder to reverse engineer.

How to Identify:

- **Unusual Code Constructs**: Look for code that behaves like a VM interpreter, where the program is executing a series of opcodes or bytecodes. This might include jump tables, switch-case structures, or complex decoding routines.

- **Uncommon File Structures**: Malware packed in a way that it looks like a virtual machine or uses non-standard instruction sets can be a clue. Look for VM artifacts in the binary, such as known VM opcodes or interpreter calls.

3. Identifying Packing Techniques

Packing is a technique used to obfuscate the contents of a binary by compressing or encrypting the code. The packed binary contains the original executable and an unpacking routine, which decompresses or decrypts the binary in memory during execution. Here are some of the most common packing techniques:

3.1 Static Packers

Static packers use algorithms like UPX, ASPack, or PECompact to compress the binary. These packers can make reverse engineering difficult by hiding the true code of the malware behind layers of compression.

How to Identify:

- **File Size Mismatch**: A significant reduction in file size compared to a typical executable of the same type could indicate the presence of packing.
- **Unusual Section Names**: Packed binaries often contain unusual or non-standard section names such as .upx, .aspack, or .textz. These can indicate that a packing tool was used.
- **High Compression Ratios**: Tools like UPX typically produce packed files with high compression ratios. Use tools like PEiD or Detect It Easy (DIE) to check the binary for common packer signatures.

3.2 Custom Packers

Malware authors often create their own custom packing tools to avoid detection by signature-based systems. Custom packers can use a wide variety of compression or encryption methods, making them harder to identify using standard packer detection tools.

How to Identify:

- **Suspicious Header Modifications**: Custom packers often modify the PE headers or other executable formats, so look for unusual or malformed headers that do not follow standard specifications.

- **Unusual Entry Points**: Custom packers might alter the program's entry point, so the malware's real code doesn't start executing until after the unpacking process. Use a debugger to identify unusual entry points or steps taken before the main code executes.
- **Emulator and Debugger Behavior**: Custom-packed malware may resist traditional debugging or emulation techniques. It may behave differently in an emulator or debugger, showing signs of anti-debugging techniques or unusual memory access patterns.

3.3 Runtime Unpacking

Some malware uses runtime unpacking, which means that the malicious code is unpacked only when it is executed. The unpacking code is typically very small, and it unpacks the malicious code into memory before jumping to it.

How to Identify:

- **Suspicious Memory Patterns**: If the malware decompresses itself in memory, you may observe suspicious memory access patterns, such as large blocks of memory being rewritten or encrypted sections being decrypted in memory.
- **Debugger Behavior**: Malware using runtime unpacking may attempt to evade detection by debugger breakpoints. In such cases, it may alter the control flow or detect the presence of debuggers. Monitoring for these changes or using tools like OllyDbg or x32dbg can help you identify runtime unpacking.

4. Techniques to Overcome Obfuscation and Packing

By understanding common obfuscation and packing techniques, malware analysts can use various strategies to bypass these protections and successfully reverse engineer the malware:

4.1 Debugging and Emulation

Using a debugger or an emulator is one of the most common ways to bypass obfuscation and unpacking. Tools like OllyDbg, x32dbg, and IDA Pro's debugger can help trace through packed code and locate the unpacking routine.

4.2 Memory Dumping

For packed or runtime-unpacked malware, capturing a memory dump after the malware has unpacked itself can provide a clear view of the executable code. Memory analysis tools like Volatility or Rekall can help extract and analyze these memory dumps.

4.3 Deobfuscation Scripts

For control flow obfuscation or string encryption, using deobfuscation scripts can be helpful. These scripts can automate the identification of common obfuscation patterns and recover meaningful data, such as function names, strings, or the original control flow.

Obfuscation and packing are key techniques used by malware authors to thwart analysis efforts. Identifying and dealing with these techniques is essential for malware analysts to uncover the true behavior of the malware. By understanding the common obfuscation methods (e.g., control flow obfuscation, string encryption) and packing techniques (e.g., static packers, custom packers, runtime unpacking), analysts can develop strategies to bypass these protections and successfully reverse-engineer the malicious code. These strategies include using debugging, memory dumping, and deobfuscation scripts, allowing analysts to ultimately understand the full scope and impact of the malware.

11.3 Extracting Indicators of Compromise (IoCs)

Indicators of Compromise (IoCs) are critical pieces of information used to detect and understand the presence of malware, malicious activities, or security breaches in a network or system. Extracting IoCs is one of the most important steps in malware analysis, as it helps security professionals identify and respond to incidents. In this section, we'll explore how to extract IoCs from malware using Ghidra and other tools, the types of IoCs to look for, and how to leverage them to enhance cybersecurity efforts.

1. What Are Indicators of Compromise (IoCs)?

IoCs are forensic artifacts or data points that suggest a system or network has been compromised by malicious activity. These artifacts can include file hashes, IP addresses, domain names, registry keys, URLs, network traffic patterns, and more. In the context of malware analysis, IoCs are used to detect specific behaviors or characteristics associated with malware, allowing defenders to identify and mitigate threats before they cause significant damage.

In malware analysis, IoCs serve two primary purposes:

- **Detection**: Help identify infected systems and potential security breaches.
- **Threat Intelligence**: Aid in understanding the tactics, techniques, and procedures (TTPs) used by threat actors, enabling defenders to better prepare for future attacks.

Extracting IoCs from malware involves identifying relevant data points during the analysis process, and in some cases, correlating these findings with external threat intelligence sources.

2. Types of Indicators of Compromise

When analyzing malware, IoCs typically fall into one or more of the following categories:

2.1 File-Based Indicators

These indicators are related to specific files that have been created, modified, or used by the malware. They include:

- **File Hashes (MD5, SHA1, SHA256):** Unique identifiers for files that can be used to quickly verify if a file has been seen before. Malware often uses unique file hashes that can be checked against malware databases or threat intelligence platforms.
- **File Names**: Specific names or patterns in file names may be indicative of a particular piece of malware. Malware often uses specific, commonly known names or deceptive names (e.g., "svchost.exe") to blend in with normal system operations.
- **File Paths**: Unusual or unexpected file locations can also be indicators. Malware may drop files in non-standard directories to avoid detection.

2.2 Network Indicators

Malware often communicates with external servers, either to receive commands or exfiltrate data. Identifying network-based IoCs is essential for understanding the malware's reach and intentions:

- **IP Addresses**: The IP addresses used by malware to communicate with command-and-control (C&C) servers can be a key IoC. These addresses can be static or dynamically generated, and may change over time.
- **Domain Names**: Malware may use domain names to reach out to external servers. These domains can be hardcoded or dynamically generated based on algorithms.

- **URLs**: Specific URLs accessed by the malware during execution are valuable IoCs. Malware often uses these to communicate with C&C servers, download additional payloads, or exfiltrate stolen data.
- **Ports and Protocols**: Identifying unusual network ports or protocols used by malware can help pinpoint its communication behavior. Certain malware types may communicate over uncommon ports to evade detection by firewalls or intrusion detection systems.

2.3 Behavioral Indicators

Behavioral indicators are patterns of activity that can signal the presence of malware based on how it interacts with the system:

- **Process and Thread Activity**: The creation of unusual or suspicious processes or threads can point to malicious activity. Malware often spawns child processes to carry out its functions or injects code into legitimate processes.
- **Registry Modifications**: Malware may create or modify registry keys to maintain persistence on the system. Keys like those under "HKEY_LOCAL_MACHINE\Software\Microsoft\Windows\CurrentVersion\Run" are often targeted by malware to ensure it starts on system boot.
- **File System Activity**: Malware often creates, modifies, or deletes files as part of its execution process. Unusual file system activity such as the creation of hidden files or the modification of critical system files may indicate the presence of malware.

2.4 Memory-Based Indicators

Memory analysis is another key method of extracting IoCs from malware. Certain malware types, especially those that use fileless techniques, leave their traces in memory:

- **Memory Dumps**: Malware that operates purely in memory without touching the disk leaves indicators that can only be detected via memory dumping tools (e.g., Volatility, Rekall). These indicators may include code fragments, strings, or function pointers that link back to the malware's behavior.
- **Injected Code**: Many types of malware inject their code into the memory space of running processes. Identifying unusual code injection into system processes, such as "explorer.exe" or "svchost.exe," can provide critical IoCs.
- **Persistent Hooks or Modifications**: Malware may modify system functions or hooks to achieve persistence. Monitoring for injected hooks in system libraries can provide insights into ongoing malicious activity.

3. How to Extract IoCs from Malware Using Ghidra

Ghidra, as a powerful reverse engineering tool, offers various features that can help analysts extract IoCs from malware. Below are the steps and techniques for extracting different types of IoCs using Ghidra:

3.1 Static Analysis: Extracting File-Based IoCs

When analyzing a binary in Ghidra, you can extract file-related IoCs such as file hashes, strings, and file paths:

- **Hashing Files**: Use tools like HashMyFiles or Ghidra's own hash generation to calculate the hashes of the malware's file. These can then be checked against external databases such as VirusTotal.
- **Strings**: Ghidra's "Search for Strings" function can help uncover hardcoded strings such as file paths, IP addresses, domain names, and more. These can be potential IoCs related to malware communication or dropped files.
- **Function Analysis**: While analyzing functions in Ghidra, look for suspicious API calls related to file operations (e.g., CreateFile, WriteFile, DeleteFile). These can point to malicious activities like file creation, modification, or deletion.

3.2 Dynamic Analysis: Extracting Network-Based IoCs

While Ghidra doesn't offer full dynamic analysis features (such as network monitoring), you can use it to track network-related IoCs by observing function calls related to network communication:

- **Network Functions**: Search for functions that interact with network protocols, such as socket, connect, send, recv, bind, etc. These functions are often used by malware for communication with external servers.
- **Domain Generation Algorithms (DGAs):** If the malware generates domain names dynamically, Ghidra's decompiler and analysis tools can help you identify the logic behind these algorithms. By extracting the domain generation routine, you can determine the structure of domains that the malware might attempt to connect to.

3.3 Identifying Persistence Mechanisms

Use Ghidra to examine the persistence mechanisms employed by malware:

- **Registry Keys**: Search for strings and code that reference Windows registry paths where persistence is commonly achieved, such as the "Run" registry key under HKEY_LOCAL_MACHINE or HKEY_CURRENT_USER.
- **Scheduled Tasks**: If malware creates or modifies scheduled tasks, Ghidra can help you locate function calls related to task creation and management.

3.4 Identifying Behavioral Indicators

Look for patterns in function calls or code that correspond to common malicious behaviors:

- **Keylogging**: Identify code related to keylogging by searching for functions that interact with the keyboard (e.g., GetAsyncKeyState, keybd_event).
- **Credential Harvesting**: Search for strings or code that indicates interaction with sensitive data such as passwords or API keys.

3.5 Memory and Runtime Indicators

While Ghidra's static analysis capabilities are robust, it's important to supplement them with dynamic analysis tools:

- **Memory Dumping**: After running the malware in a controlled environment, use tools like Volatility or Rekall to analyze memory dumps and correlate them with findings from Ghidra.
- **Code Injection**: Ghidra can help identify injection techniques by analyzing the code for suspicious API calls related to memory allocation (VirtualAlloc, WriteProcessMemory, etc.) and system function hooking.

4. Using IoCs in Threat Detection

Once IoCs are extracted, they can be used in various ways to enhance cybersecurity defenses:

- **Threat Intelligence Platforms**: Submit IoCs to threat intelligence platforms like MISP, OpenDXL, or commercial vendors to improve detection and response.
- **SIEM Systems**: IoCs can be integrated into Security Information and Event Management (SIEM) systems to automatically alert security teams when suspicious activity is detected.

- **Endpoint Protection**: Use IoCs to update endpoint protection systems to detect and block malicious files, domains, or IP addresses.

Extracting Indicators of Compromise (IoCs) is a crucial part of malware analysis. Through careful static and dynamic analysis, you can identify a range of IoCs that point to the presence of malware and its activities. Ghidra provides a comprehensive suite of tools to facilitate this process, including the ability to uncover file-based IoCs, network indicators, persistence mechanisms, and behavioral patterns. By understanding these IoCs and how to extract them, security professionals can strengthen their ability to detect, respond to, and mitigate threats in a timely and effective manner.

11.4 Understanding Common Malware Behavior Patterns

Understanding common malware behavior patterns is key to identifying, analyzing, and mitigating threats. Malware often follows certain predictable strategies to achieve its goals, such as maintaining persistence, stealing sensitive information, or establishing communication with a command-and-control (C&C) server. Recognizing these patterns early in the analysis process can help reverse engineers and security professionals detect malicious activity before it spreads or causes significant harm.

In this section, we will explore the most common malware behavior patterns observed during the reverse engineering process. We will focus on how malware typically behaves when it infects a system, the tactics it employs to achieve its objectives, and how reverse engineers can identify these behaviors to gain deeper insights into malware functionality.

1. Persistence Mechanisms

One of the primary goals of most malware is to maintain a presence on an infected system. This often requires the use of persistence mechanisms to ensure that the malware can survive system reboots, user actions, or attempts to remove it. Common persistence techniques include:

1.1 Modifying Startup Locations (Registry Keys and Startup Folders)

Malware often places itself in the system's startup locations to ensure it executes each time the system boots. These locations include:

- **Windows Registry**: Malware often creates or modifies registry entries in places like HKEY_LOCAL_MACHINE\Software\Microsoft\Windows\CurrentVersion\Run or HKEY_CURRENT_USER\Software\Microsoft\Windows\CurrentVersion\Run. These registry keys are checked by Windows at startup, and adding a reference to the malware's executable ensures it runs on every boot.

- **Startup Folders**: In some cases, malware places a copy of itself in the startup folders (C:\Users\<User>\AppData\Roaming\Microsoft\Windows\Start Menu\Programs\Startup), which can trigger execution upon login.

1.2 Service Installation

Malware may install itself as a Windows service to run in the background without user intervention. Services are typically hidden from normal user activities and can be set to run with elevated privileges. They are often used to ensure the malware runs persistently, even in restricted user environments.

1.3 Task Scheduler

Some malware uses the Windows Task Scheduler to schedule tasks that run the malware at regular intervals or trigger it in response to specific system events. Task Scheduler is a legitimate tool, making it harder for basic antivirus systems to detect malicious use.

1.4 Bootkits and Rootkits

In some cases, malware may install a bootkit or rootkit. These types of malware embed themselves within the system's boot process or the operating system kernel, making them extremely difficult to detect or remove. Bootkits load before the operating system and can take control of the system at a very low level, while rootkits hide the presence of malware or alter the operating system's normal behavior.

2. Network Communication and C2 (Command-and-Control)

Another common behavior of malware is establishing communication with a command-and-control (C2) server. This communication can take different forms and serve a variety of purposes, from receiving instructions to exfiltrating stolen data. Malware typically uses one or more of the following techniques for C2 communication:

2.1 Hardcoded Domain Names and IP Addresses

Many malware programs rely on hardcoded domain names or IP addresses to contact a C2 server. These domains and IPs are often embedded within the malware's code or configuration files. This allows the attacker to control infected systems by sending commands or receiving data without relying on dynamic methods like Domain Generation Algorithms (DGAs).

2.2 Domain Generation Algorithms (DGAs)

Some malware uses domain generation algorithms (DGAs) to dynamically generate domain names that can be used for C2 communication. These algorithms create a series of domain names based on specific algorithms, often using factors like the current date, making it harder for security systems to block the malware's communication channels. Analysts can reverse engineer the algorithm to predict future domains and block the malware's traffic.

2.3 Peer-to-Peer (P2P) Communication

Advanced malware may use peer-to-peer (P2P) networks to eliminate reliance on a central C2 server. P2P malware operates in a decentralized fashion, where infected machines communicate directly with each other rather than with a single C2 server. This technique makes it more challenging for defenders to disrupt the communication network, as each infected machine can act as both a client and a server.

2.4 Encrypted or Obfuscated Communication

Many malware programs use encryption or obfuscation techniques to hide the contents of their communications. This makes it difficult for security tools to inspect traffic and detect malicious activity. By using protocols like HTTPS, TLS, or custom encryption, malware authors attempt to evade traditional detection methods that rely on inspecting unencrypted network traffic.

2.5 Use of Legitimate Services (e.g., Social Media, Cloud Services)

Some sophisticated malware use legitimate online services (such as social media platforms, cloud storage, or content delivery networks) for C2 communication. By leveraging well-known and trusted services, this malware can blend in with normal traffic and evade detection by firewalls or intrusion detection systems.

3. Evasion and Anti-Analysis Techniques

Malware often employs a variety of tricks to avoid detection, analysis, and removal. These evasion techniques make it difficult for analysts and security systems to identify, study, or stop the malware. Common anti-analysis techniques include:

3.1 Code Obfuscation

Malware developers frequently obfuscate their code to make it harder to understand. This may involve renaming functions and variables to random strings, hiding logic through encryption, or using complex control flow structures. Obfuscation can confuse reverse engineers and automated analysis tools, significantly complicating the reverse engineering process.

3.2 Anti-Debugging Techniques

Malware often includes anti-debugging measures to detect when it is being analyzed in a debugger or reverse engineering environment. These techniques can trigger delays, prevent certain actions, or alter the behavior of the malware when a debugger is attached. Examples of anti-debugging methods include checking for the presence of debugger-specific processes, inspecting the system for virtualization environments, or using time-based checks to detect slow execution.

3.3 Virtual Machine (VM) and Sandbox Detection

Many malware programs are designed to detect whether they are running in a virtual machine (VM) or a sandbox environment. Virtual machines are often used by analysts to safely execute malware for analysis, so malware authors take steps to identify such environments and alter their behavior to avoid detection. Malware may check for the presence of common VM drivers or perform timing checks to detect the artificial environment.

3.4 Delayed Execution or Self-Destruction

To avoid detection during initial analysis, some malware delays its execution or triggers a self-destruct routine if it detects an analysis environment. This tactic makes it difficult for analysts to observe the malware's full range of behavior. Malware may execute its malicious payload only after a certain amount of time has passed or upon detecting certain conditions, such as a specific environment or a particular set of user actions.

4. Data Exfiltration and Theft

One of the primary objectives of many malware strains is data theft. Whether it's stealing personal information, intellectual property, or login credentials, exfiltrating data is often the ultimate goal. Common data theft methods include:

4.1 Keylogging

Keylogging is a common technique used by malware to capture keystrokes and record sensitive data, such as login credentials or credit card numbers. The malware often uses APIs that hook into the system's input devices, such as keyboards, to record every key press.

4.2 Credential Dumping

Malware may attempt to harvest credentials by accessing password databases, browser caches, or by exploiting insecure applications. Once it gains access to these credentials, it can send them back to the C2 server for further use, often facilitating additional attacks or identity theft.

4.3 File Exfiltration

Malware may search for files containing sensitive data, such as documents, databases, and configuration files, and then upload them to a remote server controlled by the attacker. This is often done using covert network protocols, or by embedding the stolen data within benign-looking network traffic to evade detection.

5. Common Behavioral Patterns and Indicators

By understanding these common malware behaviors and analyzing them in context, reverse engineers and security analysts can detect patterns that help identify threats more efficiently. Key behavioral indicators include:

- Unusual or suspicious system modifications, such as unexpected file or registry changes.
- Unexpected network activity, particularly traffic to known malicious domains or IP addresses.
- Fileless or memory-resident malware, which operates without touching the file system, making it harder to detect.
- Abnormal system performance, such as sudden spikes in CPU or memory usage, indicative of ongoing malicious processes.

Recognizing common malware behavior patterns is critical for efficient reverse engineering and timely detection of threats. By understanding how malware typically behaves—whether through persistence mechanisms, network communication, evasion tactics, or data exfiltration—security professionals can more effectively identify malicious activity and protect systems against potential damage. Familiarity with these patterns allows for faster, more targeted responses, and improves the overall security posture of the organization.

11.5 Case Study: Analyzing a Real-World Malware Sample

In this section, we will walk through a case study of analyzing a real-world malware sample using Ghidra. This example will demonstrate the reverse engineering process, from initial analysis to extracting key insights, identifying malicious behavior, and outlining the steps taken to mitigate the threat. We'll focus on a malware sample that represents a typical piece of ransomware, which is a type of malware that encrypts a user's files and demands a ransom for decryption.

Disclaimer: This analysis is for educational purposes only. Never analyze or interact with malware on live systems or environments without proper precautions. Always use isolated, controlled environments like sandboxes or virtual machines for analysis.

Step 1: Setting Up the Environment

Before diving into the analysis, it is essential to ensure a secure and isolated environment to prevent the malware from spreading or causing damage. In this case, we will use a virtual machine (VM) running an operating system (e.g., Windows 10) with Ghidra installed. A network monitoring tool (like Wireshark) can be useful to track network traffic, while an antivirus or endpoint detection system (in a non-production environment) will allow us to monitor for alerts.

Important Considerations:

- Set up a VM that can be easily restored after each analysis.
- Use Ghidra's isolated environment and limit the malware's ability to contact external servers.
- Disable the internet connection for the VM during initial analysis to prevent communication with any command-and-control (C2) servers.

Step 2: Importing the Malware Sample into Ghidra

The first step in Ghidra is to import the binary malware file. In this case, the malware is a Windows executable (.exe) that has been packed or encrypted to make it difficult to analyze. Once we import the file, Ghidra will prompt us to run an initial analysis, which typically includes disassembling and identifying function boundaries and symbols in the binary.

- **File Type Identification**: During the import process, Ghidra automatically detects the file type (e.g., PE for Windows executables). If necessary, we can manually specify the format.
- **Initial Analysis**: Ghidra provides several analysis options, including disassembly, function identification, and symbol recovery. It's often best to allow Ghidra to run a full analysis initially, though we can customize the options based on the specific needs of our investigation.

Step 3: Static Analysis and Identification of Key Features

After importing and performing the initial analysis, the next step is static analysis. This involves exploring the code without executing it. Ghidra provides various views of the malware, such as disassembly, decompilation, and the program's structure. In this case, we will focus on identifying key functions and looking for known patterns that may indicate ransomware behavior.

Key Points of Focus:

- **Entry Point**: The entry point is typically where the malware begins execution. We can identify it by looking for a specific function, often called _start, main, or WinMain in Windows executables.
- **String Analysis**: Many malware samples contain hardcoded strings that reveal important information such as error messages, file names, or URLs. In this case, we may find strings related to encryption (e.g., "AES encryption"), file extensions, or ransom notes ("pay X amount to decrypt your files").
- **Imports and APIs**: Malware often uses specific Windows API functions to perform malicious actions. For example, CreateFile, ReadFile, WriteFile, CryptEncrypt, CreateMutex, and InternetOpen are common in ransomware and other malware. We can identify these imported functions in the Ghidra import section and analyze how the malware uses them.

Ransomware Behavior Indicators:

- **File Encryption Logic**: Many ransomware variants encrypt user files and append specific extensions (e.g., .locked). In the disassembly view, we can look for functions that might be performing file operations on the system's directories or file system. Additionally, identifying encryption algorithms like AES or RSA will be a strong indicator of ransomware.

- **Mutex Creation**: Ransomware often creates a mutex to ensure that only one instance of the malware runs at a time on the infected machine. This prevents multiple instances of the malware from conflicting or interfering with each other.

Step 4: Dynamic Analysis (Running the Malware in a Controlled Environment)

Dynamic analysis allows us to observe the malware's behavior while it is running. It is performed in a controlled environment like a sandbox or a VM. In this case, we'll execute the malware and monitor its activity.

Monitoring Tools:

- **Network Monitoring**: Use Wireshark or a similar tool to monitor network traffic. Ransomware often attempts to connect to a remote server to send stolen data or receive encryption keys. By analyzing network traffic, we can discover whether the malware is trying to contact a C2 server.
- **File System Changes**: Monitor the file system for any new files, file modifications, or encrypted files. Ransomware typically encrypts documents, spreadsheets, images, and other user files.
- **Registry Changes**: Malware may modify registry keys to ensure persistence or alter system configurations. Tools like Regshot or Process Monitor can help track these changes.

Dynamic Observations:

- **File Encryption**: During execution, we will observe the encryption process as it locks files with specific extensions. We might see new files appear in the system or the creation of ransom notes.
- **C2 Communication**: If the malware contacts a remote C2 server, we may see the transmission of data such as stolen credentials or encrypted files.
- **File System Encryption Details**: After execution, files in the system will likely be encrypted, and we can identify which algorithms the malware uses. For example, we may see AES keys hardcoded in the binary or observe its encryption logic in the disassembly view.

Step 5: Analyzing Ransom Note and Decryption Mechanism

Once the malware has encrypted files, it often leaves a ransom note demanding payment in exchange for the decryption key. This note may be displayed on the user's screen, dropped in a specific directory, or sent as an email. It may contain information on how to pay the ransom and instructions for obtaining the decryption key.

Decryption Logic: In many cases, malware will use a public-private key pair for encryption. The malware typically encrypts files using a public key, while the private key is stored securely on the attacker's C2 server. By analyzing the malware's code and identifying any hardcoded keys or network traffic, we can gain insights into the encryption algorithm and possibly find ways to decrypt the files.

If the malware uses symmetric encryption (e.g., AES), the decryption key may be stored locally or transmitted to the C2 server during execution. By identifying the encryption and decryption logic in Ghidra, reverse engineers may be able to reconstruct the key or figure out ways to recover the encrypted files without paying the ransom.

Step 6: Mitigation and Countermeasures

After fully analyzing the malware, the next step is to apply mitigation strategies. In the case of ransomware, mitigation might include:

- **Disabling the Malware**: Kill the malware process using tools like Task Manager or Process Explorer, or quarantine it in a sandbox to prevent further damage.
- **Restoring Encrypted Files**: If the malware uses AES or RSA encryption, the possibility of file recovery depends on whether the encryption keys are recoverable. In some cases, security researchers may have developed a decryption tool.
- **Blocking Communication Channels**: Once C2 servers and IP addresses are identified, blocking outbound traffic through a firewall can prevent further malicious communication.
- **System Restoration**: In some cases, restoring from backups is the most efficient way to recover from a ransomware attack.
- **Lessons Learned**: This analysis shows the power of reverse engineering tools like Ghidra in identifying the functionality of ransomware. By carefully examining the malware's code, behavior, and network activity, we can gain valuable insights that aid in mitigating the impact of such attacks.

Through this case study, we've demonstrated how to analyze a real-world ransomware sample using Ghidra. From static and dynamic analysis to understanding encryption techniques and C2 communication, reverse engineering allows analysts to uncover key information that can help defend against future attacks. By combining the power of Ghidra with strategic analysis, reverse engineers can play a crucial role in identifying, understanding, and countering malware threats effectively.

Chapter 12: Firmware Reverse Engineering

In this chapter, we explore the specialized field of firmware reverse engineering, where you'll learn how to analyze firmware images, extract valuable information, and understand embedded systems. We'll guide you through the process of obtaining and importing firmware binaries into Ghidra, and teach you how to identify key components like bootloaders, operating systems, and device-specific code. You'll learn techniques for analyzing the file system, extracting embedded files, and understanding how the firmware interacts with hardware. We'll also cover methods for disassembling and decompiling firmware code, as well as recognizing common firmware vulnerabilities, such as buffer overflows or weak cryptographic implementations. Additionally, we'll dive into advanced techniques for reverse engineering custom protocols, drivers, and security mechanisms found in embedded devices. By the end of this chapter, you'll have a solid foundation in firmware analysis and be equipped to handle the unique challenges of reverse engineering embedded systems and IoT devices.

12.1 Introduction to Firmware Formats and Architectures

Firmware is a type of software that provides low-level control for a device's hardware. It is typically embedded into hardware components such as routers, printers, and IoT devices, and is responsible for tasks such as device initialization, configuration, and operation. Unlike traditional software, which is typically updated regularly, firmware is often tightly coupled to hardware and can remain unchanged for long periods. However, due to its critical role in the operation of devices, firmware can become a target for reverse engineers seeking to understand, exploit, or patch vulnerabilities in embedded systems.

Understanding firmware formats and architectures is a critical skill in the realm of reverse engineering, especially as more devices become interconnected and vulnerable to cyberattacks. This section will provide an introduction to common firmware formats and the various architectures they support. By understanding the structure and common features of firmware, reverse engineers can more effectively analyze it and gain insight into how these devices work or how they might be exploited.

1. Firmware Formats: The Building Blocks

Firmware typically exists in binary form and is packaged in a format that makes it easy to be loaded onto a device's non-volatile memory (such as flash memory or EEPROM). Several different firmware formats exist, each tailored to the needs of a specific device or platform. Below are the most common firmware formats encountered in reverse engineering:

1.1. Raw Firmware Images

A raw firmware image is the most basic form of firmware and is simply a byte-for-byte representation of the firmware. Raw firmware images do not have any specific headers or file structures, making them relatively simple to manipulate but also harder to identify in terms of their contents.

- **Characteristics**: These firmware images usually contain code, data, and other resources that are directly loaded into memory without any intermediate processing. The structure is straightforward but lacks a clear descriptor, so the contents need to be examined manually.
- **Example**: Many microcontroller-based devices, such as simple embedded systems, may use raw firmware images.

1.2. U-Boot Bootloader

U-Boot is a common open-source bootloader used in embedded systems, particularly for ARM-based devices, routers, and single-board computers. U-Boot allows a system to load its operating system and initialize hardware on boot.

- **Characteristics**: U-Boot firmware images usually have a well-defined header that can be recognized by reverse engineers. These headers typically contain information about the firmware version, target architecture, and the image's start and end addresses.
- **Example**: U-Boot images are frequently used in routers and IoT devices.

1.3. Intel Hex Format

The Intel Hex format is a text-based file format used to represent binary data in ASCII. It is used by many microcontrollers, especially older embedded systems, as it allows firmware to be represented in a way that can be easily read and written by both human operators and programs.

- **Characteristics**: The Intel Hex format breaks down binary data into lines of ASCII text, where each line represents a chunk of memory, often with a checksum to verify data integrity. This format is commonly used for firmware images that are loaded onto microcontrollers via serial connections.

- **Example**: Devices like old embedded systems or custom microcontroller-based systems might use the Intel Hex format.

1.4. Firmware Tarballs and Archives

Many firmware images are distributed as compressed archives, typically in formats like .tar, .zip, or .gzip. These archives can contain various firmware components, such as bootloaders, kernel images, configuration files, and more.

- **Characteristics**: In a compressed format, the firmware can be split into multiple files, allowing for easier extraction and analysis of individual components. Reverse engineers often unpack these firmware images to isolate specific sections of the firmware, such as the bootloader or application code.
- **Example**: Firmware updates for routers, cameras, or smartphones might be distributed as .tar or .zip files.

1.5. SquashFS and JFFS2

SquashFS and JFFS2 (Journaling Flash File System) are common file systems used for embedded Linux systems. These file systems allow firmware to store files in a compressed or flash-optimized format, enabling efficient use of storage in devices with limited memory.

- **Characteristics**: SquashFS is a read-only compressed file system, while JFFS2 is a journaling file system designed for flash memory devices. Both formats allow multiple files, configuration settings, and binaries to be packed into the firmware image, providing a full operating environment for the device.
- **Example**: Many modern routers and embedded Linux devices, such as wireless access points, run on SquashFS or JFFS2 file systems.

2. Firmware Architectures: Understanding the Target Platform

Firmware architecture refers to the underlying hardware platform or processor architecture that the firmware is designed to work on. Different architectures have different instruction sets, memory layouts, and hardware interfaces, which can make reverse engineering firmware for various architectures a challenge. Understanding the architecture is key to properly analyzing firmware and identifying key components, such as the bootloader, operating system, and application code.

2.1. ARM Architecture

ARM (Advanced RISC Machine) is the most widely used processor architecture in embedded systems. It is known for its low power consumption, efficiency, and widespread use in smartphones, tablets, IoT devices, and more.

- **Characteristics**: ARM processors are RISC-based, meaning they execute simpler instructions that are faster and require fewer resources. The ARM architecture is highly customizable, and devices may include proprietary extensions or variations, such as ARMv7, ARMv8, and ARM64.
- **Example**: Most modern smartphones, routers, and Raspberry Pi devices are powered by ARM-based processors.

2.2. MIPS Architecture

MIPS (Microprocessor without Interlocked Pipeline Stages) is another widely used architecture in embedded systems, particularly in networking hardware like routers and set-top boxes.

- **Characteristics**: MIPS is a RISC architecture known for being easy to implement and efficient, though it is less commonly used in smartphones and tablets compared to ARM. MIPS has a simple instruction set that is well-suited to embedded systems.
- **Example**: Many home routers, digital TVs, and other networking devices use MIPS processors.

2.3. x86 Architecture

x86, developed by Intel, is a complex instruction set computing (CISC) architecture that is primarily used in personal computers and servers. Although less common in embedded systems than ARM or MIPS, it is still present in some embedded platforms that require high processing power.

- **Characteristics**: x86 processors have a complex instruction set and support a wide variety of operating systems and applications. These processors are typically more powerful than ARM or MIPS processors but consume more power and generate more heat.
- **Example**: x86 processors are commonly found in high-performance embedded systems such as industrial controllers or kiosks.

2.4. PowerPC Architecture

PowerPC (Performance Optimization with Enhanced RISC – Performance Computing) was developed by IBM and is another RISC architecture used in embedded systems. It is still used in some legacy devices and applications.

- **Characteristics**: PowerPC processors are known for their robustness and versatility in both embedded systems and personal computing environments. However, their use has diminished in favor of ARM in recent years.
- **Example**: PowerPC was used in early game consoles like the Nintendo GameCube and some automotive and industrial control systems.

2.5. RISC-V Architecture

RISC-V is an open-source processor architecture that has gained significant traction in the embedded systems space due to its flexibility and licensing model. It is still relatively new compared to ARM and MIPS, but it is gaining popularity.

- **Characteristics**: RISC-V offers an open and extensible instruction set architecture (ISA) that can be customized to meet specific requirements. The architecture supports both 32-bit and 64-bit implementations, and its open nature allows developers to modify it to suit their needs.
- **Example**: RISC-V processors are being adopted in academic research, low-cost embedded systems, and IoT applications.

Understanding the various firmware formats and architectures is crucial for anyone involved in reverse engineering, especially when dealing with embedded systems. Whether you're analyzing firmware from a router, IoT device, or industrial controller, a solid grasp of the underlying formats and hardware architectures will help you navigate the firmware analysis process more effectively. With tools like Ghidra, reverse engineers can unpack, analyze, and modify firmware images to gain insights, identify vulnerabilities, and even enhance device functionality. In the following sections of this chapter, we'll dive deeper into the specific techniques used to analyze and reverse engineer firmware, using these foundational concepts to guide the process.

12.2 Preparing Firmware Files for Analysis

Before diving into the actual reverse engineering process of firmware, it is essential to properly prepare the firmware files for analysis. This step ensures that you can work with the firmware effectively, avoid common pitfalls, and streamline your analysis workflow.

Preparation involves extracting, identifying, and organizing the firmware files in a manner that allows for optimal analysis with tools such as Ghidra. In this section, we'll cover the steps involved in preparing firmware files, focusing on extraction, identifying file structures, and dealing with common issues.

1. Extracting Firmware from Devices or Sources

The first step in preparing firmware for analysis is obtaining the firmware image itself. Firmware can be extracted from devices directly, downloaded from a manufacturer's website, or even obtained through various public repositories. Depending on the source, the extraction process will differ.

1.1. Extracting Firmware from Devices

Firmware is often embedded into the non-volatile memory of devices, such as flash chips or EEPROMs. To extract it, you may need to connect the device to a specialized reader or use a method like JTAG (Joint Test Action Group) or UART (Universal Asynchronous Receiver-Transmitter) to access the raw memory.

- **JTAG**: JTAG is a hardware interface that allows you to communicate directly with the device's internal components. You can use it to dump the entire firmware from the device's flash memory.
- **UART**: UART can be used to interface with a device through serial communication. It is particularly useful for devices with limited access points or those lacking JTAG.

Extraction tools vary based on the device's architecture and the interface used. Popular tools include flash programmers like Bus Pirate, Chipsec, or OpenOCD. Make sure to verify the firmware's integrity after extraction using checksums or hashes.

1.2. Downloading Firmware from the Manufacturer's Website

If direct extraction is not feasible, manufacturers often provide firmware files on their websites, particularly for routers, IoT devices, and other embedded systems. These firmware updates are usually in binary or compressed formats (e.g., .img, .tar, .zip).

When downloading firmware from a manufacturer's website:

- Ensure you are getting the correct version for your analysis.
- Some manufacturers provide versioning and changelogs that can help you understand what changes have been made in the firmware.

- Be cautious of counterfeit websites or rogue sources, as malicious firmware could be introduced this way.

1.3. Using Public Repositories

Public repositories, such as OpenWRT, DD-WRT, and others, maintain large databases of firmware for various devices. These can be particularly useful for researchers or reverse engineers who need to analyze common device types and architectures.

- Repositories are valuable because they often host multiple firmware versions, allowing you to compare different builds and configurations.
- These repositories also make it easier to cross-reference specific firmware versions with security vulnerabilities or patches.

2. Identifying and Extracting Useful Parts of the Firmware Image

Once you've obtained the firmware image, the next step is to understand its internal structure and identify the relevant parts for analysis. Firmware images often contain multiple components, including bootloaders, file systems, configuration data, and application binaries.

2.1. Recognizing Common File Formats

Firmware images are not always a single binary file; they often contain various parts bundled together in a single archive or compressed image. Some of the most common file formats you'll encounter in firmware analysis include:

- **Raw Binary Images**: Simple byte-for-byte copies of the firmware without a file system.
- **Filesystem Images**: These are typically compressed or packed file systems such as SquashFS or JFFS2. These file systems contain all the files and binaries that the firmware runs on a device.
- **Bootloader and Kernel Images**: In many cases, the firmware image will include the bootloader and the kernel as separate components.
- **Configuration Data**: Some firmware images contain configuration files that control device behavior or settings.

Using tools like binwalk, you can automatically detect and extract common file formats from the firmware image. Binwalk is a powerful tool for analyzing binary files, and it is especially useful for extracting embedded file systems or compressed components.

2.2. Extracting Embedded File Systems

One of the most important tasks in firmware analysis is extracting the file system from the firmware image. Many devices use compressed file systems (e.g., SquashFS, JFFS2), which house the operating system and application binaries.

- **SquashFS**: This is a common compressed read-only file system used in embedded devices. It is designed for storing and retrieving large amounts of data in a highly compressed format.
- **JFFS2**: A journaling file system designed for flash-based storage. It is often used in embedded Linux-based devices.

To extract these file systems, you can use tools like:

- **binwalk**: Automatically identifies compressed and embedded file systems within a firmware image and allows you to extract them.
- **7zip**: Sometimes useful for decompressing firmware components, including SquashFS images.
- **mounting a file system**: After extracting the file system image, you may need to mount it on a local machine (e.g., using Linux's mount command) to inspect its contents.

2.3. Decompressing and Extracting Encrypted or Obfuscated Firmware

Some firmware images might be encrypted or obfuscated to prevent analysis. These types of firmware require additional steps to decrypt or reverse the obfuscation methods.

- **Encryption**: If the firmware is encrypted, you'll need to find the key or method used for encryption. Sometimes, the key is stored within the device itself or can be extracted by probing the system during runtime (e.g., via debugging or emulation).
- **Obfuscation**: If the firmware is obfuscated (e.g., through packing or code modification), reverse engineering techniques such as unpacking or static analysis are needed. Tools like unpacker scripts and dynamic analysis techniques can help you de-obfuscate the firmware.

3. Organizing the Firmware Files for Analysis

Once you've extracted the components of the firmware image, it's essential to organize them in a way that facilitates your analysis. A good organization will help you quickly access relevant files and avoid confusion during the reverse engineering process.

3.1. Organize by Components

Divide the extracted firmware into logical components such as:

Bootloaders

- File systems (e.g., SquashFS, JFFS2)
- Executable binaries (e.g., kernel images, application files)
- Configuration files
- Logs and metadata (if available)

3.2. Hashing Files for Integrity Check

After extracting the firmware, it is recommended to compute and record hashes (such as SHA-256) for all key components. Hashing serves several purposes:

- Verifying the integrity of extracted files.
- Allowing for comparison across different firmware versions.
- Ensuring the authenticity of the files (e.g., confirming that the extracted firmware matches the original).

3.3. Documenting and Annotating Findings

As you prepare the firmware for analysis, take notes on any observations regarding unusual file formats, encryption techniques, or obfuscation methods. Keeping a record of these findings will help during the analysis process and can also serve as a reference for future firmware reverse engineering tasks.

4. Common Pitfalls and Troubleshooting

While preparing firmware files for analysis, there are several common issues that you may encounter:

- **Corrupted Firmware Images**: Sometimes, firmware files may become corrupted during download or extraction. Always verify the integrity of the firmware using checksums or hashes.

- **Unsupported Formats**: Certain firmware formats may not be immediately recognizable by tools like Ghidra or Binwalk. In these cases, manual inspection and custom extraction scripts may be necessary.
- **Compression and Packing**: Firmware images are often compressed or packed, which can make them more challenging to analyze. Be prepared to use specialized unpacking tools or techniques to extract the files.

Preparing firmware for analysis is a crucial step in the reverse engineering process. By properly extracting, identifying, and organizing the components of a firmware image, you set yourself up for success in analyzing the system. Whether dealing with raw binary images, compressed file systems, or encrypted firmware, understanding how to handle these files is fundamental to uncovering the inner workings of embedded devices. Once your firmware is prepared, you can proceed to more advanced analysis tasks, such as identifying vulnerabilities, understanding device functionality, and modifying the firmware for your needs.

12.3 Identifying Key Firmware Components

When analyzing firmware, one of the most important steps is identifying the key components that make up the firmware image. Understanding these components allows you to gain insight into how the device works, and more importantly, where potential vulnerabilities or points of interest may lie. Firmware images are often structured in a way that different parts serve different roles, such as bootstrapping the device, managing hardware interactions, or running application code. In this section, we will discuss the key firmware components commonly found in embedded device firmware, how to identify them, and their significance in the reverse engineering process.

1. Bootloaders

The bootloader is one of the most critical components in any firmware image. It is the first piece of code that runs when the device is powered on or reset, and its primary job is to initialize hardware, load the operating system, and set up the environment for application code to run. Understanding the bootloader is crucial for both vulnerability analysis and device recovery (e.g., if the device becomes bricked).

1.1. What Is a Bootloader?

- **Primary Role**: Initializes hardware (CPU, memory, peripherals) and loads the operating system or firmware image.

- **Secondary Roles**: May perform basic security checks, handle recovery mode, or provide a user interface for recovery or debugging.

1.2. Identifying Bootloaders

Bootloaders can often be identified by their unique structure, which includes startup routines and hardware initialization code. They typically don't contain user-facing features and are relatively small compared to the rest of the firmware.

- **Size**: Bootloaders are usually much smaller than the operating system or application code.
- **Signatures**: Many bootloaders have recognizable entry points or signatures in their binary code, such as specific instructions for hardware initialization or common start-up routines.

Some common bootloader types include U-Boot, RedBoot, and Coreboot. Identifying the bootloader helps you understand the device's startup sequence and security mechanisms (such as secure boot).

2. Kernel Images

The kernel is the core part of the firmware that interacts directly with the hardware and manages system resources, such as memory, processing power, and peripheral devices. The kernel image often includes the device's operating system (OS), which could be a stripped-down version of Linux, a real-time operating system (RTOS), or other embedded OSes.

2.1. What Is a Kernel Image?

- **Primary Role**: Manages hardware abstraction, processes, memory, file systems, and device drivers.
- **Security Functions**: Controls access to critical system resources and may enforce security policies such as user authentication or encrypted file storage.

2.2. Identifying Kernel Images

Kernel images are typically much larger than bootloaders and often contain a compressed binary or an image file that can be unpacked. The kernel will contain a variety of drivers and system utilities necessary for interacting with the underlying hardware.

- **File Signatures**: The kernel is often a large binary file with specific patterns or signatures that identify it as the core part of the firmware. For example, in Linux-based systems, you may find the string Linux within the first few bytes of the kernel.
- **Compression**: Kernel images are often compressed (e.g., using gzip, bzip2, or LZMA) to save space. It's important to know the compression type to properly decompress and inspect the kernel.

3. File Systems

The file system is the structure that stores all of the device's data, including system files, application code, configuration files, and user data. The file system is often embedded within the firmware image and can be compressed or encrypted. Extracting and analyzing the file system is crucial for gaining a deeper understanding of how the device operates.

3.1. What Is a File System?

- **Primary Role**: Provides a structure for storing files, directories, and metadata that the operating system and applications rely on to function.
- **Storage Locations**: Includes files for system configuration, applications, logs, user data, and system libraries.

3.2. Identifying File Systems

Embedded devices typically use specialized file systems designed for flash-based storage, as these are more durable and efficient than traditional hard drives. Some common file systems include:

- **SquashFS**: A read-only compressed file system often used in Linux-based embedded devices.
- **JFFS2**: A log-structured file system used for flash memory storage in embedded devices.
- **UBIFS**: A flash file system designed for larger flash devices with wear-leveling and power-loss recovery features.

By using tools like binwalk or foremost, you can identify and extract the file system from the firmware image.

4. Configuration Files

Configuration files are used to define settings that control the behavior of both the operating system and application programs. These files can store parameters such as network settings, device behavior, security policies, and other critical information that influences how the device interacts with its environment.

4.1. What Are Configuration Files?

- **Primary Role**: Store system parameters and user preferences.
- **Examples**: Network settings (IP addresses, DNS configurations), device settings (GPIO configurations, power management), and user data (access control lists, encryption keys).

4.2. Identifying Configuration Files

Configuration files are typically stored in the file system and can be recognized by their plain-text or structured formats (e.g., JSON, XML, INI, YAML). These files are often small in size and can be easily edited to change device behavior.

- **Location**: Often found in specific directories (e.g., /etc/ in Linux-based systems) or as part of the root file system.
- **Content**: These files usually contain readable text, sometimes encrypted or encoded for security purposes.

Understanding configuration files is important for identifying security flaws (e.g., weak passwords, insecure default configurations) or discovering hidden features (e.g., backdoors).

5. Application Binaries

The application binaries are the actual executable code that runs on the device, providing the user-facing features and functionalities. These can include services, APIs, and applications that allow users to interact with the device. Reverse engineering these binaries is crucial for understanding how the device operates and for identifying potential vulnerabilities.

5.1. What Are Application Binaries?

- **Primary Role**: Provide functionality to the device, from managing user input to handling network communications.

- **Types**: These may include network services, web servers, user interfaces, or proprietary applications running on the device.

5.2. Identifying Application Binaries

Application binaries can be identified by their file types and sizes. In Linux-based systems, they are often executable ELF (Executable and Linkable Format) files, while in other systems, they may be PE (Portable Executable) or Mach-O files. These binaries often have unique entry points or symbols that can help you identify key parts of the application code.

- **File Types**: Look for ELF (Linux), PE (Windows), or Mach-O (Mac OS) files in the firmware's file system.
- **Entry Points**: Look for recognizable function names, strings, or external dependencies that hint at the purpose of the binary.

6. Drivers and Libraries

Firmware images also often contain various device drivers and libraries that facilitate interaction between the operating system and hardware components. Drivers provide the necessary instructions for handling peripheral devices like network interfaces, USB ports, and sensors, while libraries provide reusable code for performing common operations.

6.1. What Are Drivers and Libraries?

- **Primary Role**: Drivers manage communication with hardware, while libraries provide shared functionality (e.g., network protocols, cryptographic operations).
- **Examples**: Ethernet drivers, Bluetooth drivers, cryptographic libraries, file system libraries.

6.2. Identifying Drivers and Libraries

Drivers and libraries are typically stored in the system's file system or as part of the kernel image. They may be identifiable by their file extensions (e.g., .ko for Linux kernel modules) or by their function (e.g., network drivers, device drivers).

Identifying key components within a firmware image is an essential step in the reverse engineering process. By understanding the structure and purpose of bootloaders, kernel images, file systems, configuration files, application binaries, and drivers, you can gain significant insights into the firmware's functionality and security. Recognizing these components early in your analysis helps you focus your efforts on the most relevant areas, identify vulnerabilities, and understand the overall behavior of the device. With the right tools and techniques, you can navigate these components efficiently and leverage them to uncover critical information about the device you are analyzing.

12.4 Dealing with Compression and Encryption in Firmware

When analyzing firmware, you often encounter compression and encryption techniques that are used to obscure or protect critical data. These techniques are employed by manufacturers to protect proprietary information, prevent reverse engineering, and make it harder to extract sensitive content from the firmware. As a reverse engineer, dealing with these layers of obfuscation is a common challenge. Understanding how to identify, unpack, or decrypt these elements is crucial for an in-depth firmware analysis. This section will provide a comprehensive guide to recognizing and overcoming compression and encryption challenges in firmware reverse engineering.

1. Compression in Firmware

Firmware images are often compressed to reduce their size and improve loading times, especially in resource-constrained embedded systems. Compressed data might include bootloaders, kernel images, file systems, or other components. Compression also helps protect sensitive data, as it increases the difficulty of extracting and understanding it without first decompressing.

1.1. What Is Compression?

Compression is a technique used to reduce the size of data for more efficient storage or transmission. It involves encoding data in a way that removes redundancies or applies mathematical algorithms to represent the data in fewer bits.

- **Lossless Compression**: The original data can be perfectly reconstructed from the compressed data (e.g., gzip, bzip2).
- **Lossy Compression**: Some data is lost during compression, and it cannot be fully reconstructed (e.g., JPEG images, MP3 audio).

1.2. Common Compression Formats in Firmware

Firmware images commonly use a variety of compression algorithms, depending on the platform or manufacturer. Some of the most common formats include:

- **gzip**: One of the most widely used compression algorithms for embedded systems. It provides fast compression and decompression speeds and is often used for bootloaders or compressed file systems.
- **bzip2**: A higher compression ratio than gzip but slower in performance. It's often used in firmware images where storage space is a concern.
- **LZMA/LZ4**: Known for achieving high compression ratios with relatively fast decompression speeds. LZMA is common in firmware, and LZ4 is used for real-time decompression in some systems.
- **SquashFS**: A read-only compressed file system used in Linux-based embedded systems.

1.3. Identifying and Extracting Compressed Firmware

The first step in dealing with compression is identifying the presence of compressed data within the firmware image. This can usually be done by looking for file signatures or magic numbers that indicate a compressed format.

- **File Signatures**: Many compression formats have a unique magic number that can be identified at the beginning of the compressed section. For example, gzip typically starts with 0x1F 0x8B.
- **Tools for Decompression**: Once you've identified a compressed section, you can use standard decompression tools or scripts to extract it. Tools like binwalk or 7-Zip can detect and decompress common formats such as gzip, LZMA, and bzip2.
- **Automated Decompression**: Binwalk is a popular tool for extracting compressed files from firmware images, as it can automatically detect and extract embedded files. Once the compression is removed, you can continue analyzing the firmware as usual.

2. Encryption in Firmware

Encryption is another common technique used to protect the contents of firmware from unauthorized access. This is particularly important for security-sensitive components such as private keys, sensitive application code, and device credentials. Encrypted data in firmware must be decrypted before it can be analyzed, which can be a significant challenge for reverse engineers.

2.1. What Is Encryption?

Encryption is the process of transforming data into an unreadable format using an algorithm and a key. Only those with the appropriate key can decrypt and recover the original data. In the context of firmware, encryption is often used to secure portions of the firmware or the entire firmware image.

- **Symmetric Encryption**: The same key is used for both encryption and decryption (e.g., AES, DES).
- **Asymmetric Encryption**: Different keys are used for encryption and decryption (e.g., RSA).

2.2. Common Encryption Techniques in Firmware

Many embedded devices use encryption techniques to protect their firmware from reverse engineering. The encryption might be applied to the entire firmware image or to specific segments like configuration files, user credentials, or firmware updates.

- **AES (Advanced Encryption Standard):** Widely used in modern embedded systems due to its security and efficiency. AES is often used for encrypting firmware components or communications between devices.
- **RSA (Rivest-Shamir-Adleman):** Typically used for public-key cryptography to secure firmware or authentication data, especially for secure boot or firmware updates.
- **XOR-based Encryption**: Some simpler devices may use XOR encryption, which is weak but still effective for basic protection in some cases.

2.3. Identifying Encrypted Sections

Detecting encryption within a firmware image can be tricky, as the encrypted data may appear as random binary data without obvious patterns. However, there are several techniques you can use to detect and analyze encrypted sections:

- **Entropy Analysis**: Encrypted data tends to have high entropy, meaning it appears as random noise with no discernible patterns. You can use tools like binwalk or entropy analysis tools to detect high-entropy sections in the firmware image.
- **Known Encryption Algorithms**: Some embedded devices may use well-known encryption algorithms such as AES. You can look for encryption keys, initialization vectors (IVs), or specific structures in the firmware that indicate encryption is being used.

- **Search for Key Storage**: Encryption keys may be stored somewhere within the firmware image, either in clear text or obfuscated. Look for key storage patterns or potential locations where keys are likely to be hardcoded.

3. Decrypting Encrypted Firmware

Once you have identified the encrypted sections of a firmware image, the next step is to decrypt it. Decrypting firmware may require a combination of methods, tools, and techniques, depending on the encryption algorithm used.

3.1. Brute-Force and Key Recovery

If you know the encryption algorithm but not the encryption key, you may need to employ brute-force or cryptographic analysis techniques to recover the key. This could involve:

- **Key extraction from device memory**: If you have physical access to the device, it may be possible to extract the encryption key from memory by analyzing the device during runtime or after rebooting.
- **Key reuse or hardcoding**: Some firmware images may hardcode the encryption key, making it easier to extract. By searching the firmware image for strings, you might uncover the key or part of the key.
- **Brute-force tools**: In some cases, brute-forcing the key is possible if the encryption scheme is weak, or the key space is small. Tools like John the Ripper can help with this process.

3.2. Leveraging Device-Specific Vulnerabilities

In some cases, devices have vulnerabilities in their encryption implementations that can be exploited to bypass encryption entirely. This might include flaws in the key generation or handling process, insecure key storage, or cryptographic weaknesses in the firmware itself.

- **Side-channel attacks**: Devices that use encryption might leak information through power consumption, electromagnetic emissions, or timing analysis, allowing reverse engineers to extract keys or sensitive data.
- **Firmware update vulnerabilities**: Some devices improperly handle firmware updates, leaving encryption keys or unencrypted portions of firmware exposed.

3.3. Decryption Tools

There are several tools available to help with decrypting firmware images. Some popular tools and techniques include:

- **Binwalk**: Binwalk can identify and extract encrypted sections of firmware and may be able to handle basic decryption tasks if the key is known.
- **Firmware decryption scripts**: Community-driven repositories and scripts often exist for decrypting specific devices or manufacturers' firmware. Websites like Exploit-DB or device-specific forums may have decryption methods or tools available.

Once decrypted, you can proceed with further analysis of the firmware, similar to the analysis process for unencrypted firmware.

Dealing with compression and encryption is one of the most challenging aspects of firmware reverse engineering. However, with the right techniques, tools, and persistence, you can overcome these obstacles. By recognizing common compression formats and utilizing tools like binwalk for extraction, and by applying cryptographic analysis to handle encryption, you can begin to analyze the core components of a firmware image. Whether you're attempting to uncover hidden data, identify vulnerabilities, or simply reverse engineer the firmware for educational purposes, understanding how to work with compressed and encrypted firmware is crucial to achieving success in the reverse engineering process.

12.5 Case Study: Analyzing an IoT Device Firmware

In this case study, we will walk through the steps of analyzing the firmware of an Internet of Things (IoT) device. IoT devices, which range from smart home products to industrial control systems, often have embedded firmware that powers their functionality. These devices can be highly vulnerable to cyberattacks due to poor security practices, limited resources, and the growing complexity of their software.

The goal of this case study is to demonstrate how to use Ghidra to reverse engineer an IoT device's firmware, uncovering its components, identifying vulnerabilities, and understanding the overall structure and behavior of the device.

1. Setting Up the Environment

Before we begin analyzing the firmware, it's crucial to set up an isolated and secure environment. Reverse engineering IoT firmware often involves working with potentially unsafe or malicious components. Here's the setup:

- **Virtual Machine (VM):** Use a VM to isolate the analysis environment. This prevents any accidental compromise of your main operating system.
- **Tool Installation**: Ensure that Ghidra is installed and fully set up. Additionally, tools like Binwalk, radare2, and Wireshark can be helpful.
- **Disabling Network Access**: If you're working with a device that has network communication capabilities, disable any network interfaces on your analysis machine to avoid accidental communication with the device or the cloud services it interacts with.

2. Obtaining the Firmware

The first step in this case study is to acquire the firmware image. In IoT devices, firmware can be obtained in several ways:

- **Official Firmware Updates**: Some manufacturers make firmware updates publicly available for download on their websites. These can often be downloaded directly.
- **Extracting Firmware from the Device**: If no firmware is available online, you may need to extract it directly from the device. This typically involves using tools such as JTAG or Serial interfaces to dump the firmware from the device's memory.
- **Firmware Extraction from the Web**: In some cases, firmware for popular IoT devices can be found in third-party repositories or databases, where researchers share firmware dumps.

For this case study, assume that the firmware has already been downloaded as a binary file from the manufacturer's website.

3. Analyzing the Firmware Image

3.1. Initial Inspection

Before diving into detailed analysis, it's important to conduct an initial inspection of the firmware image:

Check the File Format: Use file command (Linux) or similar tools to determine the file type. The firmware image might be a raw binary or it could be a compressed archive (e.g., gzip, xz, or tar). For this case, the firmware is assumed to be in raw binary format.

file firmware.bin

Look for Compression or Encryption: Use Binwalk to scan the firmware for common compression or encryption techniques, which are prevalent in IoT firmware. If the firmware is compressed, Binwalk can extract the compressed sections for further analysis.

binwalk firmware.bin

3.2. Extracting the Filesystem

Many IoT firmware images contain compressed or packed files, which hold the actual software and configuration of the device. After running Binwalk, if the firmware contains a filesystem (e.g., squashfs, ext4, or yaffs2), it can often be extracted and mounted for analysis.

For example:

binwalk -e firmware.bin

This command will extract the compressed file system and place it in a directory where it can be accessed. The next step is to inspect the extracted filesystem.

4. Disassembling and Decompiling Code

4.1. Import the Firmware into Ghidra

Once the firmware has been extracted, the next step is to open it in Ghidra for reverse engineering. You would typically import the binary into Ghidra by creating a new project and selecting the firmware binary for analysis. Ghidra will automatically attempt to identify the processor architecture (e.g., ARM, MIPS) and offer default settings for analysis.

4.2. Identify Key Functions and Components

After performing the initial analysis in Ghidra, you can begin identifying key functions and components within the firmware. IoT devices often have embedded web servers, communication protocols (e.g., MQTT, HTTP), and custom firmware features like Bluetooth or Wi-Fi management.

- **Disassembly**: Using Ghidra's disassembler, analyze key sections of the firmware where the code is executed, including bootloaders and initialization code.
- **Decompiler**: Use Ghidra's decompiler to understand higher-level logic of the functions. For example, you might encounter functions related to network communication, such as opening sockets or sending HTTP requests.

If the firmware includes a web server, look for function names or code patterns that deal with HTTP requests, authentication, and any device controls accessible via the web interface.

5. Identifying Vulnerabilities

A crucial part of reverse engineering IoT firmware is identifying vulnerabilities that could be exploited. Below are some common vulnerabilities you may encounter when analyzing the firmware of an IoT device:

5.1. Hardcoded Credentials

One of the most common vulnerabilities in IoT devices is the use of hardcoded credentials (username and password pairs). These credentials can often be found in configuration files, source code, or embedded strings within the binary.

Search for Strings: Use Ghidra's search function to look for any plaintext strings like "admin", "password", or "root". This can help uncover weak default credentials.

strings firmware.bin | grep "admin"

5.2. Insecure Communication

Many IoT devices use insecure communication protocols like HTTP or unencrypted MQTT to communicate with other devices or the cloud. Look for functions that handle communication, and check whether SSL/TLS encryption is used. If the device uses plain HTTP, it's vulnerable to man-in-the-middle attacks.

Unencrypted Traffic: If you find network-related functions (e.g., socket(), connect(), send()), verify if the device encrypts sensitive traffic. If not, this could be a serious vulnerability.

5.3. Buffer Overflows

IoT devices often suffer from buffer overflow vulnerabilities, where data exceeds the allocated buffer space and overwrites adjacent memory. Check for functions that handle user input, such as web form fields or command-line arguments. Look for unsafe memory operations like strcpy or sprintf, which are common sources of buffer overflow vulnerabilities.

Function Analysis: Identify functions handling user input (e.g., from web forms, network requests, etc.). Check whether they perform bounds checking before copying data into buffers.

6. Debugging the Device

6.1. Setting Up Debugging Tools

Once you've identified potential vulnerabilities, it may be useful to debug the device or simulate its behavior. If you have physical access to the device, you can use JTAG or serial debugging to trace execution in real time.

Hardware Debugging: Using tools like OpenOCD or JTAGulator, you can directly connect to the device and monitor its behavior during boot and execution.

6.2. Emulation

If hardware debugging is not possible, emulating the firmware in a virtualized environment (such as QEMU) can allow you to simulate how the code runs on the target platform. Ghidra's built-in support for emulating different architectures can also assist with this process.

In this case study, we've demonstrated the core steps involved in analyzing the firmware of an IoT device using Ghidra. We explored how to obtain the firmware, extract its components, and reverse engineer its functionality. By identifying key functions, examining vulnerabilities like hardcoded credentials and insecure communication, and using debugging tools for deeper analysis, you can uncover security flaws in IoT firmware. As IoT devices become increasingly integrated into our daily lives, being able to effectively reverse engineer and secure these devices is crucial for protecting against potential threats in the Internet of Things.

Chapter 13: Crackme Challenges and CTFs

In this chapter, we dive into the exciting world of Crackme challenges and Capture The Flag (CTF) competitions, where you'll apply your reverse engineering skills to solve real-world puzzles and challenges. Crackme challenges are designed to test your ability to bypass protections, reverse engineer code, and crack software licenses, while CTFs provide a competitive environment where participants solve a series of reverse engineering and cybersecurity challenges. We'll guide you through solving a range of Crackme problems, from simple keygen creation to more complex challenges involving obfuscation, encryption, and anti-debugging techniques. You'll also learn how to approach CTF reverse engineering tasks, including binary exploitation, decryption challenges, and vulnerability discovery. By dissecting these challenges, you'll sharpen your analytical thinking and refine your Ghidra skills in practical, hands-on scenarios. Whether you're preparing for a CTF event or tackling Crackme challenges for fun or learning, this chapter equips you with the tools and techniques needed to succeed in these reverse engineering challenges.

13.1 Introduction to Reverse Engineering Challenges

Reverse engineering, particularly in the context of software and binary analysis, is a crucial skill in fields like cybersecurity, malware analysis, and software development. However, despite its importance, reverse engineering is often a complex and challenging task. It requires a combination of technical expertise, creativity, and patience to fully understand and dissect software, hardware, or firmware. This chapter will explore the common challenges encountered by reverse engineers and provide insights into overcoming them.

Reverse engineering challenges can arise due to a variety of factors, including obfuscation, encryption, lack of documentation, and the sheer complexity of modern software systems. These obstacles can make it difficult to analyze code efficiently or gain a full understanding of how a system operates.

One of the primary challenges in reverse engineering is dealing with obfuscation and anti-reverse engineering techniques. Developers often use methods such as code obfuscation, packing, and encryption to make it more difficult for reverse engineers to understand the code. These techniques are particularly common in the case of software protection, where the aim is to prevent piracy or reverse-engineering attempts.

Additionally, reverse engineers often work with poorly documented or undocumented systems. Many times, they are analyzing legacy systems, malware, or proprietary software with little to no information about how it is structured or designed. In these cases, reverse engineers must reverse the entire design from the ground up, which can be a time-consuming and error-prone process.

Another challenge is dealing with multi-layered architectures. Modern software and systems often consist of numerous interconnected components that may involve different languages, frameworks, and architectures. Reverse engineers need to work with not only the compiled binaries but also any accompanying hardware or firmware. Analyzing such systems requires proficiency in a variety of tools, techniques, and environments.

Moreover, time constraints and the need for efficient analysis often add additional pressure. In situations such as malware analysis or penetration testing, reverse engineers may need to identify vulnerabilities and provide solutions quickly before a threat can spread or be exploited.

In this chapter, we will delve deeper into these challenges, explore the tools and strategies used to overcome them, and provide guidance for becoming a more effective and efficient reverse engineer. We will focus on techniques that help in making reverse engineering tasks manageable, and we'll highlight real-world examples to demonstrate how reverse engineers approach and resolve the problems that arise. Whether you're dealing with encrypted or obfuscated code, analyzing complex systems, or navigating time-sensitive challenges, understanding the nature of these obstacles will provide you with the knowledge and confidence to tackle them head-on.

13.2 Strategies for Solving Common Crackme Problems

Crackme challenges are popular exercises in reverse engineering and cybersecurity that are designed to test the skillset of individuals attempting to crack or bypass software protections. These challenges often involve a program that requires reverse engineering to unlock a specific functionality, such as finding a correct password or key, bypassing a registration mechanism, or unlocking a hidden feature. Solving Crackme problems is an excellent way to sharpen your reverse engineering abilities and deepen your understanding of software protection mechanisms.

This chapter will explore common types of Crackme challenges and the strategies employed to solve them. The focus will be on analyzing the program using tools like

Ghidra, IDA Pro, and other reverse engineering software to examine the logic and find solutions.

1. Understanding Crackme Challenges

Crackmes generally consist of two main components:

- A protected executable: This is the binary that implements some form of protection or challenge.
- A challenge: The goal is typically to bypass or solve a problem, such as:
- Finding the correct password
- Unlocking a feature by generating a key
- By-passing a trial period in the software

While the binary may appear simple at first glance, the protection mechanisms inside can vary significantly. These protections are usually designed to make it difficult for a user to reverse engineer the program or understand its internal workings.

2. Common Crackme Protection Mechanisms

Before diving into strategies, it's essential to recognize the most common protection mechanisms employed in Crackme challenges:

- **Password checks**: Programs often require a password input, and the challenge is to determine the correct password by reverse engineering the validation logic.
- **Keygen (Key Generation):** A program may require a unique key based on certain inputs, and the challenge is to figure out how the key is generated by analyzing the program's logic.
- **Anti-debugging**: Some Crackmes contain mechanisms designed to detect if the program is being debugged, either by looking for a debugger or by triggering different behaviors when under analysis.
- **Code obfuscation**: Developers often intentionally make the code harder to understand, using techniques such as junk code insertion, function inlining, or renaming variables to obscure their true meaning.
- **Cryptography**: Some Crackmes use encryption algorithms or hashing techniques to store or verify data, which must be reverse-engineered to expose sensitive values.

3. Strategies for Solving Crackme Problems

3.1. Static Analysis (Disassembly and Decompilation)

Static analysis involves examining the program without running it. This is often the first step in solving Crackme problems, as it allows you to understand the structure and logic of the program before attempting to interact with it.

- **Disassembly**: Use disassemblers like Ghidra or IDA Pro to convert the binary code into assembly language. Look for functions related to input validation, password checks, or other protective measures. For instance, if the Crackme requires a password, a key function to look for is one that compares user input against a stored value or a computed hash.
- **Decompilation**: Ghidra's decompiler can turn the assembly code into higher-level C-like code. This is useful for understanding logic, function flow, and especially for identifying key locations where inputs are validated or manipulated. Decompiled code can often reveal function calls, loops, and conditions that are critical for solving the Crackme.

3.2. Dynamic Analysis (Debugging and Tracing)

Once you've identified key functions using static analysis, dynamic analysis (running the program under a debugger) can help you understand how it operates during runtime. Tools like GDB (GNU Debugger) and Ghidra's debugger integration are crucial for this stage.

- **Breakpoints**: Set breakpoints at strategic locations, such as places where the program checks for a correct password or key. This allows you to step through the code and observe how the input is processed and compared.
- **Watchpoints**: These are useful when you need to monitor the value of specific variables or memory locations, such as the password or key stored in the program.
- **Function Tracing**: Trace through function calls to understand the flow of the program. This is particularly helpful when dealing with keygen-type challenges, where you need to follow the flow that leads to the generation of the correct key.

3.3. Identifying and Bypassing Anti-Debugging Techniques

Many Crackme challenges employ anti-debugging measures to prevent reverse engineers from using debuggers to analyze the program. These techniques can include checks for debugger presence, timing checks, and system-specific flags. Overcoming these measures requires patience and creative approaches:

- **Disabling Anti-Debugging**: Use debuggers like OllyDbg, x64dbg, or Ghidra's Debugger to identify and bypass anti-debugging checks. Look for system calls or functions like IsDebuggerPresent, CheckRemoteDebuggerPresent, and NtQueryInformationProcess that are used to detect if the program is being debugged.
- **Timing Attacks**: Some programs use timing checks to detect whether the debugger is slowing down execution. To bypass this, you can use debugging tools that allow you to manipulate timing, or you can patch the binary to remove or alter the timing logic.
- **Virtual Machine Detection**: Some Crackmes check if they are running in a virtual machine (VM), which is commonly used in reverse engineering environments. You can bypass this by using VM detection tools or by modifying the binary to eliminate these checks.

3.4. Brute-Forcing the Solution

If static and dynamic analysis do not provide an immediate solution, brute-forcing can be a fallback option, though it is time-intensive and often inefficient for more complex Crackmes.

- **Automating Inputs**: If the Crackme requires a password or key and the valid input space is small (e.g., simple character strings), you can write scripts to automate the process of submitting potential solutions.
- **Keygen Generation**: For Crackmes that generate a key from a known algorithm, try reverse-engineering the key generation algorithm and replicate it to generate the correct key. This involves understanding how inputs like user names or IDs are transformed into keys.

3.5. Patching and Modifying the Binary

In some cases, you may not be able to find the solution through analysis alone. Instead, modifying or patching the binary directly can help you bypass checks or unlock features.

- **NOPing Out Code**: In many cases, the program contains protective checks, such as password validation functions. You can replace the instructions in these functions with NOP (No Operation) instructions to effectively disable them, allowing you to bypass the protection.
- **Patching Logic**: If the Crackme involves key validation, modify the assembly or decompiled code to make the key check always succeed (e.g., by changing the conditional check to always return true).

Crackme challenges are an excellent way to hone your reverse engineering skills, providing opportunities to solve real-world problems encountered in cybersecurity. Whether you're analyzing a simple password check or trying to bypass complex encryption, the strategies outlined in this chapter—such as static and dynamic analysis, anti-debugging techniques, brute-forcing, and binary patching—are essential tools in your reverse engineering toolkit.

By practicing these techniques and continuously refining your approach, you'll become more adept at recognizing patterns in protected software, understanding complex logic, and efficiently cracking even the toughest challenges. Remember, each Crackme challenge is an opportunity to learn, and overcoming these obstacles will prepare you for more advanced reverse engineering tasks, such as malware analysis, vulnerability discovery, and exploitation.

13.3 Analyzing and Bypassing Simple Software Protections

In reverse engineering, one of the most common tasks is analyzing and bypassing software protections that prevent unauthorized access, modification, or use of a program. These protections are often employed by developers to prevent piracy, cracking, and unauthorized use of their software. Simple software protections can include mechanisms like license key validation, trial version limitations, and simple anti-tampering checks. While more advanced protections exist, these simpler protections still require careful analysis to overcome.

This chapter will cover common types of simple software protections and provide strategies for identifying and bypassing them. By mastering these techniques, reverse engineers can better understand how protections work and develop the skills needed to remove or bypass them when necessary.

1. Common Simple Software Protections

Before delving into the strategies for bypassing software protections, it is important to understand the types of protections that are frequently used in simple software:

License Key Validation: A typical protection involves validating a user-provided key against an internally stored value, often through a hashing or encryption process. The challenge is to understand the algorithm used and provide the correct key.

Trial Version Limitations: Many applications restrict access or functionality after a certain time period or number of uses. This protection often involves tracking usage counters or time stamps, and bypassing it usually involves identifying and altering these limitations.

Anti-Tampering Measures: Simple anti-tampering techniques might check for modifications to the software or compare file hashes to ensure the binary has not been altered. If a file is modified, the software might refuse to run or exhibit strange behavior.

Obfuscation: While not as complex as full-fledged obfuscation techniques, some developers use basic obfuscation to make the code harder to analyze. This can include renaming functions, variables, or applying junk code to mislead reverse engineers.

2. Analyzing License Key Validation

License key validation is one of the simplest yet most common protection mechanisms. In this method, the software will require the user to input a key that must match an internal value, which can be stored in a hardcoded array or generated dynamically based on some algorithm. The goal is to reverse the validation process to identify the correct key or bypass the check altogether.

2.1. Static Analysis: Identifying the Key Validation Function

Start by disassembling the binary using a tool like Ghidra or IDA Pro. Look for functions related to string comparison or data validation, which are commonly used in key validation. A typical function might compare the user input to a pre-defined key or check the result of a mathematical operation based on the input.

In many cases, the function will compare the key provided by the user to a hardcoded string, or it might use a simple checksum or hash function. To locate the key validation logic, search for functions that use common string comparison or hash algorithms like strcmp, memcmp, or md5.

2.2. Dynamic Analysis: Tracing the Key Validation

After identifying the key validation function, you can use a debugger to step through the code at runtime. Set breakpoints or use a watchpoint to monitor when the input key is being processed. This allows you to see how the program evaluates the user input and compare it to the expected value.

If the key validation function uses a hash or checksum, you can trace the calculation to see how the input is being transformed. In some cases, this might involve reversing a cryptographic hash or a mathematical formula to identify the correct key.

2.3. Bypassing Key Validation

Once you've located the key validation code, there are a few ways to bypass it:

- **Patching the Validation**: If the validation checks are simply comparing values, you can modify the binary to force the comparison to always return true. For example, by changing a conditional jump (e.g., JE or JNE in assembly) to always jump, you can bypass the need for a valid key.
- **Generating the Correct Key**: If the program generates the key dynamically (e.g., via a hashing function), reverse the logic and replicate it to generate the correct key.
- **Patching the Key Check**: Another common method is to modify the binary to disable the key check entirely. This could involve NOP'ing out the function that verifies the key, allowing the software to skip this step.

3. Bypassing Trial Version Limitations

Many applications have trial versions that limit functionality after a certain period or number of uses. These limitations are often implemented via a time check or a usage counter that is stored in memory or written to a file. The goal in these scenarios is to find and modify the time check or counter to either disable it or reset it to a value that allows continued use of the application.

3.1. Static Analysis: Locating the Time Check or Counter

Start by analyzing the binary to locate the section of code that checks the trial period or usage count. Look for strings related to time functions (e.g., GetSystemTime, time, localtime, etc.), or search for global variables that may hold the trial period count or expiration date.

If the application uses a file or registry key to store the expiration data, locate and analyze these files to find the relevant values. Look for strings or calls related to writing, reading, or modifying the expiration data.

3.2. Dynamic Analysis: Observing Time/Usage Checks

Use a debugger to monitor the execution of the software. Set breakpoints at the time-checking function or when the usage counter is checked. Observe how the program behaves when it detects an expired trial or the maximum number of uses.

If the software compares the current system time to a predefined trial period, it may be possible to modify or bypass the check by manipulating the system time using a debugger or patching the binary to always return a valid time.

3.3. Bypassing the Trial Check

- **Patching the Counter**: If the counter is stored in a memory location, you can use a debugger to modify this value during runtime. Set the counter value to an arbitrary large number or reset it to zero to effectively reset the trial period.
- **Modifying the Time Check**: You can also modify the time-checking function to always return a value that indicates the trial period has not expired. This may involve NOP'ing the time comparison check or replacing the conditional jump with one that always passes.

4. Overcoming Anti-Tampering Measures

Some simple software protections rely on anti-tampering techniques to detect whether the binary has been altered. The most common form of anti-tampering is the use of file integrity checks, where the program compares the hash of the executable with a known, hardcoded hash. If the hashes do not match, the program may refuse to run or display an error message.

4.1. Identifying Anti-Tampering Functions

Static analysis can help identify anti-tampering measures by searching for functions related to file hashing (e.g., SHA256, MD5, or CRC32). Look for system calls or function calls that compare the checksum of the binary to a known hash.

4.2. Modifying the Integrity Check

Once you've located the tamper detection code, use a debugger to trace the logic that compares the hash. You can bypass this check by either patching the code to disable the comparison or modifying the hardcoded hash to match the altered file's hash.

Alternatively, you can remove or disable the integrity check altogether by NOP'ing out the relevant function, allowing the software to run despite the modification.

Bypassing simple software protections involves a combination of static and dynamic analysis to locate the protection mechanisms and understand how they work. Once you have identified the relevant protection code—whether it's license key validation, trial limitations, or anti-tampering mechanisms—you can apply techniques like binary patching, key generation, or counter modification to bypass these protections.

The methods described in this chapter form the foundation of reverse engineering for software protections. As you gain experience, you will develop a deeper understanding of how these protections work and become more adept at overcoming them. The skills learned here can be applied to a wide variety of reverse engineering tasks, including cracking commercial software, analyzing malware, and understanding software protections in general.

13.4 Practical Workflow Tips for Competitive Scenarios

In the world of reverse engineering, particularly within the context of Capture The Flag (CTF) challenges and competitive reverse engineering scenarios, efficiency and methodical approaches are key. These environments typically involve solving multiple problems under tight time constraints. Thus, developing a structured workflow for tackling reverse engineering problems can significantly improve both speed and accuracy. In this section, we will discuss practical workflow tips specifically for competitive scenarios, providing you with tools and strategies to excel in time-sensitive environments like CTFs and cracking challenges.

1. Organizing Your Tools and Environment

Before diving into the reverse engineering process, it's important to ensure that your workspace is optimized for speed and organization. The tools and environment you use will directly impact your efficiency during a challenge.

1.1. Prepare a Toolset and Environment

- **Pre-configured VM/Environment**: Set up a virtual machine or dedicated environment where all your tools are pre-installed and ready to go. Tools like Ghidra, IDA Pro, Radare2, OllyDbg, and x64dbg should be installed and updated. Having everything ready beforehand prevents wasted time during the competition.
- **Organize Tools and Scripts**: Have a predefined set of scripts or utilities (e.g., Python scripts for automation or memory analysis) that you can easily reuse across

multiple challenges. This could include things like pattern recognition scripts or automation for repetitive tasks.

- **Use a Version Control System**: If you're working in a team or need to track changes to your work, use version control like Git. This helps manage the evolution of your solutions and keeps your work organized. You can also track progress across different phases of the challenge.
- **Custom Shortcuts and Profiles**: Make use of custom hotkeys, macros, and profiles in your tools (Ghidra, IDA Pro, etc.) to speed up tasks like searching for functions, viewing cross-references, or navigating large codebases. Pre-configuring your environment this way saves precious seconds in competitive scenarios.

2. Structured Reverse Engineering Process

While each challenge is different, following a structured and repeatable process allows you to remain efficient under pressure. These steps can be adjusted depending on the problem type (binary analysis, crackme challenges, network analysis, etc.), but a basic process remains the same.

2.1. Static Analysis First

- **Start with the Basics**: Begin by opening the binary in your disassembler or decompiler. Look at the file type (PE, ELF, Mach-O), identify the architecture (x86, x64, ARM), and check for any odd characteristics or known patterns. Knowing the file format helps in understanding what you're dealing with.
- **Identify Entry Points**: Locate the program's entry point (e.g., main() or WinMain() in Windows) to begin tracing the flow of execution. This is a key starting point for understanding how the program behaves.
- **Search for Strings**: Quickly search for hardcoded strings within the binary that could be useful, such as error messages, license keys, or prompts. These can often reveal critical parts of the code, including checks for input values.
- **Function Analysis**: Once you've identified key functions and areas of interest, perform detailed function analysis. Use Ghidra or IDA Pro to recognize function prologues and entry points. Cross-references, function names, and symbol analysis can help you map the logic in the program.

2.2. Dynamic Analysis for Deeper Insights

- **Set Breakpoints and Watchpoints**: If you're dealing with a complex challenge, set breakpoints at strategic points, such as user input functions or calls to critical libraries. This helps you observe how data flows through the program at runtime.
- **Monitor Input and Output**: Track how the software interacts with external inputs (files, network requests, etc.) and outputs (error codes, results). In a CTF environment, this can lead you to hidden parts of the challenge, like bypassable checks or validation procedures.
- **Emulate or Debug in Parallel**: If the binary is complex and static analysis doesn't provide immediate answers, emulate the code or use debugging tools like x64dbg to trace the execution flow and capture runtime behavior.

3. Time Management and Prioritization

In competitive reverse engineering, managing your time effectively is just as important as your technical skills. Efficient time management ensures that you spend just the right amount of time on each task, rather than getting stuck on one part of the challenge for too long.

3.1. Break the Problem Into Smaller Tasks

- **Divide and Conquer**: Instead of tackling the entire binary at once, break down the problem into smaller, manageable sections. Focus on isolated components (like input validation or license key checks) first, then proceed to more complex parts (e.g., cryptographic or anti-tampering checks).
- **Prioritize High-Impact Areas**: Identify high-priority areas of the binary that are more likely to contain the flag or key pieces of information. These might include authentication routines, key verification, or other user-interactive components. If you're unsure where to start, focusing on areas that impact functionality tends to be a smart bet.

3.2. Know When to Move On

- **Avoid Tunnel Vision**: It can be easy to get caught up in trying to analyze every little detail, but this can be counterproductive in a timed challenge. If you find yourself stuck on a problem, move on and revisit it later with fresh eyes.
- **Use Time Windows Efficiently**: Set short, timed sessions (e.g., 30-minute blocks) for specific tasks like disassembly or debugging. After each session, assess your progress and decide whether to move on to the next area of the challenge or continue further with the current task.

4. Collaboration and Teamwork

In team-based reverse engineering challenges (like those in CTFs), teamwork and collaboration are essential to success. These competitions often allow participants to work in groups, and distributing tasks effectively is crucial to finishing quickly.

4.1. Divide Tasks Based on Expertise

- **Specialized Roles**: If you're working as part of a team, divide tasks based on each member's expertise. For example, one person might handle static analysis, another may work on dynamic analysis, while a third might focus on scripting or automation tasks. This minimizes overlap and speeds up the overall process.
- **Collaborative Communication**: Ensure that team members communicate frequently and effectively. Use tools like Slack, Discord, or GitHub to share findings, exchange insights, and keep track of your collective progress. Proper documentation of each step helps keep everyone aligned.

4.2. Shared Resources

- **Shared Virtual Machines**: In a team, it's important to work on a shared virtual environment or repository, so everyone has access to the same version of the challenge and tools. This avoids issues related to version differences and ensures everyone is working with the same context.
- **Script and Report Sharing**: Share reusable scripts, solutions to sub-problems, and detailed write-ups on each reverse engineering step. This helps everyone avoid redundant work and speeds up the overall analysis.

5. Handling Common Roadblocks

Even the best reverse engineers will encounter roadblocks during a competition. Knowing how to handle these effectively is a key part of the competitive mindset.

5.1. The Power of Documentation

Keep a record of what you've tried, what you've learned, and any potential leads. Documentation will help you to avoid repeating failed steps and can give you insights when revisiting a challenge later.

5.2. Seeking Help from the Community

If you're stuck, the reverse engineering community is often willing to help. Many CTF platforms have forums or channels where you can ask for guidance or share techniques. However, always try to solve as much as possible on your own first to ensure you're truly learning and developing your skills.

Having a structured and organized approach is crucial when facing competitive reverse engineering challenges. By preparing your environment, developing a clear workflow for analyzing binaries, managing your time effectively, collaborating with your team, and overcoming roadblocks, you set yourself up for success. Whether you're participating in a CTF competition or solving reverse engineering puzzles in a crackme challenge, these tips will help you streamline the process and increase your chances of success under time pressure.

13.5 Case Study: Solving a Sample Crackme with Ghidra

In this case study, we'll walk through the steps involved in solving a typical crackme challenge using Ghidra. Crackme challenges are designed to test your reverse engineering skills by presenting a binary executable that you need to analyze and bypass protection mechanisms, often by finding a correct password or key. These challenges provide an excellent opportunity to practice skills such as disassembly, debugging, and decompilation.

This case study will focus on a simple crackme, with the goal of identifying how to bypass its security check and gain access to the correct flag or value. We'll go step-by-step, from setting up Ghidra to the final solution, illustrating key concepts, techniques, and tips along the way.

1. Setting Up the Challenge

Before we begin, we first need to prepare the Ghidra environment and import the crackme binary. For this case study, we will assume the binary is a 32-bit executable designed for Windows (PE format), and we'll be solving the challenge to find the correct password validation routine.

1.1. Importing the Binary

- Open Ghidra and create a new project.
- Go to File > Import File and select the crackme binary.

- Ghidra will analyze the file and prompt you for the necessary format (PE, ELF, etc.). Ensure it selects the correct architecture (x86) and proceed with the default settings for the initial analysis.
- After Ghidra finishes analyzing the file, navigate to the CodeBrowser tool to start working with the binary.

2. Initial Analysis: Exploring the Binary

Once the file is imported, it's time to begin analyzing the binary's structure and behavior.

2.1. Inspecting the Entry Point

- In the CodeBrowser, locate the entry point of the program (often the main() function).
- The entry point is where execution begins. Start by looking at the program's flow to get a general idea of its operation.
- In our crackme example, the entry point will likely contain a call to a password-checking function or a series of validation checks before the program continues its normal flow.

2.2. Locating Functions of Interest

Use Ghidra's auto-analysis features to identify functions in the binary. You'll see that Ghidra automatically identifies standard library calls (like printf, scanf, etc.), as well as any custom functions written by the developer.

- **Search for strings**: The crackme will likely contain strings like "password", "incorrect", or "try again", which will give us clues about the locations to focus on.
- **Function analysis**: Identify the function responsible for comparing the user input to the correct password. This could be done via functions like strcmp, or custom comparison routines.

At this point, you'll probably come across a function that performs the password validation. It may look something like this:

cmp eax, [password]
jne invalid_password

This indicates that the program is comparing the user's input (stored in eax) to a correct value stored in memory. The program jumps to an invalid password handler if they do not match.

3. Disassembly and Decompilation

Now that we have a general understanding of the binary's flow, we can proceed with disassembling and decompiling the code to reveal higher-level details.

3.1. Using Ghidra's Decompiler

- In Ghidra's CodeBrowser, right-click on the function responsible for password checking (for example, validate_password) and select Decompile.
- Ghidra will provide a C-like decompiled version of the assembly code, which will be much easier to understand. Look for the part of the code where the user's input is compared to the expected password.

A possible decompiled snippet might look like this:

```
int validate_password(char *input) {
   if (strcmp(input, "secret123") == 0) {
      return 1;  // Success
   } else {
      return 0;  // Failure
   }
}
```

Here, the program is comparing the user's input to the hardcoded string "secret123". Our goal is to bypass this check, either by providing the correct input or modifying the binary to accept any input.

4. Debugging and Dynamic Analysis

At this point, we have an understanding of how the program works. To confirm our assumptions and find out more about the protection mechanism, we can proceed with dynamic analysis and debugging.

4.1. Setting Breakpoints

- Set a breakpoint at the function responsible for the password check (validate_password).
- Launch the binary in a debugger like x64dbg or OllyDbg, or use Ghidra's debugger integration if you prefer.
- Run the program until it reaches the password validation function.

Once it hits the breakpoint, you can inspect the registers and memory. Specifically, look at the value stored in eax, which holds the user's input during the comparison.

4.2. Monitoring Execution Flow

Run through the function and confirm that the password check is indeed comparing the user's input to the hardcoded value "secret123". This dynamic analysis can help verify if there are any additional checks or anti-debugging mechanisms in place, which might require further bypass techniques.

5. Modifying the Binary: Patching the Password Check

Having identified the password comparison function and confirmed that it is hardcoded, we can proceed with modifying the binary to bypass the password check.

5.1. NOPing Out the Check

One way to bypass this password check is by "NOPing" (No Operation) the comparison instruction, which essentially removes the check entirely. Here's how to do that:

- In Ghidra's CodeBrowser, locate the line where the comparison cmp eax, [password] occurs.
- Modify the binary by replacing this instruction with NOP instructions. NOPs simply do nothing, allowing the program to skip over the comparison.
- Save the modified binary.

5.2. Patching the Program

Alternatively, we could patch the binary by altering the comparison logic. Instead of comparing the input to "secret123", we can make it always return success, regardless of the input provided.

- Locate the jne invalid_password jump instruction and modify it so that it always jumps to the success routine, no matter what.

- After patching the binary, you can reload it in Ghidra and check if the changes have been applied correctly.

6. Verifying the Solution

At this point, we have either patched the binary or identified the correct password. To verify the solution, run the modified or patched binary.

- If you've NOPed out the password check or bypassed it, you should be able to input any value and still get a valid result (usually a message indicating success).
- If you've manually identified the correct password, simply input the correct value ("secret123") into the program and see if it proceeds past the password check.
- If successful, the challenge will be completed, and you'll have solved the crackme!

7. Conclusion and Reflection

This case study demonstrates how to approach solving a simple crackme challenge using Ghidra. By following the steps of importing the binary, analyzing the program's structure, disassembling and decompiling the code, and performing dynamic analysis, we were able to identify the password validation logic. Finally, we bypassed the protection either by patching the binary or finding the correct password.

Reverse engineering challenges, like crackmes, provide a hands-on opportunity to apply various techniques and tools like Ghidra for analysis and modification of binaries. With practice, these steps will become second nature, helping you solve increasingly complex reverse engineering puzzles and gain deeper insights into how software works under the hood.

Part V: Mastering Ghidra

Part V is dedicated to helping you become a true expert in Ghidra by unlocking its advanced capabilities and fine-tuning your reverse engineering skills. In this section, we'll cover topics that take you beyond basic usage and delve into mastering the tool's full potential. You'll explore advanced analysis techniques, such as working with more complex architectures and specialized file formats, and discover customization options that allow you to tailor Ghidra to your specific needs. We'll also dive into plugin development and extending Ghidra's functionality with custom scripts to enhance your workflow and analysis capabilities. By the end of this part, you'll be able to confidently use Ghidra as a powerful tool for tackling even the most challenging reverse engineering tasks, fully utilizing its features to their maximum potential. Whether you're analyzing complex software, developing custom solutions, or contributing to the Ghidra community, Part V will equip you with the expertise needed to master the tool and take your reverse engineering skills to the next level.

Chapter 14: Extending Ghidra

In this chapter, we explore how to extend Ghidra to meet your unique reverse engineering needs by developing custom plugins and scripts. Ghidra offers a highly flexible environment that allows users to add new features and automate tasks using Java and Python (Jython). You'll start by learning how to set up the development environment and create simple scripts that interact with Ghidra's API. We'll guide you through the process of developing custom plugins that can be integrated directly into Ghidra, allowing you to extend its functionality, automate workflows, and add new analysis tools. You'll also learn how to leverage Ghidra's scripting console to run and test your scripts in real-time, saving you time and improving efficiency. Additionally, we'll explore how to share your custom solutions with the community and how to integrate third-party libraries to enhance Ghidra's capabilities. By the end of this chapter, you'll have the skills to build custom plugins, automate tasks, and adapt Ghidra to your specific reverse engineering needs, taking your proficiency to an advanced level.

14.1 Writing Your First Custom Plugin

Creating custom plugins in Ghidra allows you to extend the functionality of the tool and tailor it to your specific needs. Whether you want to automate repetitive tasks, enhance analysis workflows, or create custom features for your reverse engineering projects, writing plugins can provide a powerful way to increase productivity. In this section, we'll go through the steps of writing your first custom plugin for Ghidra.

1. Understanding Ghidra Plugins

Before diving into writing a plugin, it's essential to understand what a plugin is in the context of Ghidra. A plugin is essentially a Java class that interacts with Ghidra's internal API to add or modify functionality. Ghidra's plugin architecture is based on the Ghidra API, which provides various classes and methods to manipulate and analyze data, interact with the program's analysis tools, and manage the user interface.

Plugins in Ghidra typically follow these steps:

- **Initialization**: The plugin is initialized and prepared to work with the user's project or session.
- **Functionality**: The plugin provides the custom functionality, which could be anything from analyzing a binary to modifying the UI.

- **Execution**: The plugin performs the tasks and interacts with the Ghidra environment, such as running analysis, manipulating data, or reporting results.

Ghidra provides several base classes that can be extended to create custom plugins, with the most common being GhidraPlugin and AbstractGhidraPlugin. Plugins can interact with various Ghidra tools, like the CodeBrowser, Decompiler, or Listing, and can be configured to run automatically or through user interaction.

2. Setting Up Your Development Environment

Before you begin writing a Ghidra plugin, you'll need to set up your development environment. Ghidra uses Java for plugin development, so you'll need a Java Development Kit (JDK) installed on your machine, along with an Integrated Development Environment (IDE) like Eclipse or IntelliJ IDEA. You'll also need to download Ghidra's Ghidra Dev Kit for plugin development.

Steps to Set Up the Environment:

- **Download and Install Ghidra**: Download the latest version of Ghidra from the official website and extract it to a location on your system.
- **Install JDK**: Make sure you have JDK 11 or newer installed. You can download it from the official Oracle website or use OpenJDK.

Set Up the Development Environment:

- Extract the Ghidra installation folder and open the ghidra folder in your terminal or command prompt.
- Navigate to the dev folder inside the Ghidra directory and run the gradle command to generate the necessary files for development.

3. Creating Your Plugin

Once your environment is set up, it's time to write your plugin. We'll start by creating a simple plugin that interacts with the CodeBrowser to display a message when a user selects a function in the disassembly view.

Steps to Create the Plugin:

Create a New Plugin Project:

- In your IDE (Eclipse or IntelliJ IDEA), create a new Java project.
- Add Ghidra's ghidra.jar and other necessary libraries from the Ghidra/Features folder to the classpath of your project.

Define the Plugin Class:

Create a Java class that will serve as your plugin. It must extend Plugin or AbstractGhidraPlugin. For this example, we will use AbstractGhidraPlugin since it provides convenience methods for interacting with Ghidra.

```java
import ghidra.app.plugin.Plugin;
import ghidra.framework.plugintool.PluginTool;
import ghidra.app.plugin.interfaces.ProgramBasedPlugin;
import ghidra.program.model.listing.Function;
import ghidra.program.model.listing.Listing;
import ghidra.util.exception.InvalidInputException;

public class MyFirstPlugin extends ProgramBasedPlugin {

    @Override
    protected void init() {
        // Plugin initialization, for example, registering actions
        System.out.println("Plugin Initialized");
    }

    @Override
    protected void dispose() {
        // Cleanup code when plugin is unloaded
        System.out.println("Plugin Disposed");
    }

    public void printFunctionDetails() {
        // Fetch the current program
        Listing listing = currentProgram.getListing();

        // Get the first function in the program
        Function function = listing.getFunctions(true).next();

        // Print details about the function
        System.out.println("Function Name: " + function.getName());
```

```
      System.out.println("Function Address: " + function.getEntryPoint());
   }
}
```

In this example, MyFirstPlugin extends ProgramBasedPlugin to interact with a loaded program. The init() method is used to initialize the plugin, and dispose() is used to clean up when the plugin is unloaded. The printFunctionDetails() method retrieves and prints the name and entry point of the first function in the program.

4. Building the Plugin

Once you've written the plugin code, it's time to compile and build the plugin:

- **Build the Project**: If you are using Eclipse, you can right-click the project and select Build Project. For IntelliJ, use the Build Project option in the menu.
- **Generate the Plugin**: After building the project, you need to package the plugin as a Ghidra-compatible .jar file. The .jar file should be placed in the Ghidra/Plugins directory.

5. Loading and Running the Plugin in Ghidra

After you've built the plugin, it's time to load it into Ghidra and test it.

- **Launch Ghidra**: Open the Ghidra application.
- **Install the Plugin**: In Ghidra, go to File > Install Extension and navigate to the directory where your .jar file is located. Select the file and click Open to install the plugin.
- **Run the Plugin**: To run the plugin, you can either:
- **Call the Plugin Manually**: Open the Ghidra Plugin Manager, find your plugin, and click Execute.
- **Add Custom Actions**: You can also add custom actions or buttons to the Ghidra toolbar or context menus, allowing the user to interact with the plugin more easily.

6. Testing the Plugin

Now that the plugin is loaded, test it to ensure it works as expected. In this example, when you run the plugin, it should print the name and address of the first function in the currently loaded program.

Open a program in Ghidra.

- Navigate to the CodeBrowser tool and select the Functions window.
- Execute your plugin and observe the output.

7. Enhancing Your Plugin

Once you've successfully created your first plugin, you can start enhancing it by adding more complex features such as:

- **User Input**: Allow the user to interact with your plugin through dialog boxes or input fields.
- **Automation**: Automate tasks like disassembly, analysis, or reporting based on user preferences.
- **UI Integration**: Create custom buttons, menus, or tool windows within Ghidra's user interface.
- **Batch Processing**: Perform bulk analysis or modifications on multiple files at once.

In this section, we covered the basics of writing a custom plugin for Ghidra. From setting up your development environment to writing, testing, and enhancing your plugin, you now have the tools to extend Ghidra's functionality to meet your specific needs. Ghidra's plugin system is a powerful way to automate tasks, create custom analysis tools, and integrate new features into the Ghidra ecosystem.

By continuing to explore the Ghidra API and learning more about Java programming, you can start building more advanced plugins and streamline your reverse engineering workflows.

14.2 Using Ghidra's Plugin Development Environment

Ghidra provides a robust environment for plugin development, which can significantly enhance your reverse engineering workflows. The Plugin Development Environment (PDE) within Ghidra is designed to help developers create, test, and deploy custom plugins with ease. By using this environment, you can quickly build plugins that interact with Ghidra's various analysis tools, such as the CodeBrowser, Decompiler, and Listing views. This section will guide you through the essential aspects of using Ghidra's PDE, from setting up the environment to testing and debugging plugins.

1. Overview of Ghidra's Plugin Development Environment

The Plugin Development Environment in Ghidra provides a comprehensive set of tools and resources to help you develop custom functionality. This environment integrates closely with Ghidra's core framework, offering seamless access to the Ghidra API and its features. The PDE enables you to:

- **Write and Build Plugins**: Ghidra supports Java for plugin development, so you will write your plugin code in Java and compile it into a .jar file for use within Ghidra.
- **Test and Debug Plugins**: Ghidra's plugin environment allows for quick testing and debugging of your code, without needing to leave the tool.
- **Deploy and Integrate Plugins**: Once your plugin is written, you can package it and install it into Ghidra for easy access and use across projects.
- **Access Plugin API**: The Ghidra API provides access to core functionalities like program analysis, disassembly, decompilation, and the Ghidra GUI, allowing you to create highly integrated plugins.

2. Setting Up the Plugin Development Environment

Before you can start developing your own plugins, you'll need to set up the development environment. Here's a step-by-step guide to getting everything ready:

Step 1: Install Ghidra

If you haven't already installed Ghidra, download the latest version from the official Ghidra website and install it on your system.

Step 2: Install Java Development Kit (JDK)

Ghidra uses Java for plugin development, so you'll need the Java Development Kit (JDK). The recommended version for plugin development is JDK 11 or newer.

You can download the JDK from the official Oracle website or use OpenJDK.

Step 3: Set Up Your IDE

While you can use any Java IDE, the two most commonly used IDEs for Ghidra plugin development are Eclipse and IntelliJ IDEA. You'll also need to set up the IDE to work with Ghidra's libraries:

- **Eclipse**: Use the Eclipse IDE for Java Developers, and ensure it's configured to work with the latest JDK.
- **IntelliJ IDEA**: Use the Community Edition or Ultimate Edition, and configure it for Java development with the JDK.

Once the IDE is installed, you'll need to import Ghidra's plugin development libraries into your project.

Step 4: Ghidra's DevKit

The Ghidra DevKit contains the necessary libraries and tools for plugin development. You can download the Ghidra DevKit from the official Ghidra repository:

- Extract the Ghidra installation folder to a directory on your computer.
- Inside the Ghidra folder, locate the dev folder. This folder contains all the resources you need for plugin development, such as the Ghidra API and utility files.
- In your IDE, link this folder to your project so that you can access the Ghidra API and other necessary libraries.

3. Writing a Basic Plugin

After setting up the plugin development environment, you can begin writing your first plugin. Ghidra plugins are written in Java, and the core structure of a Ghidra plugin involves creating a class that extends either AbstractGhidraPlugin or GhidraPlugin. The AbstractGhidraPlugin class is commonly used because it simplifies interaction with the Ghidra tool and provides convenience methods for managing plugin actions.

Here's a simple example of a basic plugin that outputs a message when activated:

```java
import ghidra.app.plugin.AbstractGhidraPlugin;
import ghidra.framework.plugintool.PluginTool;

public class HelloWorldPlugin extends AbstractGhidraPlugin {

    @Override
    protected void init() {
        // Initialize the plugin, run setup tasks here.
        println("Hello, World! Plugin initialized.");
    }
```

```
    @Override
    protected void dispose() {
        // Clean up when the plugin is unloaded
        println("Hello, World! Plugin disposed.");
    }

    public void sayHello() {
        // Output a simple message to the console
        println("Hello from the Ghidra Plugin!");
    }
}
```

In this example:

- The plugin extends AbstractGhidraPlugin and implements two main methods: init() and dispose().
- The sayHello() method prints a message to the Ghidra console when called.

4. Running and Debugging Plugins

Ghidra provides a powerful environment for testing and debugging plugins. Once you have written your plugin, it's important to verify that it behaves as expected. There are two main ways to run and debug your plugin in Ghidra:

Step 1: Running the Plugin

To run your plugin in Ghidra:

- **Compile Your Plugin**: In your IDE, build the plugin into a .jar file.
- **Install the Plugin**: In Ghidra, go to File > Install Extensions and navigate to the location of your .jar file. Select the plugin to install it.
- **Run the Plugin**: You can then execute your plugin either via the Plugin Manager or via custom actions in the Ghidra UI. If your plugin creates a custom action, you'll see it in the Ghidra toolbar or menu.

Step 2: Debugging the Plugin

To debug your plugin, Ghidra supports integration with external debuggers like Eclipse or IntelliJ IDEA. You can set breakpoints in your code and run the plugin in debug mode to track down issues:

- **Configure the Debugger**: In your IDE, configure the debugger to connect to the Ghidra instance running your plugin.
- **Set Breakpoints**: In your Java code, set breakpoints where needed.
- **Run in Debug Mode**: Launch Ghidra in debug mode from your IDE. The IDE will catch breakpoints and allow you to inspect the state of your plugin during execution.

5. Using the Plugin Manager

The Plugin Manager in Ghidra is an essential tool for managing plugins within the Ghidra environment. Through the Plugin Manager, you can install, enable, disable, or uninstall plugins. Here's how you can use the Plugin Manager for plugin development:

- **Opening the Plugin Manager**: Navigate to Window > Toolbars > Plugin Manager. This window lists all available plugins, including the ones you've written.
- **Installing Plugins**: Use the Install Extension button to add custom plugins that are packaged as .jar files.
- **Running the Plugin**: After installation, you can directly run the plugin from the Plugin Manager or assign custom actions to run it from Ghidra's toolbar or menus.

6. Packaging and Deploying Your Plugin

Once your plugin is working correctly, you may want to share it with others or deploy it across different systems. Ghidra makes it easy to package and deploy plugins:

- **Package Your Plugin**: Once development is complete, export your plugin as a .jar file. This file contains all the necessary classes and resources needed for the plugin to function within Ghidra.
- **Distribute Your Plugin**: Share the .jar file with others, or deploy it on multiple machines by adding it to the Ghidra/Extensions folder or through the Plugin Manager.

7. Advanced Features and Extending Functionality

As you become more familiar with Ghidra's plugin development environment, you can start exploring more advanced features:

- **Creating Custom User Interfaces**: Ghidra allows you to create custom UI components, such as buttons, menu items, and dialog boxes, to interact with the user.
- **Automating Tasks**: You can automate complex tasks, such as program analysis, batch processing, or report generation, using custom plugins.
- **Interacting with Other Tools**: Ghidra plugins can also interact with external tools like debuggers, disassemblers, or emulators to extend functionality.

Ghidra's Plugin Development Environment (PDE) provides a robust platform for creating powerful plugins that can significantly enhance the functionality of Ghidra's reverse engineering tools. By setting up the development environment, writing your plugin, and testing it within Ghidra, you can tailor the tool to suit your specific needs. As you become more experienced with the Ghidra API, you'll be able to develop more complex and specialized plugins to automate processes, improve workflows, and integrate new features into your reverse engineering projects.

14.3 Extending Existing Tools with New Features

Ghidra is a versatile and open-source reverse engineering platform that allows users to analyze software and perform detailed security assessments. While Ghidra comes with a rich set of built-in tools, it also provides extensive opportunities to extend and customize its functionality to meet specific needs. In this section, we'll explore how to enhance Ghidra's existing tools by adding new features and improving current capabilities.

1. Understanding the Extensibility Model of Ghidra

Ghidra's design is built around an extensible architecture that allows you to easily integrate new features and tools. The key to this extensibility is its modular design, which divides its functionality into discrete modules or "tools" that can be modified or extended. Here are some of the core ways you can extend Ghidra:

- **Plugins**: These are the primary way of extending Ghidra. A plugin is a self-contained module that adds new functionality, such as a new analysis tool, custom views, or additional features.
- **Scriptable Interface**: Ghidra provides an API that can be used to automate tasks and interact with the tool programmatically, enabling custom scripts that can extend the tool's capabilities.

- **Ghidra API**: Ghidra exposes its core functionality through a rich set of APIs, which provide access to the decompiler, analysis framework, disassembly tools, and much more.

By utilizing these mechanisms, you can extend existing tools in Ghidra to add additional features, enhance usability, or support specific workflows.

2. Extending the CodeBrowser Tool

The CodeBrowser is one of the most frequently used tools in Ghidra, providing a rich environment for navigating and analyzing binaries. Many Ghidra users have specific needs that aren't met by the default functionality, such as additional analysis options, custom views, or integration with other tools. To extend the CodeBrowser, consider these approaches:

Custom Views for Code and Data

You can create custom views within the CodeBrowser tool to present specific information that might not be available by default. For example, you could add a view that shows the execution flow of functions in real-time or a view that overlays additional metadata about certain variables or functions.

Example steps to add a custom view:

- **Create a Plugin**: Develop a new plugin that adds the custom view to the CodeBrowser window.
- **Modify the GUI**: Use the Ghidra GUI framework to add panels or docking windows that display the new information.
- **Hook Into Existing Analysis Tools**: Utilize existing analysis functions, like the decompiler, function discovery, or data flow analysis, to populate the custom view with meaningful data.

Improving Function Navigation

In large projects, finding specific functions or pieces of code can be cumbersome. You can extend the CodeBrowser to add new navigation tools that make it easier to locate functions, structures, or even specific references in the binary.

- **Implement Search Features**: Enhance the search capabilities by adding custom filters or search options to locate functions, variables, or data structures faster.

- **Create Quick Navigation Shortcuts**: Add new keyboard shortcuts or context menu actions that allow users to quickly jump to a function or data reference.

By integrating these new features into the CodeBrowser, you can improve the efficiency and user experience for reverse engineers working with large binaries.

3. Enhancing the Decompiler

The Decompiler is one of Ghidra's most powerful tools, transforming low-level assembly code into high-level language code that's easier to understand. However, it may not always provide perfect decompilation, especially for complex or obfuscated binaries. Extending the decompiler's functionality can lead to more accurate or tailored results.

Improving Decompilation Accuracy

You can enhance the decompiler by adding support for specific instruction sets or architectures that Ghidra's default decompiler might not handle well. For example, Ghidra can decompile many common architectures (like x86, ARM, etc.), but adding support for niche or less-common instruction sets could be a powerful extension.

Example steps:

- **Write a Custom Decompiler Pass**: Modify or extend the decompiler to handle specific instruction patterns more accurately. This could include specialized handling of custom or obfuscated opcodes.
- **Support for Uncommon Architectures**: If you are dealing with hardware or firmware using a less-supported architecture, extend the decompiler to handle that architecture and provide better results.
- **Enhancing High-Level Output**: Customize how the decompiler outputs high-level code, by adding specific comments, variable names, or restructuring code in a more understandable way.

Adding Post-Decompilation Enhancements

Once the code has been decompiled, there are several ways you could enhance the output. You could add a post-processing step that:

- **Automatically Renames Variables and Functions**: Use patterns or heuristics to rename variables and functions based on their usage in the code, making the output more readable.

- **Highlight or Annotate Code**: Add automatic annotations or color coding to highlight specific sections of code that might require further attention, such as suspicious or complex routines.

These extensions can significantly improve the quality of the decompiled output, making it easier for analysts to understand the original intent of the binary.

4. Extending the Debugger Tool

Ghidra provides a debugger that allows you to interact with live running programs. However, there are certain features that may not be available by default, such as integration with specific debuggers, enhanced control over execution flow, or deeper integration with certain hardware platforms. By extending the Debugger Tool, you can add valuable functionality.

Integrating Third-Party Debuggers

One of the most common extensions to the Ghidra debugger is integrating third-party debuggers such as GDB or WinDbg. This integration allows users to debug programs in their native environments while taking advantage of Ghidra's analysis tools.

Steps to integrate GDB:

- **Create a Plugin for GDB**: Develop a Ghidra plugin that interfaces with GDB, providing the ability to debug binaries while also leveraging Ghidra's analysis capabilities.
- **Custom Debugging Interfaces**: Enhance Ghidra's debugger with custom interfaces that allow users to control execution flow more intuitively, set breakpoints, or inspect variables in real-time.

Improving Debugger Functionality

You can also extend the Ghidra debugger by adding features that help with specific tasks, such as:

- **Automating Breakpoint Management**: Extend the debugger to automatically set breakpoints on certain types of functions or routines, based on predefined patterns or signatures.

- **Real-Time Data Collection**: Implement the ability to collect runtime data, such as memory access patterns, register values, and function call traces, and present them in a more organized manner.

These extensions can make debugging in Ghidra more powerful and versatile, and they help analysts interact with binaries at a much deeper level.

5. Integration with External Tools

Ghidra is a powerful standalone tool, but often reverse engineers rely on external tools for specific tasks. For instance, you might want to integrate Ghidra with external fuzzing tools, static analyzers, or network monitoring tools. Creating custom plugins that interface with external tools can significantly expand Ghidra's functionality.

Integrating with External Analysis Tools

You can extend Ghidra's analysis tools by adding the ability to run external static analysis tools like Flawfinder or RIPS directly within Ghidra's interface. This can be particularly helpful when performing security assessments or vulnerability research.

Network and Protocol Analysis Integration

You could also integrate Ghidra with network protocol analyzers such as Wireshark or tcpdump. This would allow you to analyze binaries that communicate over networks and enrich your analysis with network data.

6. Packaging and Distributing Your Extensions

Once your extensions are ready, Ghidra provides several ways to distribute and deploy them to users:

- **Plugin Manager**: You can package your extended tool as a plugin and share it through Ghidra's Plugin Manager.
- **Scripting Extensions**: If your extension is based on a script or automation task, you can create a script bundle and share it via Ghidra's script manager.
- **Custom Extension Installation**: Alternatively, you can manually distribute and install your custom extension via Ghidra's Extensions folder.

Extending Ghidra's existing tools with new features is a powerful way to tailor the software to your specific reverse engineering needs. By developing custom plugins, enhancing the decompiler, integrating third-party tools, or improving debugging functionality, you can build a personalized workflow that helps speed up analysis and increases the accuracy of your results. With Ghidra's open-source nature and robust API, the possibilities for customization are virtually limitless, enabling you to leverage the tool for a wide range of reverse engineering and cybersecurity tasks.

14.4 Publishing and Sharing Your Extensions

Once you've developed custom extensions for Ghidra, whether it's a plugin, script, or tool, the next step is to share it with others. Publishing and distributing your extensions not only allows you to contribute to the Ghidra community but also ensures that your work can benefit other reverse engineers, cybersecurity professionals, and developers. In this section, we will cover the different ways you can share your extensions, ensure their proper usage, and get feedback from the community.

1. Preparing Your Extension for Distribution

Before publishing your extension, it's essential to ensure that it is properly packaged and documented. This step ensures that users can easily understand how to install, configure, and use your extension.

Creating a Proper Package

You can package your extension in the following ways:

- **Plugin**: If you've written a plugin, you need to bundle it into a .zip or .tar.gz file that contains all the necessary files (e.g., .class files, configuration files, and resources). Ensure the plugin is properly named, versioned, and includes any dependencies it may have.
- **Script**: For scripts, simply include the script files (in Java, Python, or other supported languages) along with any documentation or configuration files required to run them. You might also want to include a versioning system to track changes.
- **Documentation**: Include a README file that describes the functionality of your extension, installation instructions, and usage guidelines. Providing clear examples and usage cases in your documentation can help users quickly understand how to use the tool. Documentation is critical to ensure that users can easily integrate and benefit from your extension.

Testing Your Extension

Before distributing your extension, thoroughly test it to ensure that it works as expected and doesn't introduce bugs or conflicts with other Ghidra functionalities. Perform the following steps:

- **Compatibility Checks**: Test your extension across different operating systems (Windows, Linux, macOS) and Ghidra versions to ensure compatibility.
- **Error Handling**: Ensure that your extension handles errors gracefully. Provide useful error messages that guide users toward resolving issues.
- **User Testing**: If possible, ask others to test your extension to get feedback on usability, functionality, and any issues they encounter.

2. Distributing Through Ghidra's Plugin Manager

One of the most straightforward methods for sharing your extensions is through Ghidra's Plugin Manager. The Plugin Manager is an internal tool in Ghidra that allows users to easily discover, install, and manage extensions.

Steps for Publishing Through the Plugin Manager

- **Host Your Plugin**: To publish your extension through the Plugin Manager, you'll need to host your plugin on a web server or a repository. This could be your own website, a GitHub repository, or another hosting service.
- **Create a Ghidra-Compatible Distribution**: Your plugin needs to be compatible with Ghidra's Plugin Manager. This includes ensuring that it's packaged in a way that Ghidra can download and install it. You may need to structure your plugin as a .zip file or provide an .xml manifest that describes the plugin's functionality and dependencies.
- **Register the Plugin**: You'll need to register your plugin within Ghidra's Plugin Manager. This involves adding metadata (name, description, version, and so on) to make it easier for users to find your extension. Ensure you keep your plugin's information updated as new versions or bug fixes are released.

Updating Your Plugin

Once your plugin is published via the Plugin Manager, you can release updates by uploading newer versions to your hosting location. The Plugin Manager will allow users to see if updates are available and automatically download and install them.

3. Sharing Through GitHub or Other Code Hosting Platforms

If you want more control over your extension and want to engage the community with open-source development, GitHub (or similar platforms like GitLab or Bitbucket) is an excellent option.

Steps for Publishing on GitHub

- **Create a Repository**: Start by creating a new repository on GitHub. This repository will house your extension files and all related documentation.
- **Upload Files**: Upload your plugin or script files to the repository. Be sure to include a well-written README.md file that provides clear instructions on how to install, use, and contribute to your extension.
- **Versioning and Releases**: Use GitHub's version control to track changes to your extension. GitHub allows you to create releases, so users can easily download specific versions of your extension, ensuring compatibility with different versions of Ghidra.
- **Licensing**: Clearly state the license under which you are releasing your extension (e.g., MIT, GPL, etc.). Open-source licensing is important for protecting both you and the users of your extension.
- **Issues and Feedback**: Use GitHub's issue tracker to collect bug reports, suggestions, and feedback. This can help you improve your extension and engage with the community.

Collaborating with the Community

Open-source platforms like GitHub allow others to contribute to your extension. You can accept pull requests from other developers, who may add new features, fix bugs, or improve your extension in various ways. This collaborative development model helps grow and refine your extension over time.

4. Sharing Through Ghidra Community Forums and Websites

Many reverse engineers and cybersecurity professionals participate in specialized forums and communities where they share knowledge, ask questions, and collaborate. Sharing your extensions on these platforms can help you reach users who are interested in using or contributing to your extension.

Popular Platforms for Sharing Extensions

- **Ghidra's Official Forum**: The official Ghidra forums often feature sections for users to share plugins, scripts, and other resources. Posting your extension on these forums allows others in the Ghidra community to easily find and use your work.
- **Reddit**: Subreddits like r/ReverseEngineering or r/Ghidra often feature discussions about reverse engineering tools, including Ghidra. Sharing your extension here can help you connect with others who may be interested in using or improving your tool.
- **Security and Reverse Engineering Blogs**: If you run a blog or contribute to one, writing a post about your extension can attract more attention. Share your work with the community through blog posts, tutorials, or articles detailing how your extension works and its use cases.

5. Promoting Your Extension

Once your extension is published, you can help spread the word by promoting it to the right audience. Effective promotion helps you get feedback and encourages others to use your tool.

Effective Ways to Promote Your Extension

- **Tutorials and Walkthroughs**: Create tutorials or video walkthroughs that demonstrate the installation and usage of your extension. Sharing these on platforms like YouTube, Medium, or your personal blog can help new users get started with your tool.
- **Social Media**: Use platforms like Twitter, LinkedIn, or Discord to announce the release of your extension. Engaging with communities and users directly can help drive traffic to your GitHub page or Plugin Manager listing.
- **Presentations at Conferences or Meetups**: If you attend reverse engineering conferences or local meetups, consider presenting your extension and how it can help others in the field.

6. Receiving Feedback and Iterating on Your Extension

After publishing your extension, it's essential to engage with users and incorporate their feedback. This iterative process will help you refine and improve your extension over time.

- **Track Issues**: Regularly monitor the GitHub issues page, community forums, or any other channels where users can report problems with your extension. Address bugs, fix issues, and implement feature requests.

- **Request Feedback**: Encourage users to provide feedback on usability and functionality. This will help you identify areas for improvement and ensure that your extension meets the needs of the community.
- **Iterate and Improve**: As you receive feedback, update your extension accordingly. Release new versions that incorporate improvements, bug fixes, and new features.

Publishing and sharing your Ghidra extension is an excellent way to contribute to the reverse engineering community and allow others to benefit from your work. By following best practices for packaging, documentation, and distribution, and by engaging with users through GitHub or other platforms, you can ensure that your extension reaches the right audience. Whether you're hosting your extension on the Ghidra Plugin Manager, GitHub, or sharing it through forums and social media, make sure to actively promote your work, listen to user feedback, and continue improving your extension for broader usage.

14.5 Staying Involved in the Open-Source Ghidra Community

Once you've developed and shared your Ghidra extension, your journey doesn't have to end there. Staying engaged with the Ghidra open-source community is not only a way to contribute back to the ecosystem but also an opportunity to learn, collaborate, and grow within the reverse engineering and cybersecurity space. In this section, we'll explore how you can stay involved, continue improving your skills, and foster connections with other developers and reverse engineers in the Ghidra community.

1. Contributing to Ghidra's Core Development

The Ghidra project itself is open-source, and the National Security Agency (NSA) encourages contributions from the community to improve and extend the tool. Staying involved in the Ghidra community allows you to contribute not only to the development of your own extensions but also to the core Ghidra project.

How to Contribute

- **Bug Fixes and Feature Requests**: If you encounter bugs or limitations in Ghidra's core functionality, you can report these on Ghidra's official GitHub repository. If you're comfortable with the tool's codebase, you may even submit bug fixes or new feature implementations.
- **Pull Requests**: If you've identified an area for improvement or want to add a new feature to Ghidra, you can fork the official Ghidra GitHub repository, make the

necessary changes, and submit a pull request. This process allows you to directly influence the development of Ghidra.

- **Documentation Improvements**: Documentation is crucial for any open-source project, and contributing to the improvement of Ghidra's documentation is a valuable way to give back. Whether it's adding new examples, clarifying instructions, or updating outdated content, documentation improvements are always appreciated by the community.
- **Testing and Review**: Contributing to testing the latest Ghidra versions or reviewing pull requests submitted by others helps maintain the stability and quality of the project.

Join Ghidra's Development Discussions

Participate in Ghidra's development mailing lists, forums, and GitHub discussions. These platforms allow you to engage with other contributors, developers, and researchers who are working on improving Ghidra.

2. Networking with Other Reverse Engineers and Developers

Engaging with the Ghidra community can open doors to opportunities for networking and collaboration with other professionals in the reverse engineering and cybersecurity fields. Building a network of like-minded individuals can help you grow as a developer, learn from others, and stay updated on the latest trends and techniques.

Forums and Online Communities

- **Ghidra's Official Forum**: This is the primary hub for discussions about Ghidra. Here, you can ask questions, share your extensions, or get involved in ongoing conversations with other users and developers.
- **Reddit**: Subreddits like r/ReverseEngineering or r/Ghidra provide an informal space for enthusiasts to share tips, tools, tutorials, and discuss reverse engineering techniques using Ghidra. Engaging in these subreddits can help you connect with a global community of reverse engineers.
- **Discord and Slack**: Many cybersecurity and reverse engineering communities have dedicated Discord or Slack channels where you can join real-time conversations, ask questions, share projects, and collaborate with others.
- **Twitter**: The reverse engineering and cybersecurity community on Twitter is active, and you can find professionals, researchers, and tool developers who are constantly sharing knowledge and insights. Follow hashtags like #Ghidra, #ReverseEngineering, and #Infosec to stay in the loop.

Attend Conferences and Meetups

Conferences and meetups are excellent places to network, collaborate, and learn from experts in the field. Participating in these events can help you gain hands-on experience and connect with other Ghidra users and developers. Some notable events include:

- **Black Hat**: A leading conference in the cybersecurity space, often featuring talks on reverse engineering and Ghidra.
- **DEF CON**: A renowned hacking conference where reverse engineering and Ghidra tools frequently come up in discussions and workshops.
- **Local Reverse Engineering Meetups**: Look for local meetups or user groups in your area that focus on reverse engineering and Ghidra. These can be great opportunities to meet like-minded individuals, exchange knowledge, and collaborate on projects.

3. Contributing to Educational Content and Tutorials

As you continue to develop your skills and knowledge in reverse engineering, sharing your expertise through educational content is a great way to stay involved in the community. Contributing tutorials, blogs, or YouTube videos can help newcomers get started with Ghidra, while also reinforcing your own learning.

Create Tutorials and Documentation

- **Write Blog Posts**: Share your knowledge and experiences by writing blog posts on reverse engineering topics, Ghidra features, or specific challenges you've overcome. These can be helpful for beginners or even seasoned experts looking for new insights.
- **YouTube and Video Content**: Produce tutorial videos on YouTube or other platforms that explain how to use Ghidra for specific tasks like malware analysis, debugging, or patching. Video content can be an engaging way to teach others, and many users turn to video tutorials for learning.
- **Contribute to Online Courses**: If you're passionate about teaching, you can contribute to online learning platforms like Udemy, Coursera, or even create your own courses. Sharing structured educational content about Ghidra helps grow the tool's user base and teaches others how to harness its full potential.

Offer Mentorship

As a member of the reverse engineering community, offering mentorship to newcomers is an excellent way to give back. You can guide others as they learn how to use Ghidra and reverse engineering techniques, helping to foster a collaborative and supportive environment.

4. Participating in Capture the Flag (CTF) Competitions and Challenges

Capture the Flag (CTF) competitions are popular events in the cybersecurity world, and Ghidra is often used to analyze challenges. By participating in CTFs, you can continue to sharpen your reverse engineering skills while staying engaged with the community.

Join CTF Teams

Many CTF teams use Ghidra for reverse engineering challenges, as it's a powerful tool for analyzing binaries and solving puzzles. Joining a team can provide you with the opportunity to collaborate with others and apply your skills in real-world scenarios.

Organize or Sponsor CTF Challenges

If you're an experienced reverse engineer, consider organizing your own CTF competition or sponsoring an existing one. Designing challenges that require Ghidra to solve them will help you stay involved in the community while also contributing to the development of the next generation of reverse engineers.

5. Keeping Up with Updates and Evolving Tools

The Ghidra tool suite is continuously updated with new features, improvements, and bug fixes. Staying involved in the Ghidra community means keeping up with these updates and evolving your skills accordingly.

Follow Ghidra's Release Notes

Whenever new versions of Ghidra are released, read through the release notes to learn about new features, bug fixes, and improvements. Staying up to date on these updates helps you make the most of new tools and capabilities within Ghidra.

Engage with Development Roadmaps

The Ghidra team often shares their roadmaps for future development. By staying informed about upcoming features, you can align your work with the latest improvements and anticipate changes that may affect your extensions or workflows.

Staying involved in the open-source Ghidra community is an enriching experience that can deepen your understanding of reverse engineering while fostering collaboration and learning. Whether you're contributing to the Ghidra project, networking with other professionals, creating educational content, participating in CTF competitions, or keeping up with the latest updates, there are many ways to remain active in the community. By engaging with the Ghidra ecosystem, you not only contribute to its growth but also continue to improve your skills, stay up to date with the latest developments, and build valuable connections with other reverse engineering enthusiasts.

Ghidra Essentials: The Complete Guide to Reverse Engineering is your ultimate companion to mastering Ghidra, the powerful open-source reverse engineering toolkit developed by the NSA. Whether you're a beginner eager to learn the fundamentals or an experienced professional looking to refine your skills, this book offers a comprehensive, practical guide to unraveling the secrets of software binaries.

Inside, you'll discover:

- **Core Fundamentals**: Understand the principles of reverse engineering and the essential features of Ghidra.
- **Step-by-Step Tutorials**: Learn to analyze binaries, navigate disassembly, and work with decompiled code.
- **Advanced Techniques**: Dive into debugging, emulation, scripting, and automation to tackle even the most complex challenges.
- **Real-World Applications**: Apply Ghidra to malware analysis, firmware reverse engineering, and competitive challenges like crackmes and CTFs.
- **Customization and Extensibility**: Unlock Ghidra's potential with custom plugins and scripts tailored to your needs.

Each chapter is packed with detailed explanations, actionable insights, and real-world examples to help you build a strong foundation and progress to expert-level techniques.

Whether you're analyzing malicious software, understanding legacy systems, or enhancing software security, Ghidra Essentials provides the tools and knowledge to achieve your goals. Step into the fascinating world of reverse engineering and let Ghidra help you uncover the hidden layers of software systems.

This is more than a guide—it's a roadmap to becoming a confident and proficient reverse engineer. Turn the page and start your journey today!

Dear Reader,

Thank you for choosing **Ghidra Essentials: The Complete Guide to Reverse Engineering**. Writing this book has been an incredible journey, and knowing that it's now in your hands is both humbling and inspiring.

Whether you are just starting out or are already an experienced reverse engineer, your commitment to learning and curiosity about uncovering the inner workings of software is truly admirable. It's readers like you who push the boundaries of knowledge and innovation in the ever-evolving field of cybersecurity.

I hope this book serves as a valuable resource in your learning journey. If even one chapter, example, or insight sparks an idea or solves a challenge for you, then the effort has been well worth it.

Reverse engineering is a fascinating art, and Ghidra is a remarkable tool that opens countless doors for exploration. Thank you for letting me be a part of your journey and trusting me to guide you through it. Your time and attention are deeply appreciated.

If you found this book helpful, I'd love to hear from you! Your feedback, insights, and stories of how you've used what you've learned here are invaluable. Feel free to reach out—I'd be thrilled to connect.

Once again, thank you for your support and for embarking on this adventure with me. Wishing you success and discovery as you unlock the secrets of software!

Warm regards,

Claudiox Mastrangelo